2007 Business & Administration
STANDARDS

Student
Handbook
Level 2 - 2nd Edition

cfa
business skills
at work

Vic Ashley & Sheila Ashley

Published by Council for Administration
6 Graphite Square, Vauxhall Walk, London, SE11 5EE
Registered charity number 1095 809

©CfA 2007

Published 2007
First edition published 2005

ISBN 978-0-9550920-4-6

Cover design, typeset, graphics and
additional photography by Richard Jane

Cover photography by Craig Jones

Printed and bound by Adare Halcyon Ltd.

Microsoft product screen shots reprinted with permission
from Microsoft Corporation.

www.cfa.uk.com
020 7091 9620

CONTENTS

INTRODUCTION

Welcome to the Second Edition of the Level 2 Business & Administration Student Handbook. This book can be used as a student resource for anyone working towards a vocational qualification based on the 2005 and now 2007 Business & Administration National Occupational Standards.

Business & Administration is a varied and important area of work. The opportunities to develop your career are endless.

Almost five million people are directly employed in Business & Administration job roles throughout the UK. Another ten million people need some Business & Administration skills to carry out a part of their job.

As technology improves the job roles in Business & Administration will change so it is important that people in business support roles continue to update their skills.

This book provides guidance to anyone working in, or studying for, a Level 2 role in Business & Administration.

The 25 chapters of this book cover the content of Business & Administration qualifications at Level 2 including:

- National Vocational Qualification (NVQ)
- Scottish Vocational Qualification (SVQ)
- Technical Certificate (TC)
- Apprenticeship programmes

The book will also help you achieve:

- Other Business & Administration Vocational Qualifications (VRQs)
- Key Skill Qualifications
- Core Skill Qualifications

We hope that you enjoy using this book as much as we have enjoyed writing it. A career in Business & Administration can be an exciting, interesting and challenging one. We hope that this book helps you on your way towards a long and rewarding career

Good Luck!!

Throughout the book you will come across the following symbols. These are there to remind you of the key points, skills needed and the types of evidence you can gather for each unit.

The likely skills needed to complete each unit of learning are listed at the beginning of each chapter. All of these skills are explained for you within the four sections of chapter 1.

Your understanding is tested in the 'What you need to know' sections in each chapter.

Each chapter also contains activities in the 'Are you ready for assessment' section that will give you valuable practice and generate evidence towards your qualification.

All of the evidence that you generate during your course can be stored on-line using *forward* ePortfolio PLUS.

For more information, please visit www.*forward*plus.net

CHAPTER 1
SKILLS AT WORK

Working in Business & Administration requires a wide range of skills. Each chapter of this book refers to the set of skills you will need to meet the requirements of that chapter.

You may find it useful to read this chapter through before starting on any of the other chapters you have chosen to study. You can then return to the individual skills identified in each chapter as you work your way through the book.

 The Business & Administration skills have been organised into four groups

Part 1 - Practical Skills

Reading, writing, using number, using technology and working safely.

Part 2 - Personal Skills

Personal presentation, interpersonal skills, listening, communicating, questioning, planning and summarising.

Part 3 - Organisational Skills

Organising, negotiating, decision making, managing resources, managing time, problem solving, resolving disagreements and team working.

Part 4 – Operational Skills

Researching, noting, analysing, designing, checking, evaluating, recording and presenting information.

PART 1
Practical Skills

Reading

You can obviously read already, otherwise you wouldn't be able to read this book. There is more to reading, however, than being able to make out the words on a page. Reading for business purposes requires you to be able to:

- Obtain relevant information from various types of documents
- Gain a general idea of the content of documents by skim-reading them
- Identify the required information from documents
- Understand the writer's meaning
- Identify the main points, ideas and lines of reasoning from text and images

Working in the field of Business & Administration you will be required to read a wide range of material from simple memos to complex reports. Some of your work will require careful reading, while some will require you only to skim through the material and pick out the points that you need. Skim-reading, however, requires the ability to understand the meaning of what you are reading. For instance, if you read 'I saw the man with the binoculars', who has the binoculars: you or the man? Misunderstanding an instruction can have serious repercussions. It would be dangerous to follow the instruction often seen on the roadside 'use both lanes' when what is meant is 'use either lane'.

There is only one way to improve your reading skills and that is to practise. This doesn't have to be hard work; try carrying a book with you and reading it on the bus or during your coffee break. If you prefer, magazines and newspapers may be an acceptable alternative. Not only will this improve your reading skills, it will increase your knowledge base.

Try to read things that contain words you won't immediately understand and make the effort to find out what they mean, as this will widen your vocabulary.

Highlight the words that you aren't sure you fully understand. Make a list of these words and when you get home or to the office, look them up in a good dictionary. Words in a dictionary are arranged in alphabetical order, so it is easy to find the word you want. The dictionary will then give the definition of the word. Sometimes this will not fully explain the meaning of the word in the context that you have read it. Another really useful source of information is a thesaurus. A thesaurus lists words alphabetically, exactly the same as a dictionary, but instead of giving definitions it gives synonyms, words which mean the same as or similar to the word you look up. This can sometimes be more helpful when searching for an alternative word. The dictionary definition of 'intelligent' for example is 'having, showing good intellect'. The thesaurus gives 'acute, alert, apt, brainy, bright, clever, discerning, enlightened, instructed, knowing, penetrating, perspicacious, quick, quick-witted, rational, sharp, smart, thinking, well-informed'. If you didn't know the meaning of intelligent, which would you find more useful?

Try the following exercises as examples of understanding what you read.

MEMO

To: Amanda Ramsey

From: Bill Smithers

Your train to London on 14.06.06 leaves Newcastle at 20.09

Does this mean:

- The train leaves at 9 minutes past 8 in the morning
- The train leaves at 9 minutes past 8 in the evening
- The train leaves at 20 minutes past 9 in the morning
- The train leaves at 20 minutes past 9 in the evening?

> For more information on forthcoming attractions at this theatre ring 0854 659369 and leave your telephone number. Somebody will get back to you.

What will happen if you ring 0854 659369?

- You can ask about forthcoming attractions
- You can ask for times of the shows
- You can leave a message and someone will call back
- You can request brochures be sent to you

INTERNATIONAL TELEPHONE CALLS

15 PENCE PER MINUTE
BETWEEN 9AM AND 6PM

**FIRST THREE
MONTHS
SUBSCRIPTION FREE***

CALL 016659 365418
TODAY TO REGISTER

*then £14.99 per month

What does this information tell you?

- You can register now or in three months
- You can only make international calls between 9am and 6pm
- You have to pay £14.99 after three months
- You have to call today to take advantage of the offer

Below you will find four book reviews, read them and answer the questions that follow.

The Scottish Story by William Waterfield
The main character, Simon Bretherton, is down-to-earth, maybe at times a little too down-to-earth. The descriptions of the countryside are very realistic and the characters almost seem like old friends. The story leads you down dead-ends with the occasional light to be seen; it will keep you spell-bound to the very end when the twist that you never saw coming hits you in the face. It all becomes very clear and you will wonder why you never saw it coming. This is one of the best books I have ever read. I sat and read it from end-to-end, it was so difficult to put down.

The Numerical Mystery by Christopher Agate
This is an outstanding example of Agate's work. His ubiquitous private detective is lead on a wild goose chase across the country on the trail of a fiendishly inventive murderer using numerical connections to taunt the, as usual, dull-witted police as they try desperately to bring his reign of terror to an end. The murders of a milkman in Manchester, a driver in Derby and a publican in Perth appear unconnected and only the lateral thinking of Achilles Crowe can unravel the mystery. The 1930's setting adds to the charm of this excellent whodunnit.

The Man in the White Coat by Phillipa Barker
If you like your romantic novels, you will love this one. It is set in the early 17th century. The romantic hero is a well-to-do man who lives in the big house on the hill, he notices Amanda when she comes to the house to become the under stairs maid. How long can she resist his charms? Does she really want to? What will the family make of it all? These questions will all be answered, but not necessarily in the way that you think. The twists and turns of their romantic encounters will keep you on the edge of your seat right up to the very, unusual and unexpected, end.

Blue Horizons by Demitri Kassakov
This book, like the others in the series, is set on an imaginary planet somewhere in the far reaches of space. The characters are drawn from a wide spectrum of alien races, yet all have clearly human characteristics and their failings and concerns will be instantly recognisable to all of us. The story follows the attempt by the United Planetary Corporation to extract valuable minerals from the planet Syrius 0 with disastrous consequences for all the inhabitants. A renegade space trader proves to be a thorn in the side of the inter-galactic corporation as he rallies the inhabitants of the endangered planet to thwart their plans.

1. Which book is set on Syrius 0?
2. Which book describes the countryside in which it is set?
3. Amanda is mentioned in which book?
4. What is Amanda's occupation?
5. Where does the murder of the milkman take place?
6. Who solves The Numerical Mystery?

7. How is Simon Bretherton described?
8. Which book has an unusual and unexpected end?
9. Why couldn't the police in the Numerical Mystery use DNA to track down the killer?
10. Which book is one of a series?

Writing

Writing for business purposes means being able to:

- Write letters, e-mails, memos and reports
- Use different formats to present information
- Use spelling, punctuation and grammar accurately
- Alter your style of writing to suit the purpose and the reader
- Proof read your writing and correct or amend as necessary

The amount of writing that you do will vary enormously depending on your job role. You may be heavily involved in producing written documents or you may only be required to make brief notes of conversations. Writing letters, e-mails, memos and reports is covered in depth in later chapters in this book, as is proofreading. In this chapter we will cover the basic skills of spelling, punctuation and grammar as these are needed by everybody.

The ability to spell is closely linked to the ability to read. The English language is more complex, irregular and eccentric than almost any other written language. It is the hardest European language to learn because of its inconsistent spelling. For this reason it is extremely difficult to learn to spell by learning rules such as 'i before e except after c'. There are so many exceptions to every rule that you are almost as likely to make mistakes by following the rules as by guesswork. The only reliable way to learn to spell is by reading enough material that you recognise when words are misspelled because they 'look wrong'. This will also help you to pick the right spelling from two or more words that sound alike. For instance if you hear 'Threw the Looking Glass' by Lewis Carroll it will sound correct, but if you see it written down it should be immediately obvious that 'Threw' has been spelled incorrectly.

Try the following exercises.

Which spelling is correct?

administration	administrashun	adminnistration
paperwate	paperweight	paperwaite
committee	comittee	commitee
minimmum	minnimum	minimum
calandar	callandar	calendar
dictionery	dictionary	dixtionary
seprate	separate	seperate
telephonic	telefonic	tellephonic
goverment	guvernment	government
invironmental	environmental	enviromental

Which word is correct?

- Read *threw/through* the document very carefully.
- I was asked to *right/write* to you *right/write* away.
- It was time to have a new *tire/tyre* fitted to the car.
- On my way to work I walked *past/passed* the cinema and I *past/passed* two people that I knew.
- The bride's mother was *complemented/complimented* on her outfit at the wedding.
- She had been invited to be a *guessed/guest* at the ceremony.
- The administrator was asked to *hire/higher* a replacement car for the salesman.
- I have been asked to *write/right* an article on *gorilla/guerrilla* warfare in the jungle.
- He had spilt paint on his new *over all/overall*.
- She booked her holiday for the last *weak/week* in September.

In much the same way as using incorrect spelling will lead to confusion in the mind of the reader, so will the use of incorrect punctuation. Accurate punctuation is essential in business writing as the meaning of sentences can be completely distorted. For instance, 'Am I looking at your work or the typists?' means something different from 'Am I looking at your work or the typist's?' Try saying these out loud, you will find that you automatically punctuate them differently when you speak.

There are a number of rules that can be learnt to help you punctuate accurately. If you remember the following, you will not go far wrong.

Capital (or upper case) letters are used to:

- Begin sentences
- Indicate proper names (Ahmed, Francesca, Belgrade, Africa)
- Begin titles (Mr., Mrs., Lord, Sir, Dr.)
- Begin days of the week
- Begin months of the year
- Indicate acronyms (RAF, CIA, FBI, MI5, RAC)

Commas are used:

- To separate words in a list (paper, pens, pencils and rubbers). Note a comma is not used before the 'and'
- Before speech (Bill said, 'I would like the letter typed today')
- In pairs to indicate part of a sentence that can be removed without changing the meaning of the sentence (Mrs. Patel, removing her earring, answered the telephone.)
- To indicate pauses in sentences ('I must finish photocopying my friend.' means something different from 'I must finish photocopying, my friend.')

Semi-colons are used to:

- Separate items in a list (The new office has the following features; central heating in the winter; air conditioning in the summer; reflective glass in the windows; wall-to-wall carpet and self-closing doors.)
- Emphasise contrasts (Byron liked to write poems; his manager preferred structured reports.)
- Link statements together (She wanted to pass her examination this year; promotion would be unlikely if she failed.)
- Add emphasis (Patrick answered the telephone; it was the Human Resources Director; he knew he was in trouble.)

Colons are used to:

- Introduce lists (Her manager asked for reports on: wages, hours worked, holidays booked, absenteeism and sickness.)
- Separate two parts of a sentence where the second part explains the first (Sales of coal had improved during November: it was the coldest month of the year.)

Hyphens are used:

- To avoid ambiguity (words such as co-respondent, re-formed, re-mark)
- When linking two nouns (Manchester-Birmingham coach) or two adjectives (Anglo-Italian heritage)
- When a noun phrase is used to qualify another noun (A self-closing door is self closing, a three-drawer filing cabinet has three drawers)
- For certain prefixes (Un-British, anti-hunting, pro-life or quasi-autonomous)
- To indicate words are to be spelled out (S-O-U-T-H-P-O-R-T)
- To avoid difficult looking compound words (coattail, belllike, deice look better and are easier to read, as coat-tail, bell-like and de-ice)

Brackets are used:

- For parenthesis. Similar to a pair of commas, brackets separate a phrase within a sentence that could be removed without altering the sense. (Mr. Muldoon (the new Managing Director) will visit the office next Wednesday.)

Full stops are used:

- To indicate the end of a sentence
- After initials or abbreviations (W. H. Smith, etc.)

Exclamation marks are used:

- In place of a full stop to indicate an exclamation (The machine went bang!)

Question marks are used:

- In place of a full stop to indicate a query (What time should I start work in the morning?)

Quotation marks are used:

- To indicate speech (Michael said, "I want you to work late tonight to finish the accounts.")
- To indicate a quote from another source (The letter from the supplier states ' that there is an outstanding balance of £48.80.')

Apostrophes are used:

- In place of missing letters (don't – do not; 'til – until; 'phone – telephone; B'ham – Birmingham.)
- To indicate possession

Possessive apostrophes follow certain rules:

- Where the noun is singular the apostrophe comes between the noun and the 's' (Carol's desk – the desk belonging to Carol)
- Where the noun is singular but ends in 's' the apostrophe still comes between the noun and the additional 's' (St. James's Square – the square of St. James)
- Where the noun is plural and ends in 's' the apostrophe comes after the 's' and there is no additional 's' (ladies' cloakroom– the cloakroom provided for ladies)
- Where the noun is plural and doesn't end in 's' the apostrophe comes between the noun and the 's' (children's books – the books belonging to children)

There is one exception to these rules and it's 'its'. This is one of the most common mistakes to make. If you mean 'it is or it has' then the correct usage is 'it's' because you are replacing the missing letters with an apostrophe; if you mean 'belonging to it' then the correct usage is 'its', without the apostrophe.

Try these exercises.

Punctuate the following:

1. what time will the train be arriving in the morning I need to get there to collect someone
2. james letter to the publisher said I want you to proof read read my manuscript carefully
3. the order for the stationer will need to include paperclips rubber bands sticky tape staples etc and photocopy paper for delivery on Wednesday
4. mr williams wife will be unable to attend the surgery on thursday as he will be in hospital
5. they were due to be in the office at 2pm as were going to have a meeting in the board room at 4pm
6. its going to be very difficult to finish the report on time as its going to be typed by its author who is not computer literate
7. today of all days the computer crashes have been unusually regular
8. the solicitors unable to see you today his wife has just delivered a note from his doctor saying hes unwell
9. I think the photocopier may well be broken it went off with a big bang
10. parents are not permitted to use the childrens door
11. information can be obtained from the citizens advice bureau between 9 and 5

Correct the following:

1. We need paper's, pencil's, rubbers', and staples.
2. Every one of the staff are invited to the meeting.
3. We want to get the 10am train?
4. In case of fire use neither the lift or the escalator.
5. When will the stationery order be delivered!
6. After the reports are finished should, we all meet in the pub for a drink.
7. Its been a long time since it's been this warm should, we open the windows.
8. Phillip has mastered the new printer hes worked out its idiosyncrasies.
9. The memo from accounts say will you forward all cheques as soon as they arrive.
10. If the diary is not kept up to date nobody will know were their supposed to be at any time.

The purpose of good grammar is to ensure that your meaning is clearly understood. There are a few simple conventions to follow. Divide up what you want to say into sentences and paragraphs. A sentence is a set of words which make a complete statement. As we have seen, sentences must start with a capital letter and end with a full stop, exclamation mark or question mark. Sentences can be of almost any length, but for clarity it is as well if they are as short as possible. As a minimum they must contain a subject and a verb.

A paragraph is a collection of sentences about a single subject. Each paragraph must contain one sentence which describes the subject of the paragraph. Paragraphs must contain at least two sentences and may be as long as is necessary to complete the subject. When a new subject is introduced, a new paragraph is begun.

Sentences are broken down into parts of speech. There are may different parts of speech in the English language but the main ones are:

- **Nouns** - A noun is the name of a thing (pencil, desk, computer, filing cabinet, clerk, supervisor)
- **Proper nouns** - A proper noun is the name of a person, a place, a day of the week or the month of the year (Joan, Islamabad, Tuesday, October)
- **Pronouns** - A pronoun is a word used in place of a noun (he, she, it, they)
- **Verbs** - A verb is a word that shows action (running, walking, speaks, reads, sits, jumped, followed)
- **Adverbs** - An adverb is a word that adds to a verb (slowly, quickly, efficiently, thoughtfully)
- **Adjectives** - An adjective is a word that describes a noun (blue, new, modern, antique, fast, pedantic)
- **Prepositions** - A preposition is a word that shows how one noun relates to another (towards, between, beside, behind)
- **Conjunctions** - A conjunction is a word that joins two other words (and, but, so, then, therefore)

Try this exercise:

Take a chapter from a book and analyse the grammar, checking that sentences and paragraphs are correctly formed. Try going through a few sentences and finding the different parts of speech that make them up.

Using number

Using number involves understanding and using mathematical information given by numbers, symbols, diagrams and charts used for different purposes.

The degree to which you will use number in your working experience will depend on the job roles you undertake. In this section we will try to cover all of the common mathematical applications that you might come across in your day-to-day work. You will find you are using mathematics all the time without realising it, so try and relate the examples given below to your everyday work.

Accuracy

In most applications absolute accuracy will be essential. For instance if you are ordering a carpet for a room 9.15m x 8.67m a carpet measuring 9m x 8.5m would not be enough. But there are times when an approximation is good enough. For instance if you are asked your annual turnover £6million is close enough if the actual answer is £6,027,136.55. This form of approximation is called 'rounding up' or 'rounding down' and the general rule is if the number after the number you are going to give as the answer is five or over round the answer up, four or less round it down.

Try these exercises.

Round the following numbers to three decimal places:

1. 2563.5568
2. 56.36894521
3. 96.969696
4. 6369.65459
5. 9.36549

Round the following times to the nearest quarter hour:

1. 09.42
2. 21.24
3. 10.56
4. 03.05
5. 08.12

Calculate the following weekly wage to the nearest pound:

1. 35hrs @ £6.37per hour
2. 16hrs @ £5.20per hour
3. 46hrs @ £14.56per hour
4. 2 days @ £126 per day
5. 20hrs @ £6.20per hour

Tolerances

Connected to the concept of accuracy is the question of tolerance. Tolerance is the amount of inaccuracy you are prepared to accept. For example printers often work to a tolerance of 10% on volume work, so if you order 10,000 copies of a brochure they will deliver 10,000 copies plus or minus 10%. It is important that an acceptable tolerance is agreed in any situation where inaccuracy may be acceptable. In the exercises above the tolerance is set by the instruction, so the tolerance in the exercise 'calculate the following weekly wage to the nearest pound' is 50p, since that is the furthest from an exact answer that is acceptable.

Probability

Probability is a mathematical way of describing the chance that something will happen. For instance, if a member of staff is off sick one week in every ten, the probability of them being off sick is one in ten. Probability theory is used in occupations such as insurance and medicine.

Try these exercises:

1. If you pick one card from a standard pack of 52 playing cards what is the probability of picking an ace?

2. If there are 25million cars on the road and 5million break-downs a year, what is the probability that an individual car will break down?
3. If there are 47million households and 13million claims for accidental damage a year, what is the probability of any one household having a claim for accidental damage?

Area and perimeter

The perimeter of a space is the distance around the outside (the black line in the drawing below). The area is the space contained within the perimeter (the grey space in the drawing).

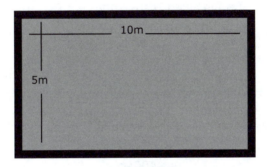

To find the perimeter of the space you must add together the lengths of all the sides. In the example above this is 10m + 5m + 10m + 5m, a total of 30m.

To find the area of the space you must multiply the length of one side by the length of the other. In the example above this is 10m x 5m, a total of 50 metres square (50m^2). This formula is only effective in a square or rectangular space.

In an irregularly shaped space you will have to divide the space into rectangles, calculate the area of each and add them together.

In the diagram below there are a total of three rectangles, one 10m x 8m and two 2m x 4m. The total area is, therefore, 80m^2 + 8m^2 + 8m^2 = 96m^2.

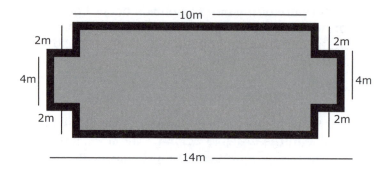

The total perimeter is 10m + 2m + 2m + 4m +2m + 2m + 10m +2m + 2m + 4m + 2m + 2m = 44m.

The area of a circle is calculated by using the formula Pi r squared which is written as πr^2. In this formula Pi = 3.14 and r = the radius of the circle, which is the distance from the centre to the edge in a straight line. So if a circle has a radius of 10m the area of the circle is 3.14 x 10 x 10 = 314 m^2.

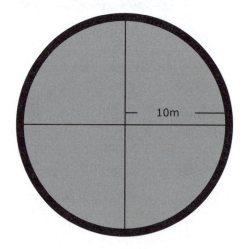

The perimeter of a circle is called the circumference. To calculate the circumference of a circle use the formula $2\pi r$, so a circle with a radius of 10m has a circumference of 2 x 3.14 x 10 = 62.8m

Averages

To find the average of a set of numbers add together all the numbers and divide by the number of numbers. For instance, from the table below, to find the average sales per day add the six sales figures together and divide by six. (269,610 ÷ 6 = 44,935).

Day	Sales
Monday	56,998
Tuesday	26,569
Wednesday	36,256
Thursday	75,556
Friday	14,984
Saturday	59,247

44,935 is the average sales per day. This is known as the mean average. There are three other expressions that are used in relation to sets of numbers such as these: mode, median and range.

Day	Number of staff
Monday	8
Tuesday	5
Wednesday	5
Thursday	8
Friday	4
Saturday	8

The mean average of the table above is the total number of staff (38) divided by the number of days (6) = 6.33.

The mode is the number which appears most often in the set, in the table above the mode is 8.

The range is the difference between the highest and lowest numbers, so in the table above the highest number is 8 and the lowest number 4 so the range is 8 – 4 = 4.

The median is the middle number of the set, so in the table above the numbers are 4, 5 and 8, so the median is 5.

Try these exercises.

Day	Number of staff	Sales
Monday	8	56,998
Tuesday	5	26,569
Wednesday	5	36,256
Thursday	8	75,556
Friday	4	14,984
Saturday	8	59,247

1. Calculate the mean average sales per head each day
2. Calculate the range of sales per day
3. Calculate the median sales per day
4. Calculate the median sales per head of staff per day

Ratios

A ratio is the proportion between one number and another, most often expressed as 'per' (miles per hour (mph), pounds per square inch (psi) for instance). So if your rate of pay is £6 per hour the ratio between your pay and your time is 6:1, if there are five people working in an area measuring 400sq ft. the ratio between space and people is 400:5, or 80:1.

Try these exercises.

1. Using the area of the circle shown in the area and perimeter section, work out the ratio of space to people if six people work in the area.
2. If you had an office space of 50m^2 and the minimum ratio of space to people is 4:1, what is the maximum number of people that can be employed in the space?

Fractions

A fraction is literally a part of a whole, for instance a half ($^1/_2$) or a quarter ($^1/_4$). They are mainly used in measuring and weighing. The number above the line is known as the numerator and the number below the line is known as the denominator.

To add fractions together they must have the same denominator. For instance to add $^1/_2$ to $^1/_4$ you must change the $^1/_2$ to $^2/_4$ then add the numerators together to give the answer ($^2/_4 + {}^1/_4 = {}^3/_4$). Remember not to add the denominators together.

To take away one fraction from another they must have the same denominator. For instance to take away $^1/_4$ from $^1/_2$ you change the $^1/_2$ to $^2/_4$ and take away the 1 from the 2 to give the answer ($^2/_4 - ^1/_4 = ^1/_4$). Remember not to take the denominators away.

To multiply fractions you simply multiply both the numerators and the denominators. For instance, to multiply $^1/_2$ by $^1/_4$, 1 x 1 = 1, 2 x 4 = 8. To give the answer ($^1/_2$ x $^1/_4$ = $^3/_8$).

To divide fractions you simply invert the second fraction and multiply the fractions. For instance, to divide ¼ by ½ invert the $^1/_2$ and multiply $^1/_4$ by $^2/_1$. 1 x 2 = 2, 4 x 1 = 4, to give the answer ($^1/_4$ x $^2/_1$ = $^2/_4$ which = ½).

Interquartile range

Statistics can be distorted by freak results either at the top or the bottom of the range. For instance calculating average monthly sales can be distorted by Christmas when sales are disproportionately high or by freak weather conditions preventing customers from reaching you, making them disproportionately low. To avoid this distortion only the interquartile range is used.

The interquartile range is found within a set of figures. In order to find the interquartile range place the figures in order from lowest to highest then divide the number of numbers into four quarters. Disregard the top and bottom quarters and work out the range of the middle two quarters. Take away the lowest figure from the highest figure to get the interquartile range.

January	14,000
February	6,000
March	15,000
April	13,000
May	17,000
June	19,000
July	18,000
August	21,000
September	16,000
October	12,000
November	10,000
December	35,000

If the above table shows monthly sales you would need to re-arrange the table into descending order by sales.

December	35,000
August	21,000
June	19,000
July	**18,000**
May	**17,000**
September	**16,000**
March	**15,000**
January	**14,000**
April	**13,000**
October	12,000
November	10,000
February	6,000

To find the interquartile range you ignore the top three and the bottom three and concentrate on the six in the middle, highlighted in bold. The grey shading shows the highest and lowest figures in this range, 18,000 and 13,000. Take the lower from the higher and the interquartile range is 5,000.

Negative numbers

A negative number is any number less than nought. They are usually written with a 'minus' sign in front of them or in brackets. An example would be this year's stationery budget is £2,500, last year's was £3,000 so this year's is -£500 compared with last year's.

To add negative numbers together you simply add the numbers together and put a minus in front so to add -101 to -879, add 101 + 879 = 980, put the minus in front to give the answer -980 or show the answer as (980).

To subtract negative numbers you change the sign of the second negative number to a positive so, to take away -3 from -6 write -6 minus –3. Change the sign on the second number to a positive and add the numbers together, so -6 + 3 = -3.

Percentages

A percentage (%) is the rate per hundred so if 20 people in every 100 who work in an organisation are on holiday, 20% of staff are on holiday. In effect a percentage is a fraction where the denominator is always 100. Therefore to add, subtract, multiply or divide percentages use the same rules as with fractions.

For instance:
- 20% + 30% = $^{20}/_{100}$ + $^{30}/_{100}$ = $^{50}/_{100}$ or 50%
- 30% - 20% = $^{30}/_{100}$ – $^{20}/_{100}$ = $^{10}/_{100}$ or 10%

However:
- 20% x 30% = $^{20}/_{100}$ x $^{30}/_{100}$ = $^{600}/_{10000}$ = $^{6}/_{100}$ or 6%

To divide:
- 20% by 30% = $^{20}/100$ x $^{100}/30$ = $^{2000}/3000$ = 66.66%

Using technology

The modern workplace is teeming with technology. It is everywhere you look. Many offices now have all of the following:

- Computers
- Printers
- Telephones
- Photocopiers
- Fax machines
- Franking machines
- Shredders
- Calculators
- Laminators

In fact it is impossible to make a cup of coffee in many workplaces, the ubiquitous coffee machine has taken over. When you put your 20p in for a cup of coffee you are using technology. This doesn't require much training (if any) and if the machine goes wrong the solution is to put an 'out of order' notice on it and go and use another one. This is not a satisfactory solution to using other forms of technology, however.

Before operating any form of technology that you have not had any previous experience of it is important that you receive training and that you read the manufacturer's manual. The manual will contain vital safety and operating information as well as a number of functions or time-saving features which you may otherwise be unaware of. Keep the manual close to the equipment for easy reference.

Remember that the equipment costs a great deal of money to replace, so treat it with respect. Where necessary, clean it after use and leave it ready for the next user.

More detailed information on using individual pieces of technology are given in later chapters of this book.

Working safely

It is the responsibility of everybody to work in such a way that they reduce the risk of harm to themselves and everybody else. This responsibility is covered in legislation which requires that you:

- Take care of your own health and safety
- Take care not to put others at risk
- Wear any protective clothing that is provided
- Take care of any fire extinguishers

You should try to work safely at all times, including when you are away from your workplace, maybe visiting another site or clients' or customers' premises. Accidents are costly, not only in terms of monetary loss to the organisation and the employee, but also in terms of the interruption of your career while recovering.

The most effective way to ensure that you work safely is to maintain good housekeeping standards. Simply putting away things when you have finished with them, closing drawers and doors behind you, not leaving boxes and cartons in gangways and making sure there are no trailing wires when you use electrical equipment will all reduce the risk to yourself and others.

If you notice any hazards in the workplace don't ignore them. If possible take action yourself to correct them, if not report them to a supervisor or the Health and Safety representative. One of the major risks is fire, so be aware of the location of fire exits and fire fighting equipment. Know what to do if there is a fire. The main priority is to save the lives of yourself, your colleagues and visitors. Saving the property comes second. The main causes of fire in buildings are electrical faults and smoking.

If any form of accident happens it must be entered in the accident book. There should be qualified first-aiders in most workplaces. Find out who they are and how you can contact them quickly in an emergency. If you are not trained in first aid avoid moving anybody who is injured, call for a first-aider or an ambulance.

If your work involves lifting anything at all, learn the correct techniques for manual handling and make sure you carry them out every time. This will reduce the risk of damaging your back or pulling muscles. Similarly if you handle any hazardous substances make sure you know what they are and the risks they pose, and how to deal with any accidents involving them.

Try this exercise.

Look around your workplace and spot any risks to health and safety. Correct those that you can immediately and report any that you cannot correct.

- Look for hazards such as loose cables, damaged carpet or wet floors
- Consider who could be harmed and how
- Think about what steps need to be taken to reduce the risks created by the hazards
- If the hazards are reduced to a minimum or removed altogether, what risk will employees still experience?
- In your view will the remaining risk be high, medium or low?
- Record your findings

PART 2
Personal Skills

Personal Presentation

Although it may be unfair, people do judge us on our appearance. Take the time to think about the way you look and the impression that you give to your clients or customers and your colleagues. Your personal presentation will send out messages about your attitude and your efficiency.

The most important aspect of personal presentation is to dress appropriately for the position that you hold. While a business suit is appropriate for working in an office, it would be totally inappropriate for a swimming pool attendant. The way you dress, the type and amount of jewellery you wear and your hair style should reflect the values of the organisation rather than your own personal taste.

There are a number of reasons for dressing appropriately:

- To identify you as a member of staff
- To avoid making colleagues feel uncomfortable
- Practicality, long hair and dangling jewellery may become entangled in equipment
- Self esteem, if you look good you feel good
- Comfort, appropriate clothing will be more comfortable to wear through the day

As well as dressing appropriately you need to think about:

- **Shoes** - Your shoes should be comfortable enough to wear all day, and always clean and polished
- **Personal hygiene** - Absolute cleanliness and the use of deodorants will show consideration to your colleagues
- **Hair** - Make sure it is clean and tidy, if your hair is long it may need to be tied back if you are using equipment such as shredders or photocopiers

Equally important is the way you behave at work. You are only at work for a few hours a day so concentrate on the reason that you are there. Treat other people the way that you want to be treated yourself. Always be polite to others as this will make it difficult for them not to be polite in turn. When you make a mistake admit it as soon as possible and accept the criticism for it. The important thing is to learn from the mistake.

Interpersonal skills

There are a range of interpersonal skills, all of which improve the quality of relationships we have with our colleagues and clients.

The first of these is self-awareness as you cannot successfully interact with others until you are aware of your own strengths and weaknesses. It is more likely that other people will recognise your strengths once you have identified them for yourself; understanding your own weaknesses will help you to work towards overcoming them.

You can become more self-aware by:

- Asking other people how they see you
- Looking at references or appraisals
- Identifying the tasks you enjoy and those you don't
- Identifying areas where you need further training

The next interpersonal skill is self-motivation. You will need to motivate yourself if you are not getting sufficient motivation from outside. Work is more enjoyable if you are motivated, there is nothing more boring than not having enough to do. Show you are motivated by keeping yourself busy. There is always something that needs doing; does somebody else need a hand with their work; are there tasks due to be done tomorrow that you could do today?

Be adaptable. Offer to help other people if they are busy and you are not. This will make you a more respected employee as well as widening your experience and your skills. If there really is nothing that you can help anybody with, possibly because you don't have the necessary knowledge, ask if you can watch a colleague carrying out a task that you have not been trained for. You can gain the knowledge to help in the future. It is important to ask in these circumstances, not just to sit and watch as this may give the wrong impression.

Being adaptable to change is one of the most important interpersonal skills at work. Most people work in environments that can change often. Sometimes every week or even every day. If you enjoy this challenge and look forward to change you will be able to support work teams effectively.

Care must be taken to display tact and diplomacy when dealing with other people. Don't give the impression that you are offering to help because you feel that your colleague is incapable of completing the task on their own. If you are responsible for allocating tasks consider the feelings of people, try not to always give the difficult or interesting tasks to the same people. Also be considerate of people's personal feelings; don't make remarks about their appearance or demeanour, they may not be looking their best because of personal problems that they don't wish to discuss. Try to let them see that you are available if they have something they want to talk about without being intrusive.

There will be times when it will be necessary to be assertive. Don't confuse assertiveness with aggressiveness. You are entitled to expect co-operation from your colleagues when you ask for assistance. If you don't receive it you will need to assert your right to ask:

- Explain why you need help
- Ask for what you really want
- Don't be tempted to use bribery
- Don't apologise for asking

This differs from aggressiveness, which is telling rather than asking, because you avoid bullying and emotional blackmail by asserting your authority.

Be realistic about what you are able to achieve. If you are asked to complete a task in an unrealistic timescale don't agree to do it when you know there's not enough time.. It is much better to explain that the target is not achievable. Give your reasons and negotiate an extended deadline or further resources. Also don't over-estimate your own abilities. If asked to carry out a task you have not been trained for, it is better to say so at the time than to attempt the task and complete it unsatisfactorily.

Try this exercise.

Complete a SWOT analysis of your interpersonal skills. This involves identifying:

- **Strengths** - What are you particularly good at when it comes to dealing with other people?
- **Weaknesses** - Where could your skills benefit from some improvement?
- **Opportunities** - What situations offer you the chance to practise your interpersonal skills?
- **Threats** - Are there any internal or external influences that make it difficult to use or improve your interpersonal skills?

STRENGTHS	WEAKNESSES
OPPORTUNITIES	THREATS

Now discuss your development needs with your manager or tutor.

Communication

Communication is a two-way process. It is the process of giving and receiving information. It is important that you exercise skill in communication so that you:

- Pass the information effectively
- Comprehend the information you are receiving
- Create the right impression
- Encourage others to communicate with you

There are a number of methods of communication including verbal, non-verbal and written. The skills required in each are different.

Verbal communication, or face-to-face communication, requires you to consider not only what you are saying but also your tone of voice, volume, clarity and speed. Your tone of voice will convey the way you feel about what you are saying; excited, angry, distressed, tired, happy, positive for example. The volume will need to be moderated according to the audience; if you are speaking to an audience in a large room you will need to speak louder than if you are speaking to one person who is close by. Clarity is important in ensuring the message is received accurately, especially if you are speaking in a language or accent that is unfamiliar to the listener. Similarly the speed at which you speak needs to be regulated according to the level of understanding of the listener.

The wording of the message will affect how well it is received and understood. Using sensory words will help communicate more effectively by creating a picture, a sound or a feeling that the listener can associate with. This is particularly useful if you are trying to persuade the listener to agree with the message. There are three main types of sensory words:

- Seeing, 'I see what you mean'
- Hearing, 'I hear what you say'
- Feeling, 'I feel good about what I hear'

Choose words that will put the message across in the way that you want it to be received; if you are unsure, use a mixture.

Non-verbal communication is also known as body language. This is the messages you send out whether you are speaking or not, by the way you sit, stand, fold your arms, and use facial expressions. Studies have shown that up to 87% of communication is made through body language.

Body language can either reinforce or take away from what you are saying. When speaking, positive body language involves:

- Good posture. Stand or sit straight
- Not fidgeting
- Not tapping your feet
- Not drumming your fingers
- Not folding your arms
- Looking at your audience
- Relaxing your facial muscles
- Not giving the impression of being bored, nervous or disinterested

Telephone communication is similar to face-to-face communication except that you are unable to see the person you are speaking to. Remember that tone of voice, volume, clarity and speed are equally as important when speaking on the telephone, because you cannot gauge the listener's reaction from their facial expression.

The way in which telephone calls are made and answered is very important. Your organisation will probably have a standard format for answering calls. Use it, it may not be your personal style but it is the company style. External callers will base their impression of the organisation on what they hear; the impression you're aiming for is friendly and efficient.

Remember to smile when you answer the phone as this will project a positive image of yourself and the organisation. Experienced communicators will always tell you they can 'hear' the smile in your voice. Do not answer the phone while eating, chewing gum or yawning.

Before making a call consider whether the telephone is the best way of communicating. Although most people nowadays carry a mobile phone, giving you access to them when they are away from their workplace, they may be in the car or on a train and variable reception or background noise may make communication difficult.

In conclusion all telephone calls whether internal or external must be given importance. Callers will receive an impression of the organisation from the way you answer the phone. Make sure you are polite, receptive and let the caller know you are listening. If you are giving information keep it relevant and accurate, if you are receiving information have a pen and paper handy. Don't 'lose' callers when transferring them or leave them to repeat themselves. Use message systems efficiently, both your own and other people's.

Try this exercise.

Here are some examples of sensory words. Which are 'seeing', 'hearing' and 'feeling' words?

sound	grasp	imagine
picture	fight	accent
voice	harmonise	colour
appearance	blunt	touch
search	image	tune in to
celebrate	hate	move
tone	speak	show

Listening

We have said that communication is a two-way process. If you don't listen to what someone is saying they are wasting their time saying it. There is more to listening than simply being within hearing distance of the message. It is possible to tell whether somebody is actively listening, i.e. making an effort to hear and understand, or simply passively listening, i.e. hearing without taking in what is being said. Passive listening involves:

- Listening but not hearing
- Switching off
- Slouching
- Not making eye contact
- Impassive expression

- Moving about restlessly
- Appearing disinterested
- Making no response

Active listening involves:

- Appearing involved
- Leaning towards the speaker
- Making eye contact
- Mirroring the speaker's facial expression
- Nodding or shaking your head
- Paying attention
- Responding with mm, yes, I say, really
- Asking for clarification

Questioning

Questions are used to elicit information. All questions can be categorised as either 'open' questions or 'closed' questions. Closed questions are those which can be answered 'yes' or 'no'. You would use a closed question if you wanted a definite answer. For instance, 'Do you want it copied?' Open questions are used if more information is needed. For instance, 'Do you want it copied in colour or black and white?' Open questions can also be used to get an opinion. For instance, 'How do you think I should lay it out?' Open questions usually begin with 'who', 'what' 'when', 'where', 'how' 'which' and 'why'.

Try this exercise.

Which of the following are open questions?

1. How many copies shall I make?
2. Do you take sugar in your tea?
3. How many sugars do you take in your tea?
4. When is the new copier being delivered?
5. Are we having a day off on Monday?
6. Can I take this down to despatch?
7. Why did you not finish the accounts yesterday?
8. Where is the paper for the printer kept?

Planning

There are a number of methods of planning your work, people who use each method will tell you it is infallible and

the only method to use. Research all the methods, settle on
the one that suits you best and, most importantly, use it.
Remember to include every task however trivial, or those
that are not included will be forgotten.

The simplest method is to make a list at the beginning of
each day of all the tasks that need to be completed or
worked on that day. Add to the list any new tasks that you
are given during the day, cross off any tasks that you
complete and carry forward any tasks that remain
incomplete. This may not mean carrying them forward to
the following day, there may be a task that you are working
on periodically, this will need to be carried forward to the list
for the next day that you are planning to work on that task.

You will need to prioritise the tasks on your list as the
chances are that you will not complete them all within the
day. Categorise the tasks as important, urgent, routine or
trivial. Some tasks will appear in more than one category in
that some routine tasks are important while some urgent
tasks are trivial. Deal with the important first, then the
urgent, but don't ignore the routine as they will become
urgent if they are not dealt with.

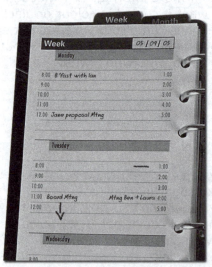

Carrying forward the uncompleted tasks will enable you to
identify those that simply never get done. This may be
because you don't like doing them or because they are too
trivial to ever become urgent. If the reason is that you don't
like doing them, try dealing with one of them as your first job
of the day and rewarding yourself with a cup of coffee when

you have completed it. Look closely at each of the tasks that are not done because they are trivial. Decide if you can delegate them to somebody else or simply stop putting them on the list as it is clearly of no importance whether they ever get done.

A supplementary method to list-making is keeping a diary, either electronic or manual. Some people use the diary to record events or appointments that are to take place at a specific time on a specific day, and keep a separate daily list of tasks; others combine the two by keeping their list in their diary. The benefit of keeping your list in your diary is that it shows in advance where there is likely to be some 'slack' in your workload so that if you are asked to agree a deadline for a task you will be able to look forward and project a completion date.

The limitation of any form of planning simply by listing tasks to be done is that it cannot adequately control complicated tasks that involve several people contributing parts to the whole over a period of time. For this sort of task you will need a separate action plan which analyses the overall task and shows which actions have to be taken when. Each action must have a starting date and a completion date. There should be milestones for key events and specified outcomes.

Choose the method that best meets your requirements, but do not use a mixture of all the methods as this will lead inevitably to confusion and tasks being missed completely. Keep your schedule of tasks to be done constantly to hand and refer to it regularly throughout the day.

Summarising

It is appropriate that this should be the last skill that we deal with in this part as it is the skill of 'abridging or stating the main points of a longer document or speech' and is usually to be found at the end of a document or conversation.

You may be asked to produce a summary of information on a subject prior to a meeting so that the person attending the meeting has all the salient points at hand without having had to read all of the information themselves.

If you are producing a complex report you will usually provide an 'executive summary', which contains the main points of the report, for the same reason, so the reader can understand the main points rather than reading the whole document. The summary appears at the beginning of the report and is the last part written.

You will also summarise conversations whether face-to-face or by telephone to ensure that both parties have understood the requirements of the other. For instance, if you were being asked to carry out a task you would summarise the conversation by saying 'so what you want me to do is...'. If you were taking an order over the telephone you might summarise by saying 'so that's four copies of Wuthering Heights in paperback and 12 copies of Great Expectations, the 1937 version, to be delivered next Wednesday'.

The purpose of summarising your work, or a conversation, is to make a short statement that confirms the main points under discussion and ensures your audience understands the situation completely.

PART 3
Organisational Skills

Organising

Organising work involves allocating tasks between the available people, deciding who is going to do what, by when, as well as organising your own work and your workspace.

The extent to which you will be involved in allocating tasks to other people will depend on your job role. You may think if you have no staff reporting directly to you, you will not be able to delegate tasks, but delegation is a skill which can be practised in any direction, upward and sideward as well as downward. The critical thing to remember is that abdication is not the same thing as delegation. If it is your responsibility to complete a task but you delegate it to a colleague, the responsibility remains yours. You need to be sure the colleague has the necessary skills and experience to complete the task successfully and you must monitor their progress so that you will not lose control of the project.

Organising your work requires discipline. It is difficult to avoid the danger of tasks being neglected because you have forgotten about them if you do not have any system of arranging the flow of work across your desk. Most people do this through the use of an in tray and a pending tray. This means that new work will be placed in the in tray rather than in an untidy pile on your desk where it can be overlooked.

At the start of each day go through the contents of your in tray and make a decision about each piece of paper it contains:

- If it requires no action, either throw it away or file it
- If it requires action, but not by you, pass it on
- If it requires action but you are not in a position to take the action today, diarise the action so that it is not forgotten and put the paper in your pending tray
- If it requires action today, put it on your to do list and return the paper to the in tray

Don't allow the pending tray to become a hiding place for tasks that you don't want to do. A task that can be put off indefinitely doesn't need doing at all.

You may be using electronic methods of organising your outstanding tasks. If you are, the process remains exactly the same, open your 'in tray' daily and make a decision on each entry. The choices remain exactly the same.

You will work much more efficiently if your workspace is well organised. Think about which files, books or reference material you use most often and place these where they are most accessible. For instance, if you keep them in a bookcase place the most often needed in the centre shelves with the things you use only occasionally at the top and the bottom.

You will spend most of your time at your desk so it is important that this is as organised as possible. If you have an L-shaped working area split the two areas so that one is free working space. Put the computer monitor in the corner of the 'L' where it will take up least space. Make sure the telephone is easily accessible and keep a message pad and pen nearby. Organise your drawers so that you know where to lay your hands on:

- Stationery
- Pens and pencils
- Telephone numbers

- Diary
- Dictionary
- Thesaurus
- Calculator
- Address book
- Regularly used documentation

Keep your desk top clear of things you are not using at the time. Always put everything away before you go home at night. You will find it much easier to get started the next day if you have a clear desk when you arrive.

Try this exercise.

Look at your workspace, are the things you use regularly in the most accessible places and the things you rarely use in the least accessible? If you work in an office with lots of desks, is yours the tidiest at the end of the day?

Negotiating

Negotiation is not about getting your own way, it is about reaching a situation where everybody gains. This is known as a win:win situation. The skill involves persuading people to agree rather than in persuading them to change their mind.

It is important to remember that in order for both parties to win, both parties will probably have to agree to lose something. The aim is a compromise that both parties feel comfortable with and if you have to lose a minor battle in order to win the war, this is a small price to pay. Decide before you begin negotiating what you are prepared to lose and what you are absolutely determined not to give up. Try to find out what the other person's 'must haves' are and what they might be prepared to sacrifice. A successful outcome is one in which both keep what they were determined to keep and give up as little as possible of what they were prepared to lose.

At the beginning of negotiation you will need to identify the issue that you are negotiating on and not confuse the problem with the people concerned. It may be that you think you can't work successfully with someone, but if you identify the reasons you think that and negotiate on the reasons, there is a chance that you will find an acceptable compromise. Too often people base their negotiation on their emotions about the issue rather than the facts.

Try to find common ground, that is areas where you both agree, rather than focussing on areas of disagreement. You will often be surprised to find that there is much more common ground than you expected. Try to keep an open-mind and listen actively to what the other person is saying; they may not take the position you are expecting and if you don't listen you may miss an opportunity.

Know when to stop. Recognise when you have achieved your main objective and that you are unlikely to gain any more by continuing and summarise the agreement before the moment passes. Sometimes there is only one moment when everybody is prepared to agree, miss it and the negotiations can go on endlessly.

The stages of negotiation are:

- State your case
- Listen to their case
- Identify common ground
- Give sensible reasons for your views
- Explain the reasons
- Overcome their objections without dismissing them or becoming aggressive
- Confirm agreement

There are people who are naturally good at negotiating, but don't worry if you come up against them; if they are really good they will want you to come out with a win situation too.

Problem solving

Problem solving is a very important activity at work. Unexpected situations are always arising. You or your colleagues can experience all sorts of problems in just one day. Employers value people who can resolve problems calmly. There are six stages to problem solving:

1. **Identify the problem** - This will often be done for you as a customer or colleague will point out that you or your department is not providing the service required. If you are monitoring your own

performance you may have recognised the fact that there is a problem before you are told.

2. **Define the effects of the problem** - If the problem has been pointed out to you by somebody else they will probably have told you what the effects are. For instance, if you have failed to meet a deadline, you will probably have been told in no uncertain terms why it was important. If, on the other hand, you have identified the problem yourself, you need to find out what, if any, the effects have been. You may have a task on your list as a priority and be surprised to find, if you fail to carry it out, that nobody actually notices. Defining the effects of the problem allow you to decide the importance that needs to be given to solving the problem.

3. **Find the cause of the problem** - This stage is not about apportioning blame but about finding out why a problem has arisen. This may require some tact and diplomacy in asking other people what their contribution has been to the problem, or may need some honesty on your own part to admit that the fault lies with you. It may be that you have failed to give the task sufficient priority or that other tasks have been added to your list and caused a backlog.

4. **Identify possible solutions** - If it is a one-off problem then a short-term solution will need to be found; either the task will have to be re-assigned or you may have to stop what you are doing and deal with the problem. Repetitive problems need a longer-term solution. When you have identified the causes you will be able to look at alternative ways of dealing with them. If in the example above additional tasks have caused a backlog, you should have advised the people involved that you would not be able to meet your deadline before the deadline was reached or advised the person giving you the additional tasks that you were unable to take them on as you already had a priority task to complete.

5. **Choose between the solutions** - As in any matter of choice you need to look at the advantages and disadvantages of each solution and identify the one that has the most advantages and the least

disadvantages. In this situation you should weigh up the advantages and disadvantages to the whole organisation rather than to yourself or your department.

6. **Plan the way forward** - If other people are involved in the chosen solution, make sure you involve them in the planning of the way forward to prevent the problem re-occurring. Get the agreement of everyone involved that the chosen solution is the best way forward; involving them in choosing the solution will ensure their commitment to its success.

Decision making

We have touched on decision making in stage five of problem solving. A decision is a choice between two or more possibilities; it is impossible to choose correctly every time so don't despair if you find yourself making the wrong choice. It is only necessary to make a decision when there is more than one possibility. If there is only one option you may decide to delay making a decision. The skill lies in evaluating the choices, making the decision for the right reasons so that even if it turns out to have been an unwise decision you will be able to justify your reasons for making it.

You will be making decisions from the moment you wake up; what shall I wear today, shall I take the car or the bus to work, what shall I have for breakfast? You may feel you make these decisions without giving them a great deal of thought, but the process you go through is the same as the process you use for making major decisions; find the advantages and disadvantages of each option and select the option with the most advantages and least disadvantages.

When making a decision between a number of choices it may be possible to eliminate some as clearly impractical. This may be because the possible solution is far too expensive, will take far too long to implement or involves too great a risk should it fail. This will leave you with a smaller list to choose from. One technique for choosing between several options is to list them and then compare each with the one above and below it, moving them up and down the list. For example, if you were asked to rank the following laptops in order of their suitability for your use:

1. Toshiba Satellite M30X-129
2. Toshiba Satellite M40-149
3. Toshiba Satellite L10-151
4. Toshiba Qosmio F10
5. Toshiba Qosmio G20
6. Toshiba Qosmio G10
7. Goodmans P50
8. Goodmans M40
9. Goodmans M20

First compare No.1 with No.2 looking at the features which matched your needs in each and if No.2 were preferable to No.1 move it to the No.1 position. Compare No.3 with No.2 and again move them to the correct relative position. Continue this process with each pair in turn until you have an agreed ranking. This is known as 'bubble up, bubble down' as each solution can finish anywhere in the list; No.9 could finish at No.1 but will have had to be favourably compared with all the other eight in order to do so.

If the decision is between a number of solutions to a problem it may be that two of the solutions are not mutually exclusive but would complement each other and work better than any single solution. Test your decision by asking a number of questions. If the answer to all the questions is 'yes' you may have found the best solution.

QUESTION	YES	NO
Does it solve the problem?		
Does it solve the cause of the problem?		
Has everybody involved agreed to it?		
Is it practical in terms of cost?		
Is it practical in terms of time?		
Is it practical in terms of people?		
Is it practical in terms of resources?		
Will it prevent the problem re-occurring?		
Have you considered all the disadvantages?		
Have you considered all the consequences?		

Remember that decisions are never final. Circumstances will change and today's best solution may not be tomorrow's. Be open to suggestions to reconsider decisions in the light of new circumstances.

Managing resources

Excluding human resources and time, the majority of resources in an office environment are equipment and stationery. The management of equipment will consist of ensuring that it is kept in good order by arranging regular maintenance, avoiding careless acts that could cause damage and carrying out necessary cleaning.

Stationery resources can be divided into items that you would expect to last for some time and consumables which are used up and thrown away. Items you would expect to last include hole-punches, staplers, calculators, staple removers, scissors, box files and filing trays for example; consumables include paper, note pads, pens, sticky tape, correcting fluid, envelopes, stamps, plastic wallets, disks.

The management of stationery resources includes ordering, receiving, storage and handling. Efficient ordering requires some form of stock control so that you can place orders when stock is needed. Most organisations will operate a maximum and minimum stock level so that, for instance, if the maximum stock level of white C5 envelopes is five boxes of 500 and the minimum is three boxes, whenever the stock level reaches three, two boxes would be ordered to restore the stock to the maximum.

When the goods arrive, check that you have received the quantity and quality that you ordered. If there are any discrepancies report them to the supplier and arrange for the necessary corrective action to be taken.

Plan where items are to be stored taking into account such variables as their weight and the frequency with which they are used. Generally put heavier goods on lower shelves than lighter ones. Rotate stock so that new deliveries are placed behind or underneath existing stock so that the old stock gets used first. You may think this is unimportant with stationery but many items have a limited shelf-life; pens will dry out, the gum on envelopes will lose its stickiness, printer cartridges will dry out. In some cases poor storage conditions will render stationery unusable:

- Envelopes that get damp will seal themselves
- Disks stored near heat or magnets will be useless
- Unwrapped paper will discolour

- Damp paper will jam the printer
- Paper not stored flat will curl
- Sticky tape if stored near heat will lose its stick
- Rubber bands kept too long will perish

When handling stationery remember that paper is a very dense material and boxes of paper may be heavier than you expect. Use correct handling methods when lifting heavy objects. Don't leave boxes in gangways where people might trip over them and don't stack boxes too high as they pose a risk of falling on passers-by as well as possibly injuring someone trying to reach the top box. Handling stationery also involves being careful in its use; if you are photocopying a large number of copies, make one copy first and check that it is correct before finding you have a large number of incorrect copies which have to be thrown away. Don't leave the tops off marker pens, correcting fluid, felt tipped pens, so that when you come to use them again they have dried out. Store paper at the correct temperature and in a dry place to prevent deterioration.

You will also need to consider security of resources; should the stationery cupboard be kept locked and items issued only in exchange for requisitions so that a check on usage can be maintained? Most people these days will have a use for stationery consumables at home and while you may think the taking of one biro or a couple of disks is not important, if every member of staff helped themselves regularly the cost of stationery would soon get out of hand.

Managing time

Time is the one resource that cannot be replaced. Although time is infinite we never have enough of it. You need to make the best use of every minute of your time at work, but this does not mean you need to be 'doing' something all the time. Time spent planning and reviewing is time well spent.

Do you know how you spend your time at work now? You probably think you spend most of your time on the important tasks that you have to complete each day, but you might be surprised to find how much time you actually spend on the trivia. You might think that a few minutes spent on an unnecessary task don't matter too much, but if you work out how much your time is worth you might be surprised. Try the following calculation:

- Multiply your monthly salary by 1.5 to allow for overheads
- Divide by four
- Divide by the number of hours you work in a week
- Divide by 60

This will give you the cost to the organisation of every minute of your time. Next time you spend five minutes staring out of the window, think about how much it has cost.

If you have kept a log of your time and analysed it you will probably find that you are spending 60% of your time on routine tasks, 25% on urgent tasks and 15% on important tasks; you should be spending exactly the opposite proportions, 60% on important tasks, 25% on urgent tasks and only 15% on routine tasks.

The chart below may help.

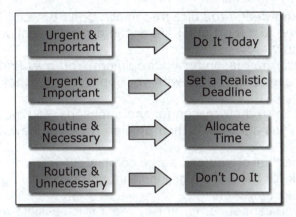

Be realistic when planning. Don't plan more than you know you can achieve, it will de-motivate both you and others involved if you consistently fail to achieve everything you have planned for the day.

Be flexible, remember 'the best laid plans of mice and men often go awry'. Demands will change and your plans will need to change to reflect the new priorities. The important thing is to re-adjust to accommodate the new demands, not just to push everything back.

Resolving disagreement

With the best will in the world you will have occasional disagreements with colleagues. Each of us is different and we all have to learn to adapt our actions to suit the situation. What works one day with one person may be completely unsuitable on another day with someone else.

We all bring our own experiences, attitudes and needs to any situation; two or more people trying to work in harmony will find that their approaches may clash because of this. This may lead to disagreement, which is not necessarily a bad thing as conflict can lead to innovation; it is the way that the disagreement is handled that decides whether the experience is positive or negative.

When you find you are in disagreement with a colleague:

- Acknowledge the disagreement. Don't pretend to agree just for a quiet life or the disagreement will simply grow
- State the reason for your opinion. You may find your colleague will agree with your opinion once they have heard it
- Listen to their reason for their opinion. You may find you will agree with their opinion once you have heard it
- If neither of you can agree completely with the other, look for the middle ground that you can both agree a compromise on
- If you cannot compromise, see if it is possible to 'agree to disagree' and carry on working
- If compromise is not possible and a solution is essential, seek mediation

From time to time you may find yourself in the position of being asked to mediate between two colleagues who have been unable to resolve disagreement between them. This is not an easy situation to be put in and you will have to:

- Be careful not to take sides. Let each have their say and try to let them find a solution
- Make sure the discussion is about the issues and not the personalities. However, it is not always possible to keep emotions out of things so allow for them
- Summarise regularly to make sure that both the protagonists understand what is being said
- Remember the object is to achieve agreement so focus everybody's efforts on this
- Be prepared to make the decision for them if after every opportunity they are unable to reach a compromise

Remember that over a period of time decisions will tend to even out; none of us wins every conflict, the important thing is not to bear a grudge when you don't get our own way but to put it behind you and move on.

Team working

A team is a group of people working collectively to achieve a common aim. You will find yourself working in a number of teams during your career, indeed if you work in a large or complex organisation you will probably find yourself working in more than one team at a time. Within the organisation you may be part of the accounts team for instance, at the same time as being part of a project team; you will also be part of a team that stretches outside of the organisation to include your contacts in suppliers, customers and contractors. As the various teams are likely to overlap it is essential that there is effective communication both within the team and between the teams.

Each member of a team has their own strengths and weaknesses and you will need to integrate those with your own if you are to work effectively.

Successful teams have the following characteristics:

- **Honesty** - Members of the team must be prepared to express their opinions openly with the rest of the team
- **Willingness** - to take on any task. There are bound to be jobs that you would not choose to do, but in a team each must be prepared to do what is needed
- **Clear objectives** - Every member of the team must understand their purpose and be committed to its achievement
- **Results oriented** - The focus in a team must be on achieving its goals rather than on the process required
- **Mutual trust** - You must be able to rely on every other member of the team to achieve their part of the whole
- **Support** - Each member of the team needs to know that if they are having difficulty completing their part they can expect help from others

Each member of a team will have their own role, utilising their individual skills to the best advantage of the team. For instance, to produce a magazine the features editor will choose the subjects to be included; writers will write the articles; sales staff will sell the advertising; graphics designers will organise the layout; sub-editors will edit the content; printers will print the magazine and the distribution manager will see that copies reach the news stands. Each will be taking their particular role because it best matches their skills.

Each team needs people to undertake one or more of the following roles:

- **Initiator** - The person who starts the whole process
- **Clarifier** - The person who turns generalisations into specifics
- **Information provider** - The person who either has the knowledge the team needs or knows where to get it
- **Questioner** - The person who raises doubts in the team and challenges assumptions
- **Summariser** - The person who doesn't add anything new but ensures the team knows how far it has got
- **Supporter** - The person who supports members of the team as necessary
- **Joker** - The person who helps the team to keep their perspective
- **Process observer** - The person who overcomes difficulties by referring to a known method

There may or may not be an appointed team leader, but the leadership role will be assumed by one or other of the team depending on the situation. Leadership is derived from power, and power comes from a variety of sources, the importance of which will vary from situation to situation.

Whatever their roles in the team it is vital that everyone knows what the goals of the team are and is kept informed of the team's progress towards achieving those goals. There are various ways of motivating team members, some organisations have set incentives while others leave this to the team leader.

In any team there will always be people you get on with better than others. There will always be some people that you just don't understand, but that doesn't mean you can't work with them. Everybody has some positive attributes, if you concentrate on those you will be able to find a way of working together.

PART 4
Operational Skills

Researching

Effective research is the searching for and bringing together of information relevant to a purpose. Usually this will be carried out in response to a request for information from your line manager or supervisor or for an internal or external customer. This request for information may be from inside or outside the organisation. If you are asked to research a subject it is important to be thorough and find all of the available information; the obscure fact that you are tempted to overlook may be the decisive factor in the decision that is made as a result of the research. At the same time you must be careful not to be sidetracked into including information that is not directly relevant to your search.

When asked to research information make sure you get clear 'terms of reference' so you know exactly what it is you have been asked for. The terms of reference should cover how much or how little information is required, by when and in what format and how the information should be reported. If in any doubt seek clarification from the person asking for the information before you waste time producing irrelevant or unnecessary information.

Once you are sure what it is you are going to research, you need to decide where you are going to research. There are four main sources of information available:

- Previous research you may have carried out
- Paper-based reference material
- The internet
- The experience of other people

Each of these has short-cuts which will reduce the time taken to research the information. You will be able to find information in previous research you may have carried out if you have kept accurate and comprehensive records of the research and properly referenced them so that the information in them can be readily accessed.

Paper-based reference material includes reference books, publications, company documents, catalogues, price lists, directories. There are short-cuts to looking up information in reference books:

- **Look in the preface** - This will help you decide whether there is likely to be useful information in the book
- **Look at the publication date** - This will tell you how up to date the information is
- **Look in the index** - Using the key word that will lead you to the pages where the subject you are looking for may be found
- **Look in the contents** - This may lead you to the chapter that is relevant
- **Look in the bibliography** - This will guide you to other books that might be useful

The Internet holds information on almost everything; the drawback is that there is so much information it can be difficult to find exactly what you are looking for. The short-cut on the internet is to use a good 'search engine'. Having chosen your search engine there are some tips for narrowing the search:

- Think of keywords you would expect to find in the article you are searching for
- Avoid using lengthy combinations of keywords
- Start with seven words
- Spell the keywords correctly
- Use a thesaurus to choose keywords
- Use lower case letters

To use the experience of other people, start with those in your own network and ask them if they have any information on the subject you are researching. Then ask if they know anybody who has any information and ask them, if necessary, to introduce you to them.

At this stage gather together all the relevant information you can find, discarding none until you have compiled all of it.

Try this exercise.

Research all the appropriate qualifications available to you in the Business & Administration field.

Analysing

Analysis is the examination of facts in sufficient detail to understand them or discover more about them. In an office environment it is used to examine information that has been gathered by research in order to draw conclusions.

A frequently used method of analysis is SWOT analysis, in which the strengths, weaknesses, opportunities and threats of a situation are compared. The strengths and weaknesses focus on the internal environment and the opportunities and threats focus on the external environment.

Analysis reduces an unmanageable volume of information to an amount that can be handled more easily. This is not necessarily done by discarding information but by combining two or more pieces of information to produce a third, allowing the original information to be discarded.

Try this exercise.

Analyse the qualifications which you researched and identify those that are most suitable for you.

Noting

A note is something that is written down, often in abbreviated form, as a record or a reminder. You may make notes during a meeting, on the bus or train on the way to work, when you are being given instructions or when taking a message.

Nobody can remember everything that is said during a meeting, or exactly what instructions they have been given, or all the details of a complex message. Rather than try, it is best to jot down notes which will enable you to recall the main points and fill in the gaps later.

If you have a difficult task to complete when you get to work you may choose to make notes during your journey to work. It is best not to try to write out whole sentences but just to write headings or keywords to remind you of the ideas you had.

Most people have developed their own individual method of note taking. Some write just the keywords and omit all of the connecting language, some write as much as they can, often abbreviating the words; for example, two people attending a meeting and making notes of a decision to increase the fees for conveyancing from £80 per hour to £90 per hour with effect from the following Monday might make the following notes:

- conveyance fees £90 Monday
- inc. fees conv. 80-90 w.e.f. Mon

Don't try to write down every word as, although you may be able to do so, the meeting will have moved on and you will have missed the next point. Even if you are able to write shorthand you cannot concentrate on taking part in the meeting and write verbatim notes at the same time.

Whatever method you adopt, it is unlikely that anybody else will be able to make sense of the notes you take. Even you may find it difficult to remember exactly what they meant after a time, so it is important that you make use of them as quickly as possible, either taking the action the notes are to remind you to take or expanding on the notes to make a fuller record.

Try this exercise.

Find a busy spot and make notes on what you see. This may be:

- A busy road junction. Note the make, model and colour of the first 20 cars that pass

- A busy bus stop or train station. Note as much as you can about the first 20 people that get off a bus or train

These are only suggestions, you can choose any situation where you can take notes on what is happening but you don't have time to write full details. Don't forget to note anything unusual that may happen while you are there.

Now imagine that an incident has occurred during your note taking and you are asked to supply the fullest possible details of every car that passed or person that was in the area. Write up a witness statement from your notes.

Designing

Designing is the planning or making of something in a skilful or artistic way. Its most common use in an administrative setting will be in creating presentations. The effective use of design will make slides more attractive and interesting.

Anything well designed will adhere to certain elements and principles. The elements of design are the things that make up the slide; the principles of design are what you do to the elements.

The elements of design are:

- Line
- Shape
- Direction
- Size
- Texture
- Colour
- Value

The principles of design are:

- **Balance** - A large shape close to the centre of the slide can be balanced by a small shape close to the edge. A large light shape will be balanced by a small dark shape
- Gradation - Gradation of size and direction produce linear perspective. Gradation of colour from warm to cool and tone from dark to light produce aerial

perspective. Gradation from dark to light causes the eye to move along the shape

- **Repetition** - Repetition with variation is interesting, without variation repetition becomes monotonous
- **Contrast** - The major contrast should be located at the centre of interest
- **Harmony** - Harmony is achieved by combining similar, related elements such as adjacent colours on the colour wheel, similar shapes etc
- **Dominance** - Dominance can be applied to one or more of the elements to give emphasis
- **Unity** - Unity refers to the visual linking of various elements

A well designed slide show will consider all of the elements and principles of design in order to add interest and make the presentation more effective. For instance red is the most exciting colour, green the most restful and blue the most cheerful so thoughtful use of colour will help you get the message across. Be careful of overuse of colours as different colours have different physical effects on the audience.

Checking

The purpose of checking is to confirm the accuracy of text, data or figures. Before sending out any form of information or irrevocably entering it into the system, it is important that you check its accuracy. Sending out inaccurate information will, at the very least, give a poor impression. At worst it could lead to serious consequences if decisions are made based on the inaccurate information. Inputting inaccurate information into a spreadsheet or database can lead to effects far more serious than the original error, for instance, if you input incorrect dosage information onto a patient's records the effects could be catastrophic.

Probably the best way to check the accuracy of text is to first use the spell check facility and the grammar check facility on your computer to pick up any blatant errors. Then print a draft copy as it is usually easier to proof read on paper than on screen. At this point you will be looking for errors that cannot be picked up electronically such as the substitution of one word for another. At the same time you will be looking for more subtle changes that may be required such as the order in which facts are presented or repetition.

When inputting data to a database it is essential that you check the accuracy before you complete a record as the database will automatically be updated on completion of each record. There is only one way to do this, and that is to input the data then check against the source document before completing the record.

Figures are probably the most difficult when it comes to checking because every single digit must be checked against the source document. Whereas words with transposed letters will stand out as incorrect, transposed figures will appear to be as accurate as correct figures. When inputting rows of figures it is a good idea to use a ruler to prevent your eye from straying from the line of figures. It may also be possible to check the accuracy of figures by estimating the outcome. For instance if the total number of hours worked in a week by an employee comes to 375 there is a strong chance that you have input the decimal point in the wrong place!

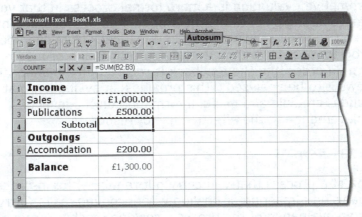

If you are using a printing calculator to total a column of figures, check the print-out against the source document, ticking each entry in case you get interrupted in the middle. If you are using a non-printing calculator input the figures twice to check that the same result is achieved.

Evaluating

Evaluating is a systematic objective examination of the way that things are done. There are two types of evaluating:

- Formative evaluation looks at the way things are being done at present to judge whether you are doing the right things in the right way
- Summative evaluation looks at a project after completion or processes after amendments have been put in place to judge their efficiency, effectiveness, impact and sustainability

You will be using formative evaluation regularly to assess all the things that you do on a day-to-day basis to see if there are any improvements that can be made. Self-evaluation involves reviewing your regular tasks to confirm that you are using the most efficient methods to complete them. External evaluation involves asking the people you do the tasks for and those you work with for feedback. They will be able to tell you if you are satisfying their requirements and give you any suggestions for how completing the task may be made easier.

Summative evaluation is a more formal process in that you are evaluating a specific project or change of process. This can be done by seeking structured feedback from everybody involved, possibly by the use of a questionnaire or feedback form, in order that the feedback is received in a manner that allows it to be analysed. This provides an evaluation that includes credible and useful information on the level of achievement and the effective use of resources.

Try this exercise.

Look at a process that you carry out regularly, for instance organising a meeting or dealing with incoming mail. Carry out an evaluation of the process, seeking feedback from all those involved and write an evaluation report.

Recording

Recording is keeping an account of something, preserved in a lasting form, e.g. in writing or electronically. The decisions that have to be made in an administrative environment are:

- **What to record** - Basically you should record anything that you may need to refer to at a later date. You will need to bear in mind the principle of the Data Protection Act 2000 which states 'personal data shall be obtained only for one or more specified and lawful purposes' when recording any personal information. The temptation is to record everything 'because it might be useful one day' so a degree of selectivity is required

- **How to record it** - Essentially there are two choices, hard copy or electronic record. Legal documents and others requiring original signatures to be retained will need to be recorded in hard copy. Most other records can be recorded electronically as hard copies can be produced should they be required
- **How to reference records for ease of retrieval** - Whether your records are in hard copy or electronic it is important that you are able to find them quickly when necessary. Hard copy records can be filed alphabetically, numerically, alpha-numerically or chronologically; electronic records can be filed in folders or directories
- **How long to record it for** - There are three criteria to consider; some records such as payroll records and VAT records for instance, must be retained for specific periods; the Data Protection Act 1998 states that personal records 'shall not be kept for longer than is necessary'; records should be kept only as long as they are useful

The overriding issue in recording anything is that the recording must be accurate; inaccurate records can cause all manner of confusion and problems for your organisation.

Presenting information

Whether you are going to present information in writing or verbally, you will need to organise your material so that your presentation has a clear beginning, middle and end. There are a number of techniques which will help you to get started:

- **List the ideas you want to cover** - For instance an announcement of a meeting may include the time and place, people involved, reason for the meeting, any preparation required and any follow-up action needed
- **Use index cards** - Write each idea on a card, lay out all the cards on a flat surface and move the cards around until you get the ideas into a coherent order

- **Use Post-it notes** - Similar to index cards except that you can stick your Post-it notes with the ideas written on onto the wall and move them about

If you struggle to start, give yourself a limited amount of time to think and, at the end of that time, write whatever you have thought of. It is as likely to be as useful as anything you will come up with if you sit endlessly waiting for inspiration.

There are a number of different ways that you can organise the ideas. Probably the most often used is to state your ideas in the order of their importance. Using this method means that:

- The recipient will understand the purpose of the communication immediately
- If not all the information is read, the most important will be
- People can make their minds up whether to read the information or not more quickly

An alternative is to organise your ideas in chronological order. This simply means putting it in date order either by listing past events starting with the earliest, or listing future events starting with the soonest.

A third option, similar to chronological, is sequential. This involves listing the events in the order in which they will occur without allocating times or dates to them.

A further method is to organise the information into two sets that can be compared with each other for instance, if recommending the purchase of a laser printer over an inkjet printer you might state the features of the laser printer followed by the comparable features of the inkjet printer.

Try this exercise:

You have been asked to write a report on the feasibility of launching a new insurance product. Below are the ideas that you have produced on your index cards, sort them into the final order that they will appear in the report.

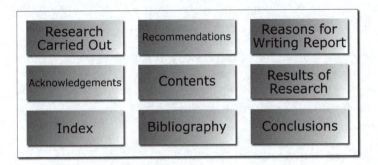

CHAPTER 2
UNIT 110 – Ensure your own actions reduce risks to health and safety

It is important that the workplace is safe and conducive to the health of everybody who works there and any visitors or customers. Any organisation with more than five employees must publish a Health and Safety Policy which should include:

- An outline of the policy
- Steps to be taken to fulfil the policy
- The legal responsibilities of employer and employees
- Information on training opportunities
- Information on how the policy will be displayed
- Plans to review and revise the policy
- Details of any relevant Codes of Practice
- Procedures for reporting accidents
- Names of those responsible for health and safety
- Reference to the organisation's rules on health and safety

No one wants to work somewhere that is unsafe, and visitors certainly don't want to feel in danger, or uncomfortable, when they enter the premises. It is your responsibility as much as anybody else's to look out for potential hazards and to observe safe working practices.

Electrical equipment in particular is a source of hazards. You should not attempt any repairs or maintenance of electrical equipment unless you are properly qualified. The hazards to be aware of include:

- Insufficient insulation
- Lack of earth connection
- Incorrectly wired plugs or sockets
- Faulty wiring
- Worn insulation
- Poorly routed cables
- Incorrect fuse rating

Any of the above can lead to fire. A single spark can start a major fire. Sometimes the danger is not immediately apparent but there are warning signs that you should be aware of:

- Plugs or cables giving off excess heat
- Flickering lights or unreliable electrical supply
- Sparking noises
- Fuses blowing frequently
- A smell of burning

Other common causes of fire include:

- Overloaded electrical sockets
- Electrical equipment not switched off and disconnected overnight
- Smoking
- Heaters

Accidents can be very costly, and in the event of serious accidents they must be reported to the Health and Safety Executive. Compensation claims have become much more common in recent years. The law recognises that people and organisations are accountable for their actions, but claims are paid for out of the organisation's profits, which in turn impact on the job security of its employees. Dangerous occurrences, which are events that didn't actually cause any injury but could have done, also have to be reported. An example of this would be a fire caused by an electrical fault leading to the building being closed for more than 24 hours.

An important part of reducing risks to health and safety is good housekeeping. This involves ensuring the offices are kept clean, light bulbs are replaced as soon as they blow, broken furniture is repaired or replaced promptly, equipment is maintained properly, worn carpets are replaced and particular attention is paid to the condition of stairs and landings. Other areas that require attention include:

- Separate toilets should be provided for men and women, these should be well ventilated, clean, in working order and easily accessible
- A ventilated space must be provided between toilets and working areas
- Provision of wash basins with hot and cold running water
- Provision of soap and towels or a hand drier
- Regular emptying of waste bins
- Provision of clean drinking water
- Somewhere to heat up and eat food and drink

It is also important to consider the customer's perception of the organisation. If a customer is involved in an accident on the premises, they are not likely to hold the organisation in high regard and may not wish to deal with them again and may even seek compensation from your employer through legal action.

When ensuring your own actions reduce risks to health and safety you will need the following skills:

- Reading
- Analysing
- Decision making
- Communicating
- Working safely
- Personal presentation

These skills are covered in chapter 1.

Health and Safety Legislation

Legislation makes health and safety at work everybody's responsibility, including yours. There are a number of relevant Acts of Parliament including:

Health and Safety at Work Act 1974 - This makes it the employer's duty to provide:

- Safe entry and exit routes in and out of the workplace
- A safe working environment and adequate welfare facilities
- Safe equipment and systems of work
- Arrangements for ensuring the safe use, handling, storage and transport of articles and substances
- Information on health and safety, instruction, training and supervision
- The thorough investigation of any accidents

It also makes it the employee's duty to:

- Take reasonable care for their own health and safety
- Take reasonable care for the health and safety of other people who may be affected by their actions
- Co-operate with his or her employer or any other person carrying out duties under the Act

Reporting of Injuries, Diseases and Dangerous Occurrences Regulations (RIDDOR) - This compels organisations to:

- Notify the Health and Safety Executive if any accidents occur which have caused serious or fatal injuries or have resulted in a lengthy period off work of an employee or employees
- Keep records of all notifiable injuries, dangerous occurrences and diseases

Control of Substances Hazardous to Health (COSHH) - These require organisations to:

- Identify any hazardous substances in use
- Eliminate the use of the substance if possible
- Substitute a safe substance where possible
- Enclose the substance so as few people as possible come into contact with it

Noise at Work Regulations - These require employers to:

- Assess noise hazards in the workplace
- Reduce noise hazards where possible
- Keep employees informed of noise hazards
- Provide ear protectors

The Management of Health and Safety at Work Regulations - These require employers to:

- Carry out risk assessments which assess significant risks both to employees and others affected by the organisation
- Keep a record of the assessment and the measures which have been identified to control the risk if there are more than five employees
- Appoint competent people to implement and monitor the health and safety arrangements
- Make arrangements to plan, organise, control, maintain and review health and safety arrangements
- Set up emergency procedures to deal with situations of serious or imminent danger
- Provide full information and training to all employees plus details of any risks involved in their work

Workplace (Health, Safety and Welfare) Regulations - These state minimum legal standards for:

- **Health** – lighting, ventilation and temperature; space and room dimensions; workstations and seating; cleanliness
- **Safety** – maintenance of the workplace and equipment, floors, windows and skylights; doors, gates and escalators; traffic routes, falls and falling objects
- **Welfare** – toilets and washing facilities; drinking water; changing rooms, rest rooms and eating facilities

Display Screen Equipment (DSE) Regulations - These apply to all who regularly use Visual Display Units (VDUs) in their work, and relate to workstations as well as the equipment. They require employers to:

- Assess all workstations for health and safety risks and lower the risks as much as possible
- Plan work activities to incorporate rest breaks at regular intervals
- Arrange and pay for eye tests and pay for spectacles or lenses if these are prescribed specifically for VDU work
- Provide health and safety training for DSE users and re-train if the workstation is changed or modified
- Provide DSE users with information on all aspects of health and safety which apply to them and measures being taken to reduce risks to their health

Provision and Use of Work Equipment Regulations - Work equipment means any type of machine, appliance, apparatus or tools used at work. They require the employer to:

- Ensure that all equipment is suitable for the task and kept well maintained
- Take into account working conditions and potential hazards when selecting new equipment
- Issue appropriate information, instructions and training on its use
- Restrict access when necessary

Personal Protective Equipment at Work Regulations - These require employers to:

- Provide suitable personal protective equipment (PPE) without charge
- Ensure the PPE is suitable and fits properly
- Ensure the PPE is maintained in good condition

- Store the PPE safely
- Provide information on its use

Manual Handling Operations Regulations - These require employers to:

- Avoid any manual handling operations in which employees could be injured
- Assess and reduce the risk of injury as much as possible
- Provide employees with information on specific loads which will help them avoid risk

Every organisation that employs more than ten people must keep an accident book. This must record:

- Details of the injured person (name, address, age)
- Details of any injury sustained
- Details of the accident (what happened, when, where)
- First aid or medical treatment given
- Names of any witnesses

When the accident book is full it must be kept for three years after the date of the last entry.

16 Report Number

16 Report Number

ACCIDENT RECORD

1 About the person who had the accident

Name Abigail Inskip

Address 10 Rosedale Ave, Norwood, London

Postcode SE19 3PN

Occupation PA to CEO

2 About you, the person filling in this record

▼ If you did not have the accident write your address and occupation.

Name Heather Bellis

Address 6 Graphite Square, Vauxhall Walk, London

Postcode SE11 5EE

Occupation Office Manager

3 About the accident *Continue on the back of this form if you need to*

▼ Say when it happened.   Date 21 / 07 / 2005   Time 1025

▼ Say where it happened. State which room or place.

CEO's office, OfA offices

▼ Say how the accident happened. Give the cause if you can.

...ang on the...

What you need to know

How the legislation applies to your job role

Whose responsibility is it to provide safe equipment and systems of work?

Where escape routes are and why they must be kept un-blocked

What hazardous substances are in use in your workplace?

How your workplace complies with the Display Screen Equipment Regulations

What is the minimum legal temperature in your workplace?

Whether Personal Protective Equipment is in use in your workplace

What is the correct method of lifting heavy objects?

Identifying hazards and evaluating risks

A hazard is a situation or an object that has the potential to cause injury, harm or ill health. A risk is the likelihood of something causing harm because the hazard, or potential hazard, exists. All organisations are required to carry out Risk Assessments which will identify where hazards exist and evaluate what the risks are. There are five steps to carrying out an efficient Risk Assessment.

STEP 1: LOOK FOR THE HAZARDS

Walk around your workplace and look at what could reasonably be expected to cause harm. Only look at significant hazards which could result in serious harm or affect several people. Ask your colleagues if they have noticed anything that might be a potential hazard, as they may have noticed something that is not immediately obvious. Look at accident records for trends or patterns to see if these can shed some light on dangers in your workplace.

STEP 2: DECIDE WHO MIGHT BE HARMED AND HOW

As well as full-time members of staff consider people who are not in the workplace full-time such as cleaners, visitors, contractors, maintenance people and, of course, customers.

STEP 3: WHAT ARE THE RISKS, WHAT IS BEING DONE?

There are probably precautions and systems in place already to reduce the risks created by the hazards that you have identified. What you have to decide for each significant hazard is whether the remaining risk is high, medium or low.

- Ask yourself whether everything has been done that the law says must be done
- If so ask yourself whether everything has been done that you would normally expect
- Then ask yourself whether there is still something practical that could be done to reduce the risk

If you find something needs to be done consider whether the hazard can be removed completely or, if not, how the risk can be controlled so that it can be significantly reduced.

STEP 4: RECORD YOUR FINDINGS

If your workplace has five or more employees the Risk Assessment must be recorded. This must show:

- The significant hazards
- Your conclusions
- That a proper check was made
- That employees who might be affected were asked
- That all obvious significant hazards were dealt with
- Precautions are reasonable
- The remaining risk is low

The written document should be kept for future reference. It will help to show that the organisation has done what the law requires.

STEP 5: REVIEW YOUR ASSESSMENT

It is not sufficient to carry out a Risk Assessment once, file it, and then forget about it until you are asked to produce it.

Things will inevitably change in the workplace; new equipment, new employees, new work practices. Anything that produces new hazards will mean a new Risk Assessment will need to be carried out.

You may feel that Health and Safety is the responsibility of someone else in the organisation, and, in fact, if you work in a reasonably large organisation there will be named people responsible for it. Remember, however, under The Health and Safety at Work Act everybody is responsible for taking reasonable care for the health and safety of themselves and others who may be affected by their actions.

If you come across a hazard that you can deal with immediately, for instance, a fire extinguisher propping open a fire-door or a carton left in a corridor, it is your responsibility to deal with it there and then. If you come across a hazard that you cannot deal with immediately for instance the fire door is padlocked, it is your responsibility to report it there and then to somebody who can deal with it.

If your organisation has appointed Health and Safety representatives and First Aiders, make sure you know who they are and how they can be contacted.

 What you need to know

Who your First Aiders are

> What should you do if you find a hole in the stair carpet?

Who your Health and Safety representatives are

> How should you deal with an unknown liquid spill on the floor in the corridor?

The five steps to Risk Assessment

> How can you contact your First Aiders and Health and Safety Representatives?

Why is it important to deal with risks immediately?

Reducing risks to health and safety

You may think that an office is among the safest of places to work, but there are many hazards in even the most modern, up to date, paper-free environment. Everyone must be involved in noticing and either dealing with or reporting any risks.

It is probable that more working days are lost through illness caused by the actual office environment than there are through injury caused by accidents at work. You may not have considered that even the colour of the walls can have a significant effect. Paint or wallpaper should be a restful shade as patterns and bright colours can cause headaches. Nylon carpets can increase the risk of static electric shocks, while windows need curtains or blinds if there is a possibility of bright sunshine on computer screens.

Lighting and furniture are important. Background lighting should be restrained, complemented with directional light over work areas to reduce eye-strain. Desks should be large enough to take all the equipment and paperwork needed and high enough to get your legs under. Chairs should have a five-star base, adjustable seats and backs that give support. Filing cabinets need to be fitted with a device that prevents more than one drawer being opened at a time.

Computers can be a major source of problems. Using a monitor, or VDU, can cause headaches, eye-strain, neck problems, repetitive strain injury and stress. Of course, it is not the computer that causes the problems, it is the use of the computer. To avoid some of these there are steps that you can take:

- Sit on an adjustable chair with your back supported. Your arms should be horizontal when on the keyboard and the monitor should be immediately in front of your eyes
- Make sure the screen is the right distance from your eyes to enable you to focus easily. If necessary change the zoom facility

- Consider using a wrist rest to prevent repetitive strain injury and a foot rest to improve your posture to reduce the risk of back, shoulder and neck strain
- Adjust the screen brightness to reduce glare
- Clean the screen regularly to prevent the need to squint
- Take regular short breaks

If you have to lift and carry things in your work such as files, stationery, etc., use correct lifting techniques. If the load is too heavy to carry, use a trolley.

- Keep your back straight, lift with the legs and bend the knees
- Keep arms close to the body
- When pushing and pulling, tuck your chin in, keep your back and arms straight
- When pushing use your front foot for balance and your rear foot for thrust
- When pulling use your rear foot for balance and your front foot with knee bent for thrust

To prevent accidents with equipment there are a few simple rules to follow:

- Don't overload filing cabinets
- Don't open more than one drawer at a time
- Don't place liquids on or near any electrical equipment
- Don't remove any safety guards
- Be careful not to get clothing, hair or jewellery caught in equipment
- If anything gets jammed in equipment don't try to free it without switching off
- Make sure you know where and how to disconnect equipment in an emergency
- Don't attempt to repair equipment unless you are sure you know how and are authorised to
- Inform your supervisor immediately if equipment breaks down or fails to work, switch it off and put an out-of-order notice on it

Common causes of injury in offices are slips, trips and falls. Make sure any spillages are mopped up immediately they occur. Always close drawers after you have used them to avoid the risk of people falling over them or walking into them. Don't leave items such as boxes and handbags where people can trip over them. Be careful that cables are not left trailing, particularly when furniture and equipment are moved. This is not only a trip hazard but can also cause damage to the cables which could lead to risk of fire or electrocution. Portable equipment can be dangerous if not properly maintained. Look out for damaged plugs, sockets and leads. Don't use chairs or boxes to stand on to reach objects on high shelves or off the top of cabinets. Always use steps and make sure they are well-maintained.

Potentially the most devastating risk is fire. The priority must be to prevent fire, and to minimise the effect should one start. To prevent fire:

- Report any faulty equipment or wiring
- Switch off any faulty equipment until it has been repaired
- If smoking is allowed ensure cigarettes are properly extinguished and ashtrays are emptied into metal bins
- Don't put papers, clothing, etc., near heaters or equipment that gets hot
- Switch off all equipment at the end of the day

To minimise the effect of fire:

- Take fire drills seriously
- Don't block fire doors or fire exits
- Don't prop fire doors open
- Know where the fire exits are
- Know where your assembly point is

- Know where fire fighting equipment is and its uses
- Know how to raise the alarm

If you discover a fire raise the alarm and follow your organisation's procedures. This may require you to evacuate the building in all circumstances or may allow for attempts to extinguish the fire if it is small. In this case you will need to know what fire fighting equipment there is and how to use it. Equipment may include fire blankets which can be used to smother the flames, buckets of sand and fire extinguishers. Fire extinguishers come in a number of types which can be identified by colour coding.

Colour	Contents	Use
Red	Water	Most fires except liquids or electrical appliances
Blue	Dry powder	Flammable liquids or electrical appliances
Green	Halon	Flammable liquids or electrical appliances but not in confined spaces
Black	Carbon Dioxide	Flammable liquids or electrical appliances but not in confined spaces
Cream	Foam	Flammable liquids

If you are the first on the scene of an accident it is important that you know how to react. If you are not a first aider it is vital that you know who the first aiders are and how to contact them quickly. There are a number of basic rules to follow:

- Is it safe for you to approach the casualty?
- Do not move the injured person
- Is the casualty conscious?
- Check to see if their airway is blocked
- Check whether they are breathing
- Check the casualties circulation by taking their pulse at the wrist or neck
- Give any first aid that you are trained to give or find your companies trained first aider
- Place the patient in the recovery position and keep them warm
- Loosen any tight clothing
- Don't offer food, drink or cigarettes
- Dial 999 for an ambulance and stay on the line so that the operator can take all of your details

You also need to know how to deal with different types of medical emergency.

- In the case of someone who is bleeding badly, elevate the wound and apply pressure with a sterile dressing
- Where someone has been burnt or scalded, run cool water over the burn. Do not pull clothing off the wound
- If someone has had an electric shock, turn off the electricity before you touch them or you are likely to get a shock as well
- If someone is choking, encourage them to cough at first. If this does not work then deliver short sharp slaps between their shoulder blades to dislodge the item

Make sure you know the limits of your ability to deal with emergencies and don't attempt anything you have not been trained or feel confident to do. In all of the cases above the casualty should go to the local Emergency Department.

What you need to know

The steps that can be taken to avoid health problems connected with the use of computer equipment

What can you do to reduce the risk of fire?

Correct lifting techniques

What type of fire extinguisher should be used on an electrical equipment fire?

Actions that can be taken to minimise the effects of fire

What type of fire extinguisher should be used on a paper fire?

Your organisation's health and safety
policy

Who should you report electrical
hazards to?

The benefits of good housekeeping

What indications might there be that an
electrical fire is imminent?

The time to decide what to do in the case of an emergency is BEFORE the emergency happens

Are you ready for assessment?

To achieve this unit of a Level 2 Business & Administration qualification you will need to demonstrate that you are competent in the following:

- Correctly name and locate the persons responsible for health and safety in your workplace
- Identify which workplace policies are relevant to your working practices
- Identify those working practices in any part of your job role which could harm yourself or other persons
- Identify those aspects of the workplace which could harm yourself or others
- Evaluate which of the potentially harmful aspects of the workplace are those with the highest risks to you or to others
- Report those hazards with a high risk to the persons responsible for health and safety in the workplace
- Deal with those hazards with low risks following workplace policies and legal requirements
- Carry out your working practices in accordance with legal requirements
- Follow the most recent workplace policies for your job role
- Put right those health and safety risks that you are able to within the scope of your job responsibilities
- Pass on any suggestions for reducing risks to health and safety within your job role to the responsible persons
- Make sure your personal conduct in the workplace does not endanger the health and safety of yourself or others
- Follow the workplace policies and suppliers' or manufacturers' instructions for the safe use of equipment, materials and products
- Report any differences between workplace policies and suppliers' or manufacturers' instructions as appropriate

- Make sure your personal presentation at work ensures the health and safety of yourself and others; meets any legal duties and is in accordance with workplace policies

(Remember that you will need the skills listed at the beginning of this chapter and that these are covered in chapter 1.)

Your Assessor will need you to produce evidence from a variety of sources. If you carry out the activities that follow they will provide some of the evidence for you.

Activity 1
Draw a floor plan of your workplace indicating:

- Fire exits
- Position of fire equipment
- Location of first aid boxes
- Location of first aiders

Activity 2
Carry out a Risk Assessment of your workplace

Activity 1
Keep a work diary over the period of a month recording any incidents, fire drills, accidents etc.

Activity 3
You are sitting at your desk working on a report. You hear a cry and a crash from the next office. You go through to investigate and find a colleague on the floor apparently unconscious. It appears that they have fallen from a chair that they were standing on and may have struck their head on the edge of a desk. What steps do you take immediately? And what further action must you take once the initial emergency has been dealt with?

Activity 4
Make a list of first aiders and health and safety representatives in your workplace, together with their location and telephone extensions.

Activity 5

Imagine you have been given the responsibility of supervising a new member of staff. Prepare a help-sheet that would tell them:

- Who to report hazards to
- Who the safety representatives are
- What to do in the event of a fire
- Where the fire-fighting equipment is
- How to operate the fire-fighting equipment
- Who and where the first aiders are
- Where the first aid box is kept
- Where the accident book is kept
- How to use correct lifting techniques

Activity 6

Which legislation covers each of the following:

- Identification of hazardous substances
- Legal standards for toilets and washing facilities
- Provision of Personal Protective Equipment without charge
- Provision of eye-tests
- Safe entry and exit routes
- Notification of accidents to the Health and Safety Executive
- The need to co-operate with employers
- Provision of training to employees on risks
- Provision of ear-protectors
- Carrying out of Risk Assessments
- The requirement to avoid any manual handling operations in which employees could be injured
- Investigation of accidents
- The need to take into account working conditions when selecting new equipment

Activity 7

Photocopy a page of the Accident Book. If you have personally entered an accident copy the relevant page, if not copy a blank page and complete it with fictional information.

Remember: Evidence will be generated for this unit while gathering evidence for all of the other units being attempted.

CHAPTER 3
UNIT 201 – Carry out your responsibilities at work

Whatever size or type of organisation you work in, you will have responsibilities that need to be carried out. These responsibilities will include the actual function of the job that you do, but also responsibilities to the person or people you report to, anybody who reports to you, the team or teams in which you work and, perhaps most importantly, to yourself.

While you will hopefully enjoy your time at work, there will be frustrations, times when demands seem unreasonable, times when you feel you are being unfairly treated; it is the way you deal with these situations that will determine how much you enjoy your time. Working as part of a team will provide you with greater demands, but offer greater scope for development than working as an individual. Responding to the demands will improve your performance as you learn from other members of the team. Similarly your colleagues will benefit from working with you as they learn from your skills and experience.

Modern organisations tend to give individuals more responsibility for their own work than was once the case. It is no longer enough not to make mistakes (or not to get caught making mistakes); everybody is now expected to be accountable for planning and organising their own work.

The successful employee is no longer the one who keeps their head down and just does what is asked of them – initiative is the key to success. Decisions are now taken by everybody, problems are dealt with at a lower level than previously, all members of staff are expected to get involved in meetings, training colleagues and bringing forward suggestions to improve efficiency.

The key to working in this environment is communication. Information needs to be exchanged continually; not only information about the work being carried out but also information on your own situation and feelings. Effective communication will also enable you to progress your career, increase your skills base, expand your personal networks, and improve your relationships with colleagues and your decision-making ability.

Giving and accepting feedback oils the wheels of communication. Feedback can be positive or negative but must always be constructive. The receiver must take on board what is said and, if positive, take it as confirmation that what they are currently doing is effective; if negative, take steps to use the feedback to improve.

 When carrying out your responsibilities at work you will need the following skills:

- Communicating
- Planning
- Managing Time
- Solving problems
- Evaluating
- Team working

These skills are covered in chapter 1.

Communicate information

The most important thing about communication is that it is two-way. It is said that 'if the learner hasn't learnt, the teacher hasn't taught'. It is equally true that if the receiver hasn't understood, the communicator hasn't communicated. The fault, however, lies equally with the receiver if they haven't asked the necessary questions.

There are, of course, various methods of communicating. The earliest is communicating verbally. In the workplace verbal communication takes place in meetings, presentations, discussions, telephone conversations and informally across the office or around the water cooler.

It is a fact of life that you will attend numerous meetings in the course of your work. You should be invited only to meetings that you can actively contribute to; if you find yourself regularly attending meetings that don't seem to affect your work, you need to inquire, politely, why you are attending them. It may be that you have a particular knowledge that may be needed at the meeting, or possibly it is seen as a developmental activity. Pay close attention to everything that is being said during the meeting and you will be able to make a contribution at some point. Speak clearly and confidently but remember that others may not agree with your views. This does not mean you are necessarily incorrect, simply that there are differing views on the subject. Your opinions have more chance of being accepted if you remain calm and polite; you are unlikely to persuade anybody by being aggressive.

Discussions are basically spontaneous meetings. They are held to resolve immediate problems or to canvas opinion before decisions are taken. The thing to remember about discussions is that they are not a means of one person simply giving information to another, they are an exchange of information. Neither party necessarily has the answer before the beginning of the discussion, by the end of the discussion hopefully both have.

Even more than meetings, you will almost certainly spend a great deal of your working life on the telephone. There are specific techniques in using the telephone; learn what these are and you will communicate much more effectively.

When making a call:

- Be clear why you are making the call
- Make sure you communicate the information that was the purpose of the call
- Say who you are and what organisation you are calling from
- Speak clearly and slowly in as simple terms as possible without being patronising
- If you have to use technical terms or pass on names and addresses repeat any words that may be difficult
- Try not to be side tracked

Remember why you made the call and make sure you get your point across. It will waste your time and theirs if you hold a meandering conversation without getting to the point. While keeping in mind that time is money remember you should be focused without being abrupt.

Answering the telephone at work is completely different from answering it at home. Your organisation will probably have a standard format for answering calls, for instance:

- Telephone rings – pick up within five rings
- Say 'Good morning/afternoon Patterson's, Anthony speaking, how may I help you?'

Use it, it may not be your personal style but it is the company style. The purpose is to provide the caller with a prompt response, not to make you run across the office.

Informal chats may or may not be about work, but they still need to be carried out politely without being aggressive or patronising. Treat others as you expect to be treated yourself. Never be rude or impolite.

Probably the most daunting form of verbal communication for most of us is giving a talk in front of a group of people. As with many things in life, careful preparation will make it seem a lot easier. If you have never given a talk, think about the kind of talk you may be asked to give. It might be a team talk to tell your colleagues about a new system or product, for instance.

You will want to know:

- Where the talk is to be given
- How long you are expected to speak
- How many people will be in the audience
- How much they are likely to know about the subject

Once you have this information you will be able to prepare the talk. If you are not confident that your own level of knowledge is sufficiently superior to the audience's, research the subject carefully. If you anticipate any questions that you might be asked you won't be asked a question you don't know the answer to. Make notes of the main points you are going to cover but don't attempt to write a script and read it out. If you need handouts prepare sufficient copies well in advance; organise any equipment such as projectors, flip charts or white boards. Practice your talk, asking someone to listen to it and give you feedback. This will also give you the opportunity to check your timing. If you have 30 minutes to give your talk you won't want it to last 15 or 45 minutes.

When the time approaches to give your talk, you will be nervous. This is a perfectly natural reaction. People whose career depends on talking to groups will tell you they are always nervous before they start. If you have prepared adequately you can re-assure yourself that 'it will be alright on the night'.

- Think about talks you have been in the audience for; what was the common feature of ones you enjoyed? It will probably be that they got off to a good start. The first few minutes will set the tone. Your audience will either get on your side or switch off

---

- Speak confidently; remember you know what you are talking about. The audience will be there to hear what you have to say
- Talk to the whole audience; don't concentrate on one person or one group. If you do the rest will lose interest. Make eye contact with as many as possible
- Avoid making jokes unless they really do add to what you are saying. If a joke falls flat your confidence will ebb away
- Some speakers prefer to stand still while they speak, others move about. Find your own style but avoid excessive movement, and particularly try not to wave your arms about too much
- Don't speak any more quickly than you would in normal conversation. You will find your nervousness will disappear after the first few minutes
- The classic format for a talk is tell them what you are going to tell them, tell them, and tell them what you have told them. In other words, an introduction, the body of the talk and then a summary
- Invite questions. If you know the answer, give it as briefly as possible. If you don't know the answer, admit it and offer to find out
- End by thanking your audience for listening. Ask someone that you trust to give you feedback on how it went. You may be surprised by the answer as it is extremely difficult to judge while you are giving the talk

There comes a point at which verbal communication is not appropriate, either because the message is complicated or because a permanent record is needed. The advantages of written communication are:

- A permanent record is produced
- Complex subjects can be covered
- Information can be amended during the preparation
- Care can be taken over the precise wording

The disadvantages are:

- Cost
- Careless content is permanently recorded
- It can be ignored
- It is more formal

There are a number of ways in which information is exchanged in writing within an organisation. (In this context e-mail is just another way of passing written information.) Relatively simple information will be communicated by memo, more complex information in the form of a report.

A memo is a formal method of conveying information from one person to another, or to a group of people. The important components are:

- Who the memo is from
- Who the memo is to
- The date
- The information

Take care to check the accuracy and completeness of the information as it is frustrating to receive a memo which requires you to telephone the sender to ask for clarification. For instance, if you are advising people that a meeting will be held on Thursday the 4th, if Thursday is actually the 5th people will need to ring to ask if you meant Wednesday the 4th or Thursday the 5th.

If you are preparing a report some research and analysis will almost certainly be necessary. The most appropriate source will very much depend on the type of information that you are researching. In general terms, however, you will be guided by your own experience of similar research and the expertise of others that you can seek advice from.

Having identified relevant information from a number of sources, you will need to bring it all together into one format. Try to sort all of the information into categories. Once you have organised your information you will be able to look at it and select the facts which will be useful in producing a report. When selecting the facts, care must be taken not to ignore those that do not seem to fit with the desired result. There is always a temptation to include facts that support a preconceived idea and ignore those that contradict it.

The process of compiling a report is:

- Confirm the purpose of the report
- Research the information
- Analyse the information
- Sort the information into an introduction, a main body, a conclusion and recommendations

- Write a first draft
- Read and amend
- Write a final copy

There is a third method of communication which is taking place all the time, although we may not be aware of it. This is non-verbal communication or 'body language'. The messages you send out when you are not speaking. The way you sit, stand, fold your arms, your facial expression, all communicate things to others. The messages may be deliberate, such as a nod or a shrug, or involuntary, such as a yawn. Reading body language will often tell you more than listening to what a person is saying.

What you need to know

Why effective communication is important

Why is it important to listen carefully?

The order in which information is presented in a report

Why is it important to ask questions?

How to take part in discussions effectively

What do you understand by the term 'body language'?

How to research information

How should you answer the telephone?

Why confidence is important when communicating

Why should you address the whole audience when giving a presentation?

How to analyse information

What preparations should you make before making a telephone call?

Plan and be accountable for your work

The key to planning your work is time management. Time is always limited and there are techniques which you can learn to help you make the most of it:

- **Prioritise your tasks** - Make a list of things you need to do and identify each as 'must do', 'should do' or 'could do'. Deal with the important, then the urgent, then the routine and finally the trivial if you have time
- **Plan your time** - Days, weeks, months and years can all be planned for. Set aside enough time to do the important and the urgent by their deadlines, but allow time for the routine and even the trivial
- **Delegate** - If you cannot do everything in the time available, ask someone else to do some of it
- **Plan meetings** - You may not be able to avoid attending them but you can try to make sure they are as brief as possible
- **Record the time you use** - This will help you identify where you have lost time
- **Deal with disruption** - If you have something important to do let it be known that you don't wish to be disturbed
- **Handle each piece of paper only once** - Don't keep thinking about dealing with something and putting it back on the pending pile
- **Control the telephone** - List the calls you need to make and make them all in a period of time set aside for telephone calls

You may feel that you are not in charge of your own time, if your boss brings you a task and requests that you do it immediately, you have no choice. This may be true, but you are able to discuss whether the timescale is realistic and to point out that completing the new task will affect other tasks that were planned. Beware of the temptation to agree to all requests, you may think it will make you indispensable, but if it means you never complete any task on time it will simply make you unreliable.

If problems occur while you are dealing with a task which may affect your ability to meet an agreed deadline, let the person you are doing the work for know as soon as possible. It may be possible to extend the deadline, or it may be necessary to get help with completing the task. If the problem is reported sooner rather than later, action can be taken. If you simply carry on in hope, by the time it is obvious that the deadline will not be met it may be too late to do anything about it.

Your colleagues would far rather you ask for help than discover that there is a backlog of work that you have been unable to complete and unwilling to admit to. The same is true of mistakes. If you own up to a mistake as soon as you discover it, everybody will be willing to help you sort it out. If you try to cover up the mistake, when the truth is uncovered there will be very little sympathy. Mistakes are much more easily remedied immediately than they are further down the line, and acknowledging that you have made a mistake is the first step towards learning from it.

Don't change established ways of doing things without consultation. It is quite possible things are done the way they are 'because we've always done it that way' and that you have come up with an ingenious improvement. On the other hand it's quite possible things are done that way for very good reasons, possibly legal, and changes may have consequences that you cannot foresee. If you have come up with an idea to improve the way things are done, take it to your supervisor and discuss whether the change is feasible.

What you need to know

Why it is important to plan your work

> Why is it important to agree realistic targets?

How mistakes can be seen as positive

> What do you understand by the term 'time management'?

Who to keep informed about progress

> Who would you report problems to?

Guidelines and procedures relevant to your work

> How do you agree realistic targets?

Codes of practice relevant to your work

> When do you report that deadlines may be unachievable?

Improve your own performance

If you were performing a piece of music or playing a sport, you would not expect to be as good the first time you tried as you will be after a period of time. The differences are practice and experience, and the same is true of the tasks you perform at work. Sports stars and musicians have coaches and teachers who analyse their performance and give them tips on how to improve. At work this is known as feedback and comes from people who have more experience than you of carrying out the tasks.

You should welcome and encourage feedback from others at work. While it is very nice to hear that you have done something particularly well, it is probably more useful to be told when you have not done as well as you might have. The important thing about feedback is that it should be constructive. If someone is to tell you that your performance is not all it might be, they need to explain what you should have done, not just tell you what you should not have done.

There will be occasions when feedback is given in a more formal way known as appraisals. There are a number of reasons for appraisals to be carried out:

- To identify your current level of performance
- To identify strengths and weaknesses
- To reward contribution to achievement of goals
- To motivate
- To identify training and development needs
- To identify potential

Appraisals are an important opportunity for supervisors and staff to discuss performance. They should be seen as a joint problem-solving exercise in which opportunities will be identified. The outcome of an appraisal will be a development plan which will identify what you need to do in order to achieve an acceptable level of performance and what opportunities there are for you to fulfil your potential.

Appraisals are usually held annually, so the development plan will aim to track your progress from where you are now to where you hope to be in 12 months time. There will need to be milestones set along the way so that you can review and amend targets. When you review your progress, if you are achieving your goals you will be encouraged, if you are not you will need to identify the reasons before it is too late to take any corrective action. A well-written development plan will enable you to:

- Concentrate on the right parts of your job
- Motivate yourself
- Build your self-esteem
- Negotiate deadlines more realistically
- Recognise how to avoid time-wasting activities
- Get evidence for any qualifications you may be working towards

The best kind of development is self-development. You are the only person who knows what you want to achieve and how much effort you are prepared to make to achieve it. You are also the only one who knows whether you really like the job you are doing now and whether you really want the responsibility that progress would inevitably bring. Therefore, you are the only person who can actually motivate you to achieve.

What you need to know

How to improve your overall performance

Why should you encourage feedback?

The opportunities for progression
available to you

What are the benefits of continuous
learning and development?

The opportunities for training available to
you

How should you receive feedback which
is not positive?

Behave in a way that supports effective working

One of the things that may be identified during an appraisal is whether your attitude is appropriate. There is a lot of difference between doing all that is asked of you to a satisfactory standard and going out of your way to do as much as possible to the highest possible standard. If you set yourself targets well in excess of those that are required of you, you will find achieving the required standards easy.

From time to time there will inevitably be changes in what is expected of you. It may be that there is new software introduced, there may be new products to get to grips with, or a long serving colleague may leave and be replaced by somebody with different skills. Any of these changes will provide new challenges for you and your colleagues. It is important that you view these challenges as opportunities rather than as problems. Your enthusiasm to embrace change will motivate others and raise morale at what might be a difficult time.

If colleagues are struggling to cope with the new situation offer to help in any way that you can. Remember it is important to be honest about how much help you can give. You will still have your own work to complete and it will not be helpful in the long run if you either jeopardise your own deadlines or put yourself under undue stress in order to help your colleagues through. The most appropriate approach is to go to your supervisor and explain that the change has produced unexpected difficulties.

If there is a new member of staff try to remember how you felt on your first few days. Make allowances for the fact that they are probably feeling nervous and uncomfortable and don't jump to conclusions about either their abilities or their attitude. Until you get to know them give them the benefit of the doubt. Their attitude to you will be very much influenced by your attitude to them. Treat them with respect and consideration and you will get the same in return.

You should also treat your employer with the respect and consideration that they deserve by being honest in your dealings with them. This means that you must be punctual, only take days off sick if you are genuinely unwell and also not 'borrow' items from the office without the consent of your supervisor. It also means that you must do your job to the very best of your ability.

 What you need to know

The importance of behaving responsibly

> Why should you treat colleagues with honesty, respect and consideration?

How to set high standards for your own performance

> How do you show you are honest, respectful and considerate?

Why it is important to embrace change

> What behaviour indicates a lack of honesty?

The importance of adapting readily to change

> Why should you always help and support others to the best of your ability?

Carrying out your responsibilities at work is no longer simply a case of meeting your job description. To be successful you will need to communicate, be positive, volunteer for extra responsibility, be loyal to your colleagues, accept constructive feedback, get on well with everybody that you meet and treat your employer with honesty and respect. This is not easy to achieve, in fact it is unlikely that anybody can achieve all of this every day, but if you set your own high standards you will achieve much more than you would have thought possible.

You only get out of the job what you are prepared to put into it

Are you ready for assessment?

To achieve this unit of a Level 2 Business & Administration qualification you will need to demonstrate that you are competent in the following:

- Actively focus on information that other people are communicating, questioning any points you are unsure about
- Provide accurate, clear and structured information confidently to other people and in a way that meets their needs
- Make useful contributions to discussions
- Confirm and read written material that contains information that you need
- Extract the main points you need from written material
- Provide written information to other people accurately and clearly
- Agree realistic targets and an achievable timescale for your work
- Plan how you will make best use of your time and the other resources you need
- Confirm effective working methods
- Identify and report problems when they arise, using the support of other people when necessary
- Keep other people informed of your progress
- Meet your deadlines or re-negotiate timescales and plans in good time
- Take responsibility for your own work and accept responsibility for any mistakes you make
- Follow agreed guidelines, procedures and, where appropriate, codes of practice
- Encourage and accept feedback from other people
- Use feedback to agree ways to improve your own work and put improvements into practice
- Agree where further learning and development could improve your performance
- Follow through a learning plan that meets your own needs
- Review your progress and update your learning plan

- Set high standards for your work and show commitment in achieving these standards
- Understand your own needs and rights
- Show a willingness to take on new challenges
- Adapt readily to change
- Treat other people with honesty, respect and consideration
- Help and support other people

(Remember that you will need the skills listed at the beginning of this chapter and that these are covered in chapter 1.)

Your Assessor will need you to produce evidence from a variety of sources. If you carry out the activities that follow they will provide some of the evidence for you.

Activity 1
You are the secretary of the works' social club and have been asked to suggest options for the outing to be held in six weeks time. The committee meeting requires you to put forward three alternatives with advantages and disadvantages, including relative cost for a group of 30 people. Prepare either a written report or a talk that you will present to the committee meeting.

Activity 2
Keep a precise log over a period of time, recording everything that you do and exactly how long it takes. Review the log and look for time that you could have saved if you had planned more effectively. Use the information to plan the next period of time, and at the end write a short account of how the planning has improved your efficiency.

Activity 3
Complete the following self-appraisal by ticking the most appropriate box against each skill. For each tick in the 'training needs' column identify an action that you can take.

	Can do	Training needs	Actions to be taken
Speak at meetings			
Join in discussions			
Answer the telephone			
Make telephone calls			
Make telephone calls			
Give a talk			
Write a report			

Write a memo			
Research information			
Prioritise tasks			
Delegate			
Deal with disruption			
Say 'no' if necessary			
Admit mistakes			
Put forward ideas			
Accept feedback			
Motivate yourself			
Set high standards			
Accept new challenges			
Embrace change			

Show the completed self-appraisal to your supervisor to check that they agree with your findings.

Activity 4

Your supervisor has advised you that a new member of staff is to start work in your department next week and has asked you to carry out their induction to the whole organisation. Prepare a check list of all the things that you will need to cover. Don't forget things like toilets, staff rooms, arrangements for lunch etc.

Activity 5

If you don't have an official job description, write one and ask your supervisor to look at it and check that it covers everything you are required to do. If you already have a written job description write one for a colleague's job by asking them to tell you what they do.

Remember: Evidence will be generated for this unit while gathering evidence for optional units at Level 2. Assessment should be planned alongside the appropriate optional units.

CHAPTER 4
UNIT 202 – Work within your business environment

The economy of the United Kingdom is a mixed economy. This means there are organisations owned by individuals as well as organisations controlled by the state. Those owned by the state are known as the 'Public Sector' and include:

- Public Corporations such as the BBC
- Hospital Trusts
- Local Authorities such as local councils, local education authorities (LEAs)

Those owned by individuals are known as the 'Private Sector' and include:

- **Sole traders** - These are individuals who are self-employed
- **Partnerships** - This is a group of two or more self-employed people who have formed an organisation together in which each is a partner
- **Private Limited Companies (Ltd.)** - Two or more people form an organisation which is registered under the Companies Act 1985. Shares in the company can be sold privately
- **Public Limited Companies (plc.)** - A company whose shares can be bought and sold on the Stock Exchange

There is a third group of organisations which differ from the Public Sector in that they are not owned by the state, and differ from the Private Sector in that they are not set up for the purpose of making a profit and are often owned by their members. These organisations form the 'Mutuality Sector' and include:

- Those Building Societies which have not yet become Public Limited Companies
- Registered charities such as the RSPCA
- Co-operative Societies which operate in much the same way as Public Limited Companies except that any profit is returned to the customers

Organisations can also be divided into the following:

- **Service Providers** - These include Public Services, financial services such as banks and insurance companies, hotels and catering, call centres etc
- **Retailers** - These include High Street shops, on-line stores such as Amazon and mail-order catalogues such as Kays. They sell products direct to the public
- **Wholesalers** - These buy products direct from the manufacturer and sell them to retailers

- **Manufacturers** - These take raw materials and make them into a product which they sell to wholesalers
- **Extractive industries** - These include farming, mining, quarrying and fishing - they extract the product from natural resources

Wherever you work you will be working in one of the three sectors and one of the five types of organisation above. If you are unclear which it is, ask. Everyone employed has responsibilities to their employer and rights which they can expect their employer to respect. These are set out in your Contract of Employment and protected by legislation including the:

- National Minimum Wage Act 1998
- Disability Discrimination Act 1995
- Race Relations Act 1976
- Sex Discrimination Acts 1975 & 1986
- Equal Pay Act 1970
- Working Time Regulations Act 1998
- Data Protection Act 1998 (Employment)
- Employment Relations Act 1999
- Employment Rights Act 1996
- Human Rights Act 1998

Your responsibilities will involve you in acting in your organisation's best interests while you are at work, taking care of your employer's property and respecting the confidentiality of information belonging to both your employer and clients or customers. Respecting confidentiality extends beyond the time spent at work to include your spare time and even after you have left the organisation. The information that you have had access to during your time at work must not be disclosed when you are out socially or when you start work at another organisation.

You will hear a lot about diversity in the workplace. Diversity means the qualities that make people unique including their race, religious beliefs, physical abilities, family background – the list is endless. There is legislation to protect the rights of employees against discrimination on grounds of:

- Ethnicity
- Gender
- Marital status
- Parental status

- Disabilities
- Sexual orientation

You can play your part in supporting equal opportunities in the workplace by treating everybody fairly, learning from other people, not ignoring others who don't treat everybody fairly and by supporting equal opportunity programmes. Treat your colleagues fairly, just as you would want to be treated.

 When working within your business environment you will need the following skills:

- Planning
- Reading
- Communicating
- Interpersonal skills
- Team working

These skills are covered in chapter 1.

Your organisation's purpose and values

Every organisation was set up with a purpose. It may be a commercial enterprise set up for the purpose of making money, a charitable organisation set up to relieve a need or meet a public service. Each organisation will also have values, the principles by which it operates. These may be to raise as much money as possible for the cause, to operate in an ethical and environmentally friendly manner, or simply be the best in their field. In order to achieve their purpose and uphold those values, the people in charge will have set aims and objectives which will need to be amended in the light of changing circumstances. This may be enshrined in a 'mission statement' which attempts to explain the organisation's purpose and values in a few words. For instance a training organisation may have a mission statement 'Helping to expand your horizons'.

Your role is to carry out your work in a way that helps your organisation to achieve its aims. For this reason you need to understand how your job fits in to the organisation as a whole. You may feel your part is unimportant but everybody has a part to play and it's the little cogs that make the big wheels turn. Remember that a complex organisation requires each member to carry out their part in the way that has been designated; if you decide that your contribution is minor and that you can change the way you carry it out without consultation, you may produce a major change in the way the whole organisation functions.

It is also important to understand that everything that you do in your job should reflect the organisation's values. Many organisations operate in an environmentally friendly way and everybody employed within that organisation is involved in that. This means reducing energy wastage, recycling, using low emission vehicles as company cars, using public transport on company business wherever possible; it can also mean considering which products are purchased for use within the organisation. If you work for an organic farmer then it would not be appropriate to order chemical fertilisers. If your job is in the public service sector, all of your actions should be aimed at serving the public.

Remember that to the public and people from outside your organisation, you represent the organisation. Their perception of your employers will be based on the impression that they are given by you. Every time you communicate with anyone you will give them an impression of the organisation you work for, whether you work on the reception desk, attend meetings or answer the phone or letters. Think about situations when you have spoken to someone from another organisation and have left with the feeling that they are not interested or couldn't care less. What was your impression of the organisation they worked for?

If you are to give the correct impression you need to know and understand your organisation's purpose and values. If you are not absolutely sure what these are ask for guidance.

What you need to know

Your organisation's purpose

> What three sectors make up the UK economy?

Your organisation's values

> What sector does your organisation operate in?

How your organisation compares to other similar organisations

> What are your main responsibilities?

How you contribute to the success of the organisation

> How are the values of your organisation relevant to your role?

How to apply values in your day-to-day work

> Who can you get guidance from on policies and values?

Employment responsibilities and rights

Your responsibilities as an employee will be laid down in your job description, your staff handbook, your letter of appointment, your contract of employment, notices on notice boards, in newsletters and policy documents. Your contract of employment will also state many of your rights as an employee, but there will be others not included in your contract.

When you first started your current job, your responsibilities will have been explained to you and you will have been issued with a job description. It is extremely unlikely, however, that you will be able to perform satisfactorily if you simply carry out the list of duties to the letter. All of us find, in practice, that there are many responsibilities attached to our jobs that are not listed on the job description (although sometimes the last item on the job description will be 'such duties as may from time to time be necessary' which is pretty much a 'catch-all'). It is much better for everybody if you are prepared to take on anything that needs doing, providing you have been trained to do it.

There are also responsibilities involved in your job that go beyond the duties required. These may be summed up as showing a positive attitude to work and involve such things as:

- Always looking your best and projecting the correct company image
- Being enthusiastic even when you're feeling a bit low
- Accepting constructive criticism
- Dealing with pressure
- Working well with other people even if you don't particularly like them
- Being punctual
- Not taking time off unnecessarily

All employers are required by the Employment Rights Act 1996 to give an employee a written statement of the terms and conditions of their employment within two months of their starting work. This is often in the form of a Contract of Employment, although legally speaking a contract exists whether it is in writing or not. The statement of employment particulars must contain:

- The names of the employer and employee
- The date employment started
- The date continuous employment started
- The rate and intervals of pay
- The hours of work
- Holidays and holiday pay
- Sickness and sick pay
- Pensions and pension schemes
- Length of notice required
- If non-permanent, the period for which employment is expected to continue or the date at which it is to end
- The job title or brief description
- The place of work

- Any collective agreements
- Disciplinary rules
- Grievance procedures

Your employment rights are also protected under the following legislation:

National Minimum Wage Act 1998

All workers are entitled to be paid at least the National Minimum Wage. The minimum hourly rate is reviewed each year by the Low Pay Commission who set rates for those aged 22 or over and those aged 18–21. Excluded from this Act are company directors, those aged under 18 and the genuinely self employed.

Equal Pay Act 1970

It is unlawful to offer different pay and conditions to men and women who perform the same type of work. This is defined as work of equal value in terms of effort and skills.

Working Time Regulations 1998

In general these impose an obligation on employers to ensure that employees:

- Work an average week of no more than 48 hours calculated over a 17 week period including working lunches, job related travel and time spent on business abroad

- Have an 11 hour continuous rest period between working days
- Have a continuous 24 hour period off work each week
- Have a break of at least 20 minutes during the day if the day is more than six hours long

Workers above school leaving age but under 18 cannot work more than eight hours a day or 40 hours a week as part of their ordinary working pattern.

Employment Relations Act 1999

Regardless of what may be written in the Contract of Employment, employees have a right to receive the following minimum periods of notice when employment is terminated:

- One week's notice for employees who have been employed for more than one month but less than two years
- Two weeks' notice for employees who have been continuously employed for more than two years, and one additional week's notice for each complete year of continuous employment up to 12 weeks for a period of up to 12 years
- At least 12 weeks notice for employees who have been continuously employed for more than 12 years

Employees must give employers one week's notice if they have been employed continuously for one month or more.

Human Rights Act 1998

This came into force in October 2000 and includes provisions on:

- Prohibition of discrimination
- Forced labour
- The right to privacy
- The right to join a Trade Union

There is other legislation which refers to employment rights. Information will be available from your human resources department, your local Citizen's Advice Bureau, the Internet or your public library.

Employers keep records on their employees which detail their attendance, time keeping, disciplinary records, appraisals, etc. Employers also keep personal details such as address, National Insurance Number, next of kin, date of birth, current rate of pay and hours worked. If any of the details alter you should inform your employer immediately. The employer is obliged to keep records regarding PAYE deductions etc.

What you need to know

Where to find your terms and conditions of employment

Are there any regulations that apply specifically to the industry you work in?

The employment legislation that affects your role

How does legislation protect the rights of both employees and employers?

Where to obtain information on employment legislation

Who would you contact if you had a grievance?

What to do if you are ill or need time off work

What information do employers keep on employees?

Maintaining security and confidentiality

Security rules are in place for your protection and the protection of your colleagues, visitors and customers. It is vital that everybody follows them. Any suspicious circumstance should be reported immediately it occurs. Security must extend to everybody who enters the building; staff, contractors, maintenance people, clients, customers and visitors. Many organisations provide their staff with badges, often containing a photograph. Some use electronic access systems which allow the staff to enter by swiping their identity card. Any genuine visitor will be carrying some form of identity which they should be willing to show when asked.

All visitors should be asked to sign in and their signature checked against their identification. You must be sure everyone in the building has a right to be there. Do not leave visitors unsupervised.

Keys to the building should be kept to a minimum, and a system put in place to record who has access to them. In the event of a problem outside of working hours it will be necessary to contact a key holder to access the building so a list of key holders will be held by the police or a private security company. Keys to internal doors, cabinets, safes, etc., should preferably be removed from the building at night or locked securely away and that key removed from the building. Safes and cabinets that contain no valuables are best left open to prevent burglars causing expensive damage forcing them open. Internal doors need to be closed to

prevent the spread of fire, but should be left unlocked if the contents of the room are not particularly valuable for the same reason.
You can help to prevent burglary by:

- Locking doors and windows
- Removing any valuable items from view
- Using any security devices available

If you are the first to enter the premises and you discover there has been a burglary:

- Telephone the police by dialling 999
- Contact your manager or the security department at Head Office
- Do not disturb any evidence

A major risk to you personally is violence. If you find someone on the premises who has no right to be there:

Do Not	Do
Put yourself at risk	Be vigilant and alert
Argue	Remain calm and polite
Be confrontational	Walk away
Give chase	Ask them their business

There are a number of steps that can be taken to minimise the risk of violence:

- Panic buttons
- Glass screens
- Two-way radios
- Improved training
- Avoiding lone working

The main protection against violence is knowing in advance what to do if you feel under threat.

A major risk to the premises is fire. The priority must be to prevent fire, and to minimise the effect should one start. To prevent fire:

- Report any faulty equipment or wiring
- Switch off any faulty equipment until it has been repaired
- If smoking is allowed ensure cigarettes are properly extinguished and ashtrays are emptied into metal bins
- Don't put papers, clothing, etc., near heaters or equipment that gets hot
- Switch off all equipment at the end of the day

To minimise the effect of fire:

- Know how to raise the alarm
- Take fire drills seriously
- Do not block fire doors or fire exits
- Do not prop fire doors open
- Know where the fire exits are
- Know where your assembly point is
- Know where fire fighting equipment is and its uses

If you discover a fire raise the alarm and follow your organisation's procedures.

A major risk to property, both the organisation's and the personal property of the staff, is theft. There is no such thing as a typical criminal. They come from all walks of life, cultures and ages. There are as many different types of criminal as there are types of people.

There is no end to the ingenuity of people who are intent on stealing from others. There are many different ways in which they will steal:

- In offices criminals will pose as visitors or customers to steal equipment and staff's personal belongings or pose as maintenance people to remove equipment
- In hotels they will collect room keys from reception after watching the guests go out or steal equipment from conference rooms or store cupboards
- In leisure centres they will steal valuables from changing rooms or staff rooms

Some criminals may even be staff members. They may feel that stealing from a large organisation is not really theft as nobody suffers, but this is not the case. The cost of theft is passed on to the customer of the organisation through higher prices or higher charges, as well as increasing insurance premiums to cover the cost of paying compensation. A further, knock-on effect of theft is that there is less profit available in the organisation to pay wages and salaries.

There are precautions that can be taken to reduce the risk of company property being stolen:

- Mark expensive equipment with the organisation's name or post code using an 'invisible' marker
- Keep a record of equipment serial numbers
- Don't turn your back on valuable equipment
- Don't assume things won't be stolen just because they are not particularly valuable
- Change the codes used to access areas regularly and especially when people who know them leave the organisation
- Sign out and sign back in again any portable equipment that is allowed to leave the building

If you see a theft taking place, or suspect that someone is stealing, there are a number of things that you can do:

- Observe their behaviour while a colleague alerts security or a manager. Try to keep them under constant observation so that they do not have the opportunity to pass on the stolen items to an accomplice
- Watch them until you are sure a theft has taken place
- Avoid confronting them if you are on your own as this leaves you vulnerable to violence
- Take a detailed description of the person in case you lose sight of them
- Above all, keep a safe distance and do not put yourself at risk

You must be aware of the limits of your authority under the law to take action against a suspected criminal. Under the

Police and Criminal Evidence Act 1984 you have the power of arrest but you do not have the authority to search people, cars or premises, only the police do.

If you search someone without their permission you are open to a charge of assault. You can request that the person empties their pockets, handbags, briefcases, etc., but you cannot insist. Always make sure you have a third person present as a witness.

Remember most criminals are opportunists, remove the opportunity and they won't be able to steal. Don't take cash or valuables to work unless you absolutely have to. If you have no choice, ask if it can be locked away somewhere safe. Keep your handbag in your sight or out of everybody else's. Don't leave your wallet in your jacket hanging on the back of a chair in an empty room. Don't leave your mobile phone on the table in the staff room. Challenge any visitors that you find in an area of the building where they are not permitted.

One of the fastest growing types of theft is the theft of information. This may be commercially sensitive information which can be stolen by one organisation from another, or personal information which can be stolen to be used fraudulently.

The information may be held on a computer, in which case it should be protected by passwords, or it may be paper copies of information, in which case care should be taken that it is not left in plain sight on desks and that it is shredded before being disposed of. Remember not to discuss confidential issues in areas where visitors or the public may be able to overhear.

Personal information about living individuals, including customers, employees, suppliers, clients or other members of the public held on computers or in some cases on paper, is covered by the Data Protection Act 1998. There are eight data protection principles which state that personal information must be:

- Fairly and lawfully processed
- Processed for specified purposes
- Adequate, relevant and not excessive
- Accurate and where necessary kept up-to date
- Kept for no longer than necessary

- Processed in line with the rights of the individual
- Kept secure
- Not transferred to countries outside the European Economic Area unless there is adequate protection for the information

If you have any suspicions that security or confidentiality is being compromised report your concerns to someone in authority. If it transpires that there was no breach, it will be better to have checked than to have ignored the situation.

 ## What you need to know

The principles of the Data Protection Act 1998

What security rules are there in your organisation?

The do's and don'ts of confronting a trespasser

How can you help prevent burglary?

How to minimise the effect of fire

What should you do if you discover a burglary?

Where your fire evacuation assembly point is

What do thieves look like?

The consequences of staff theft

What action should you take if you suspect someone of stealing?

Your powers under the Police and Criminal Evidence Act 1984

Why do people steal information?

Supporting sustainability

Supporting the sustainability of the business involves:

- Keeping waste to a minimum
- Recycling waste wherever and whenever possible
- Disposing of hazardous waste effectively
- Following procedures for equipment maintenance
- Making the best use of technology

Resources are relatively expensive, so you should take care to waste as few as possible. While it is essential to have sufficient stock, care must be taken to avoid over-ordering, which may result in obsolete stock if equipment changes. The biggest source of waste in an office comes from over-printing and over-copying. Always check for errors first before printing a large number of documents.

Almost all waste generated in an office can be recycled, in many cases saving money on replacements. Think before you throw anything away. Remember to shred any confidential documents before recycling. Any hazardous waste must be dealt with in accordance with the Control of Substances Hazardous to Health (COSHH) Regulations.

It is important to know what each piece of equipment in the office is used for, and what other materials are required, in order to use it in the most efficient way.

Don't expect to know how to use equipment without being shown or trained. A valuable resource in getting to know an unfamiliar piece of equipment is the operating manual. This contains the most efficient and cost-effective way of using the equipment. A lot of time can be saved by following the manufacturer's operating instructions. The manual contains vital safety and operating information which, if ignored, can invalidate the warranty. There may also be a number of functions or time-saving features that you will not discover by chance. The manual will usually include a troubleshooting guide, so that when the equipment doesn't work you can quickly find out why. Keep the manual close to the equipment for easy reference.

What you need to know

How to keep waste to a minimum

What materials does your organisation recycle?

The procedures in place for the maintenance of equipment

What are the requirements of COSHH?

The most efficient way of using various items of office equipment

Where are the operating manuals kept?

Supporting diversity

The dictionary definition of diversity is 'the state of being different'. You should deal with diversity by remembering that everybody should be shown the same respect. People with disabilities or the elderly may require help with access to the building. Visitors, of both genders, with young children may require baby-changing facilities.

Hearing impaired colleagues may need more visual aids. Visually impaired colleagues may need documents in large print or in audio format. Also be aware that English may not be someone's first language.

These are some examples of dealing with diversity. Don't make up your mind about somebody based on appearance, accent etc. People have different requirements, help with access, help with reading, help with understanding, but the important thing to remember is they are all colleagues and should be shown the same respect.

Many workplaces today are far more diverse than in the past. You may well find yourself working with colleagues from a wide range of cultures and abilities. It's in the best interests of everybody that you understand what is meant by Equal

Opportunities. For employers Equal Opportunities is about good business practice and can:

- Reduce costs
- Improve efficiency
- Lower staff turnover
- Improve customer relations

For employees it means they are judged on merit, ability and past performance and covers:

- Recruitment
- Promotion
- Training
- Benefits
- Dismissal

Your organisation will probably have an Equal Opportunities programme which will be designed to:

- Improve team success through respect and dignity for all
- Reduce stress levels and therefore absenteeism
- Improve safety performance
- Reduce recruitment costs
- Increase sales through staff commitment
- Widen the customer base

Employers can make these programmes more successful by:

- Outlawing discrimination and harassment
- Treating everybody equally
- Providing advice and training
- Offering flexible working time
- Handling complaints promptly

Discrimination may be direct or indirect. Direct discrimination means treating people less favourably because of their gender, ethnicity or sexual orientation etc. For instance selecting a male for the supervisor's position ahead of a better-qualified female because the majority of the staff are male and traditionally the role has been male.

Indirect discrimination occurs when a rule or practice discriminates against a particular group unintentionally, for instance stating that everyone applying for a job must have been to public school when there is no good reason for this.

Harassment is an unwelcome or offensive remark, request or other act that discriminates against a person by harming his or her job performance or satisfaction. Sexual harassment is a criminal offence. Other types of harassment may be criminal, for instance:

- Offensive jokes, remarks or insults based on ethnicity, nationality or other characteristics
- Bullying
- Threats, verbal or physical abuse
- Threatening or discriminating against someone for reporting a breach of the law

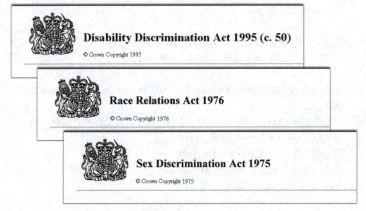

Disability Discrimination Act 1995 (c. 50)
© Crown Copyright 1995

Race Relations Act 1976
© Crown Copyright 1976

Sex Discrimination Act 1975
© Crown Copyright 1975

If you feel you are being discriminated against or harassed you are advised to tell the person involved that you find their behaviour offensive and want it to stop. If you feel you have been unfairly treated in terms of pay or promotion, ask for the decision to be reconsidered. If you feel unable to talk to the other person involved directly speak to their line manager. Make sure you have kept a record of what has happened and when.

The following legislation addresses Equal Opportunities at work:

The Sex Discrimination Acts 1975 & 1986

These Acts prohibit discrimination against people based on their gender or marital status. It covers two main areas:

- **Recruitment** - This includes the job description, the person specification, the application form, the short-listing process, interviewing and final selection
- **Terms and conditions** - This includes pay, holidays and working conditions

Direct sex discrimination involves refusing to consider somebody for a job because of their gender, for example refusing to consider a male for a job that is traditionally perceived as a female role. Indirect sex discrimination involves making it more difficult for one gender or for married people to be considered for a job, for instance if a condition of employment was willingness to regularly move home which would discriminate against married applicants as they would find this more difficult.

Race Relations Act 1976

This Act prohibits discrimination against people based on their race, colour, nationality or ethnic origin. It covers:

- Recruitment
- Training
- Selection
- Promotion
- Dismissal

Racial discrimination may be direct or indirect.

Disability Discrimination Act 1995

This Act prohibits discrimination against people based on their disability. It describes a person with a disability as 'anyone with a physical or mental impairment which has a substantial and long-term adverse effect upon their ability to carry out normal day-to-day activities'.

Employment Rights Act 1996

This Act is about the terms and conditions of employment. It could apply to sex discrimination as it covers the right to return to work after maternity leave.

Health and Safety at Work Act 1974

This Act could apply to a case of bullying that affects a person's health or safety.

Other forms of discrimination may be unlawful even though no specific law prohibits them, for instance discrimination based on age or HIV infection. However, even these will be subject to new legislation by 2006.

Equal Opportunities at work come down to changing the attitude of people about colleagues who are different from themselves and making the best use of the organisation's human resources. Equal Opportunities policies have the potential to bring out the best in people.

What you need to know

The definition of diversity

What is the difference between direct and indirect discrimination?

The benefits of Equal Opportunities policies to employers

What are the purposes of Equal Opportunities programmes?

The benefits of Equal Opportunities policies to employees

How does harassment differ from discrimination?

The main provisions of the Sex Discrimination Acts 1975 & 1986

How can Equal Opportunities programmes be made more successful?

The main provisions of the Race Discrimination Act 1976

Can you think of some examples of discrimination?

The main provisions of the Disability Discrimination Act 1995

Who should you tell if you feel you are being harassed?

The benefits to you of working effectively within your organisation are that you will be given more support, bigger challenges and greater opportunities. While it is important to know your employment rights it is more important to understand and fulfil your responsibilities. If you welcome the opportunity to work with as wide a range of people as possible you will learn to do things differently as other people's skills and experience will enhance your own. Keep your workplace, yourself and your colleagues safe by considering security as a priority and keep information secure by preserving confidentiality. As a result the whole organisation will work more effectively.

Everyone needs the chance to realise their full potential. This will lead to economic prosperity

Are you ready for assessment?

To achieve this unit of a Level 2 Business & Administration qualification you will need to demonstrate that you are competent in the following:

- Work in a way that supports your team's objectives
- Follow the policies, systems and procedures that are relevant to your role
- Put relevant organisational values into practice in all aspects of your work
- Work with outside organisations and individuals in a way that protects the image of your organisation
- Seek guidance from others when you are unsure about objectives, policies, systems, procedures and values
- Access information about your employment rights and responsibilities
- Carry out your responsibilities to your employer in a way that is consistent with your Contract of Employment
- Understand your employment rights
- Seek guidance when you are unsure about your employment responsibilities and rights
- Keep waste to a minimum and follow procedures for recycling and the disposal of hazardous materials
- Follow procedures for the maintenance of equipment
- Make best use of technology to work in an efficient way
- Interact with other people in a way that is sensitive to their individual needs and respects their background, abilities, values, customs and beliefs
- Learn from other people and use this to improve the way you work and interact with others
- Follow your organisation's procedures and legal requirements in relation to discrimination legislation
- Maintain the security of property in a way that is consistent with your organisation's procedures and legal requirements
- Maintain the security and confidentiality of information in a way that is consistent with your organisation's procedures and legal requirements

- Report any concerns about security and confidentiality to an appropriate person

(Remember that you will need the skills listed at the beginning of this chapter and that these are covered in chapter 1.)

Your Assessor will need you to produce evidence from a variety of sources. If you carry out the activities that follow they will provide some of the evidence for you.

Activity 1
If your organisation or department has a mission statement, explain in writing how this is reflected in the way that you and your colleagues carry out your responsibilities. If there is no mission statement, write one in discussion with your colleagues.

Activity 2
Write an account of your organisation's purpose and values explaining how these fit into the sector in which your organisation operates.

Activity 3
Your department is to recruit a new office junior. The Human Resources department has asked for a job description, person specification and a written statement of terms and conditions. You have been asked to supply these.

Activity 4
You have been asked to give a 15 minute talk at the next team meeting on 'Diversity in the Workplace'. Prepare the notes for the talk being sure to include as many forms of diversity as possible, not just those you have personal experience of. Rehearse the talk with a colleague and get feedback on its content.

Activity 5
Find out what security procedures there are in place in the building that you work in. Suggest improvements that could be made to offer better protection to the premises, people and property. Show these suggestions to your line manager and ask them to write a witness testimony on your report as it may not be acceptable to show your report to your assessor as it may contain confidential information.

Activity 6

Research Employment Legislation and write a report on how it impacts on your job role.

Activity 7

List the equipment in use in your office and prepare a maintenance schedule to cover it.

Activity 8

Research the waste produced in your organisation and look for ways to reduce the cost of its disposal.

Remember: Evidence will be generated for this unit while gathering evidence for optional units at Level 2. Assessment should be planned alongside the appropriate optional units.

CHAPTER 5
UNIT 203 Maintain customer relations

Maintaining customer relations is about knowing your customers and meeting their needs and expectations, whether your customers are internal or external. Customers will judge the organisation on the care they receive from everybody that they interact with. You may think you are not directly involved in providing customer service as you do not have direct face-to-face contact with your organisation's customers, but many activities influence the impression that the customer will receive of your organisation's customer care standards:

- The sales department must make it easy for a customer to make a purchase or place an order. Confirmation of receipt of order must be prompt and the customer kept informed of any delays in despatch
- The accounts department must provide suitable methods of payment, send out prompt and accurate invoices, provide an accessible system for querying invoices and customer-friendly credit facilities
- The despatch department must provide a flexible delivery service, contact the customer promptly in case of any changes to delivery arrangements and check the quality of the goods before despatch
- The after-sales department must be available when customers need them and provide a prompt and reliable service in the event of problems

- The complaints department must make it easy for customers to complain, respond promptly to complaints, keep records to identify trends and take action to reduce recurring problems

Hopefully most of your customers will be happy with the service you provide, but from time-to-time some may be unhappy, disappointed or even angry about the situation. The way you deal with these customers will reflect on the organisation you work for. The Supply of Goods and Services Act 1982 sets the minimum that the customer is entitled to, but many organisations will go further to keep their customers happy. Other legislation that may affect your dealings with customers includes:

- The Consumer Credit Act 1974 which regulates the way that credit can be offered to customers
- The Consumer Protection Act 1987 which prohibits the sale of dangerous goods
- The Estate Agents Act 1979 which governs accounts in respect of clients' money
- The Property Mis-descriptions Act 1991 which prohibits false or misleading statements of property by estate agents or builders
- The Trade Descriptions Act 1988 which regulates the description of goods and false claims for services
- The Unsolicited Goods and Services (Amendment) Act 1975 which controls the supply of unsolicited goods and demands for payment
- The Unfair Contract Terms Act 1977 which makes unfair contract terms void

There is also a variety of legislation specific to different occupations. You need to make yourself aware of the legislation that applies to your particular organisation. Personally, you must be vigilant in your dealings with your customers, within the limits of your authority, in offering a solution. You will need to know who to refer the problem to when this limit is reached. Even the most customer-friendly organisation can only be reasonably expected to go so far.

When maintaining customer relations you will need the following skills:

- Interpersonal skills
- Questioning
- Listening
- Negotiating
- Managing time

These skills are covered in chapter 1.

Know your customer

One of the most common questions asked within an organisation is 'who are my customers?' The answer is, usually, 'anybody you supply goods or services to'. Customers may be internal to the organisation or external. Customers are the reason for your work, not an interruption to it. They are the life-blood of the organisation, and without them there would be no organisation.

Remember it is far easier to lose a customer than to gain a new one. Many organisations spend a great deal more time, effort and money in attracting customers than they do in retaining the ones they have already. This can be a serious mistake.

It is your responsibility to build positive working relationships with your customers which will ensure that they remain loyal. Get to know your customers and their expectations. Discover how they would like to be addressed, what products or services they regularly buy and how often. When a customer is unsure of their needs, use open questions to help them clarify exactly what they want. Use 'active listening' to make sure you fully understand their requirements. Remember the aim is to reach a win:win situation that satisfies the organisation's needs as well as the customer's needs. When you feel you have reached an agreement, summarise the conversation and confirm by repeating it back to the customer. If the customer feels valued they will give you the opportunity to put right any problems that may occur.

 What you need to know

Who your customers are, both internal and external

> Do you have a list of regular customers?

What you can offer potential customers:
- Products and services
- Terms and conditions

> Could you explain to a new member of staff how to find customers' terms and conditions?

Ways to make customers feel valued

> Do you know your organisation's policy on discounts?

How to address your customers

> What would happen to your job if you had no customers?

The legislation that applies to your organisation

> How does your department impact on

the level of customer care provided by
your organisation?

The impact other departments have on
customer care

Do you know what products or services
your regular customers order?

Meet your customers' needs and expectations

'The customer is always right'. Despite this, customers will
not always know what they want, (even if they do they may
not find it easy to explain). You will have to listen carefully
to what they say and ask intelligent questions such as:

- How many?
- What colour?
- For delivery by when?
- Smoking or non-smoking?
- Single or return?
- What denominations would you like the money in?
- When did you buy it?
- How long would you like the warranty for?

In order to identify and confirm your customer's needs it is
important to listen actively to the customer's responses, but
you must also take note of what they *don't* say. There is a
risk that they will see you as the expert and not want to
disagree with you although your suggested solution may not

actually match their needs. They may not want to give the real reason if they are dissatisfied.

Summarise the outcome of the conversation, this will give the customer a chance to confirm or deny your understanding of what has been agreed. It will probably be a good idea to write down the details of the agreement either as you go along or immediately afterwards. Your job is to give away as little as possible while the customer reaches a point at which they are happy.

When you believe you have met the customer's needs and expectations and that the service has been delivered on time, you will still need to follow up with the customer to check their needs and expectations are met. It is possible that despite your best efforts to ensure that everybody understood what had been agreed, the customer is still not happy with the service you provided. Your organisation may have a formal method for obtaining the customer's confirmation that they are satisfied. If not, a verbal check may be sufficient.

What you need to know

Whether your organisation has a formal method for obtaining confirmation that the customer is satisfied

> How do you deal with a situation where you have checked that the customer is satisfied and they have surprised you by saying 'no'?

The consequences of failing to check that the customer is satisfied

> If you were asked to produce 4,000 copies of a ten-page document back-to-back, bound and four-hole punched, when would you check that you are meeting the requirements?

What the limit of your authority is when negotiating with customers

Who would you approach when you reach the limit of your authority?

How to summarise a conversation to confirm agreement

How can you tell if somebody is actively listening to you?

Systems and procedures

When you know what will satisfy the customer, agree with them exactly what is going to happen and when. This may require you to liaise with other departments in order to agree the timescales and procedures that need to be followed and the quality standards to be achieved. Make sure you have the commitment of everybody involved that they will play their part in achieving the target of meeting the agreement. The customer has placed an order with your organisation in preference to others who could have supplied their needs.

If you do not keep your side of the bargain the customer will feel disappointed with the service your organisation has provided. Having agreed with the customer and other departments what is going to happen, you will have to take the necessary steps to ensure that you meet your commitments. Where problems arise that put the timescales or quality agreed at risk, action needs to be taken to make every effort to get back on target.

Where, despite your best efforts, it is clear that the deadline is not going to be met, this is the time to advise the customer. This will involve phoning the customer, apologising that there is a problem, explaining the effect this will have on the agreement and re-negotiating the agreement. They are not going to be happy, but they are going to be even more unhappy if you wait until the deadline arrives and then tell them that it is not going to be met.

What you need to know

The functions of other departments that
will be involved in delivering the promised
service to the customer

> If you were asked to arrange a delivery
> to the Isle of Man, would you know
> when the customer could expect it?

The quality standards your organisation
works to

> How would you calculate the charge for
> a delivery to Llantwit Major?

How to obtain the commitment of other
departments

> Who do you have to liaise with to
> arrange a delivery?

What action to take if deadlines are not
going to be met

> If you find you are unable to meet an
> agreed deadline, when should you tell
> your customer?

Who to inform if an agreed timescale
cannot be achieved

> Why is it important to inform your
> customer that you cannot meet the
> deadline agreed?

Dealing with complaints

Whatever your role in the organisation, you may have to deal
with problems over customer care. Customer care is about
the systems, procedures and the whole organisation's
approach to the customers. This will include:

- Sales and order systems
- Accounts and invoice systems
- Delivery systems
- After sales service
- The customer complaints process

You will need to know how to resolve a complaint or who to refer it to where it exceeds your authority. Failing to carry out the solution within the agreed timescales may be the final straw in the eyes of your customer. To reduce the effect of this it will be necessary to agree with the customer at this stage what will happen if you fail to carry out the agreed service. You must always bear in mind the limits of your authority.

How you handle complaints will decide whether it is the last time you ever see the customer or if they are happy to return regularly in the future. There are some important 'do's and don'ts':

- Do listen to what they say
- Don't try to have the last word
- Do empathise with how they feel
- Don't show that you are annoyed
- Do apologise for the inconvenience
- Don't raise your voice
- Do tell the customer what action you are taking
- Don't say you are unable to do anything
- Do learn to value complaints
- Don't turn your back on a customer

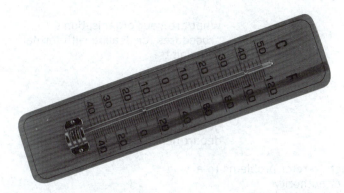

Aim to resolve the complaint promptly in order that the customer feels important. Accept responsibility for the problem. To the customer, you represent the organisation. Remember to leave the customer feeling that they were right. Never argue with a customer, you cannot win.

Your organisation may have a department for dealing with customer complaints, or a customer service desk, or the manager or supervisor may handle complaints. You need to know who deals with complaints in your organisation. It may be necessary to involve a supervisor or the Customer Care department, but you should do this yourself – DON'T expect the customer to go and find someone who can deal with them.

Once you have collected as much information as possible from the customer, give a clear explanation of the complaint to your colleague to help them solve the problem. Never ask the customer to repeat themselves, this will only further annoy them. Handing the complaint over effectively and efficiently will not only help your colleague to resolve the matter, but will also help the customer feel more confident that their complaint is being taken seriously and that they, and their custom, are valued.

 ## What you need to know

The legal implications of dealing with customer problems

> What are your organisation's procedures for dealing with formal complaints?

The types of problems that could arise

> What sort of complaints may be generated by the accounts department?

How and when to refer problems to a higher level of authority

> Why should an organisation welcome complaints?

In conclusion every customer, whether internal or external, must be treated as if they were the most important person in the organisation. Your purpose must be to satisfy their requirements. Business can be lost if you do not have the correct relationship with your customers. Make sure you know and follow your organisation's procedures for dealing with both orders and complaints. If you deal with every customer request efficiently and effectively there will be no cause for complaint. While you may not personally be able to go quite this far in your organisation, the successful management of customer relations will go a long way towards reducing complaints. It is a lot cheaper and less stressful to prevent problems than it is to deal with them.

Remember if there were no customers there would be no organisation

Are you ready for assessment?

To achieve this unit of a Level 2 Business & Administration qualification you will need to demonstrate that you are competent in the following:

- Build positive working relationships with customers
- Identify and confirm customer needs and expectations
- Agree timescales, quality standards or procedures to follow
- Provide services to agreed timescales and quality standards
- Check customer needs and expectations are met
- Resolve or refer customer complaints in a professional manner and to a given timescale

(Remember that you will need the skills listed at the beginning of this chapter and that these are covered in chapter 1.)

Your Assessor will need you to produce evidence from a variety of sources. If you carry out the activities that follow they will provide some of the evidence for you.

Activity 1
If the company you work for has a list of regular customers, find a copy. If it doesn't, create one.

Activity 2
You are working alone on the reception desk at a hotel. It's 9.00am and you have been on duty since 4.00am without a break. There is a queue of guests, some wanting to check out, others seeking directions to a function being held in the hotel conference room that morning. There is an atmosphere of discontent spreading through the queue. Suddenly a customer pushes her way to the front and starts demanding to see the manager, shouting about the poor service, the lack of hot water in her room, the quality of the breakfast, the litter in the car park and the disgraceful price charged for drinks in the bar. None of this is your fault, but you have to deal with the irate customer, while not making the situation worse by holding up the other guests who are still waiting to be dealt with.

How do you deal with the situation?

Activity 3
Keep a work diary over the period of a month recording all of the complaints you deal with and how you resolved them.

Activity 4
According to research what percentage of customers are lost through bad customer service?

What two-word phrase is used to describe an outcome that is satisfactory to all concerned?

Who must be involved in agreeing timescales to provide a solution to a customer delivery problem?

Other than customer service related complaints, what type of complaints may you be required to deal with?

True or false, the customer must be informed immediately if a delay occurs in resolving their complaint?

What is the most important reason to contact your regular customers?

Activity 5
Visit a local solicitor's office and pick up a leaflet on conveyancing.
- Read the leaflet carefully and ask someone to explain any areas that you don't understand
- Explain the service offered to a friend or colleague as if you worked for the solicitors and they were a potential client

Activity 6
While in your local town centre look around and find examples of good customer relations.
- Price promises
- Easy access for disabled customers
- Vegetarian options on menus
- Family friendly environment

Activity 7
Write an account of what is meant by active listening, explaining how this affects the management of customer relations.

Remember: While gathering evidence for this unit, evidence **may** be generated for units 110, 201, 202, 206, 209, 216, 219 and 225

CHAPTER 6
UNIT 204 – Manage diary systems

One of the most important activities in an office is planning and organising schedules, both your own and other people's. This can be done using various types of diary depending on the information that needs to be kept. In a busy office people's plans are constantly being changed it is essential that someone co-ordinates these changes, communicating with everybody who is affected to avoid confusion and time-wasting errors. If you are responsible for arranging meetings and appointments for somebody else, remember to leave them time for routine matters such as dealing with the post and other day-to-day responsibilities. Also remember to allow time for them to travel from one appointment to another.

Probably the most common form of diary in use in an office is still the 'page-a-day' book. This has the advantage of enabling you to record appointments and meetings that need to be attended during the day and on the same page recording your 'to-do' list. As the diary can be locked away at the end of the day it is possible to enter confidential information but if you use the diary for this purpose it is important to make sure that you do lock it away if you leave your desk. Regular events, deadlines, jobs carried forward can all be recorded but remember to keep it brief to avoid confusion. Make all entries accurately and clearly in pencil to make changes easier. You might find it useful to divide the page into two sections, one containing appointments and the other the 'to-do' list.

Another form of diary commonly found in offices is the 'wall planner'. This usually covers a whole year with spaces for each day. They are usually laminated so that, providing the correct type of pen is used, changes can be made neatly. Alternatively, coloured stickers can be attached to give a graphic display of information. Wall planners are used for long-term planning such as staff holidays, as they allow you to see at a glance whether too many people are on holiday at the same time, or if the week you want off is available. Planners are also useful for displaying deadlines for projects, and for planning promotions or events. Obviously confidential information should not be displayed on a wall planner unless it is in a room that has restricted access.

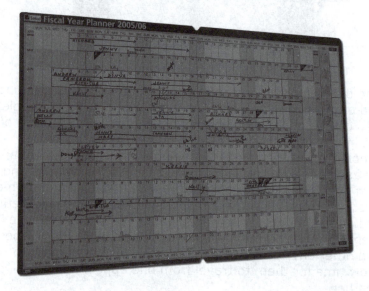

The most up-to-date form of diary is an electronic planner, which is maintained on a computer, palm top or electronic organiser. The advantages of this are:

- Regular events can be scheduled by being entered only once and the computer will update the system
- Reduced paperwork
- They can be set to display a reminder on screen that an appointment is imminent
- They can be shared by people in different locations
- They can be password protected so that confidential information cannot be seen by unauthorised people
- They can be connected to databases for easy access to telephone numbers etc
- They can highlight potential conflict of arrangements

- Some more-advanced electronic diaries can even invite colleagues to attend meetings by e-mail, and receive their acceptance or apologies automatically

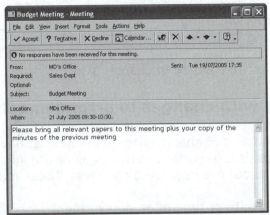

As with all innovations there are some disadvantages:

- The risk of a system failure making all of the information unavailable or, even worse, losing all of the data
- The fact that a desk top computer is not portable
- Not everybody is computer literate yet
- There is always the danger of the diary being subject to hacking

Whatever form of diary you choose to keep, be aware of the dangers of maintaining two or more versions. While this may be convenient from the point of view of being able to carry the paper version with you and still have all the advantages of the electronic system, it is vital that any changes made to one are made to the other as soon as possible to avoid confusion.

When managing diary systems you will use the following skills:

- Questioning
- Listening
- Analysing
- Planning
- Organising

- Problem solving
- Decision making
- Negotiating
- Recording
- Communicating
- Using technology

These skills are covered in chapter 1.

Dealing with changes to arrangements

If you are asked to change arrangements that have already been made, it is important to obtain all of the information you need about the requested changes. These may include:

- The date or time of an appointment
- The location of an intended meeting
- The names of the attendees
- The duration of the appointment

Requests for amendments may be made by telephone, fax, e-mail, letter or verbally. You will need to confirm that you have fully understood the requested changes.

You may receive a number of requests simultaneously to amend existing arrangements. These will need to be prioritised so that you can ensure that you carry these out in such an order that changes to imminent events are made first. Changes to arrangements for next week can be made after changes to tomorrow's schedule have been dealt with.

You may be asked to make a change which on the face of it appears to be minor, for instance to change an appointment from 0900 to 1000. However the impact could be significant and have major implications for existing commitments. All other appointments for the rest of the day could be delayed. You will need to go back to your original plans to check what other arrangements will be affected by the requested change.

When you identify that a requested change will have implications for existing entries, you will need to make alternative arrangements. To solve any possible problems you will probably have to contact a number of people to advise them that the arrangements have had to be altered, and negotiate revised schedules with them. This may need a

deal of tact and diplomacy to avoid giving the impression
that something more important has come up.

What you need to know

What implications a change in
arrangements might have

How might you receive amendments to
a diary?

How to prioritise tasks

Why should you amend tomorrow's
schedule before next week's?

How to negotiate tactfully

What are the advantages of an
electronic diary?

How to use electronic diary systems

Why is it important to confirm that you
have understood requested
amendments?

How to use a wall planner to organise
staff holidays

Whose diary are you responsible for?

What confidential information you deal
with

What types of diary systems does your
organisation use?

Communicating revised arrangements

When you record changes that have been agreed in the diary
remember to amend anything that is affected by later
arrangements. It is particularly important to delete
appointments that have been cancelled, as it is embarrassing
to turn up when you are not expected. If you are using an
electronic planner this may update other people's diaries
automatically.

It is important to communicate the agreed alterations to schedules to all those who may be affected. This may be done by letter, telephone, fax, e-mail or verbally, and needs to be completed even where networked diary software is in place. You can guarantee that at least one person won't look at their diary until the alert lets them know they should have been somewhere!

Bear in mind when deciding which method of communication to use that issues of security and confidentiality need to be heeded. Arranging meetings for Royalty, politicians or celebrities, for instance, will have security implications. Meetings between people from different organisations may be confidential, as may disciplinary or grievance interviews.

If you do not keep the diary up-to-date, it is of no use to anybody. In fact it is worse than no diary at all, as people will rely on the information in the diary. Make sure all changes are made as soon as possible after they have been agreed. Check regularly and where mistakes happen, investigate the reasons and take steps to prevent them re-occurring.

 What you need to know

The procedures that are in place to notify attendees of schedule changes

What problems may occur when alterations are made to a schedule?

Why alterations must be updated as soon as possible

What steps would you take to deal with the problems?

The importance of ensuring that the diary is kept up to date

Why should you take security implications into account when organising a diary?

The efficient planning and organising of diaries contributes to the smooth running of the office and indeed, the whole organisation. You may think keeping a diary is a trivial part of your daily routine, but imagine the chaos there would be in the office if everybody had to remember where they should be when, and what they should be doing at any given time. Whichever type of diary you keep, coping with the changes to arrangements and making sure that everybody has the latest information is an important responsibility.

A diary that is not kept up to date is just a book

Are you ready for assessment?

To achieve this unit of a Level 2 Business & Administration qualification you will need to demonstrate that you are competent in the following:

- Obtain the information you need about requested diary entries
- Make diary entries accurately and clearly
- Prioritise requested changes
- Identify the implications of any changes for existing entries
- Solve problems by negotiating alternative arrangements
- Record agreed changes in the diary
- Communicate agreed changes to those affected
- Keep the diary up-to-date

(Remember that you will need the skills listed at the beginning of this chapter and that these are covered in chapter 1.)

Your Assessor will need you to produce evidence from a variety of sources. If you carry out the activities that follow they will provide some of the evidence for you.

Activity 1
What are the advantages of electronic planners over a manual diary?

What is a diary alert?

If you keep a paper diary, how long are they stored after the end of the year?

Activity 2
The Human Resources Director has rung to say she won't be in today due to illness. She has a number of appointments in her diary. What methods would you use to re-arrange them?

Activity 3
Keep a work diary over the period of a month recording amendments you have made to your diary system.

Activity 4
Taking into account security and confidentiality, print or photocopy
selected pages from your diary system.

Activity 5
You are responsible for keeping the diary of the Sales Manager of a
building contractor. The diary below is his current schedule for 21st July

Thursday 21 July

09	Budget meeting with MD (MD's Office)
10	
11	Client Meeting at MRA
12	
13	Lunch with Lydia Cluskey (Lydia's Office)
14	Finance meeting with Ben
15	Sales Dept meeting (Adam Bone's Office)
16	Disciplinary Hearing with Annabelle Hawkins
17	Drinks with Andrew & Cameron (The Rose)

**At 4.00pm on 20th July, the Managing Director's secretary rings to
advise that the meeting scheduled for 09.30am tomorrow has
been rearranged for 11.00am.**

**The meeting with MRA has been organised for the past six weeks
and they are a valued supplier.**

How do you deal with the alteration to the schedule?

Remember: While gathering evidence for this unit, evidence
may be generated for units 110, 201, 202, 205, 209, 211,
212, 213, 216, 219, 224 and 225.

CHAPTER 7
UNIT 205 – Organise business travel and accommodation

When your colleagues are planning business trips you will be required to organise their travel, accommodation and any meetings that they are planning to attend. You will need to know when the trip is taking place, where to and for how many people. The effectiveness of their trip will be greatly enhanced if arrangements are made efficiently within the budget allowed.

There are a number of issues to take into consideration when organising business travel. To schedule the trip you will need to work in reverse from the time and date that meetings are scheduled allowing for actual travelling time, remembering that there are always likely to be delays; any time zone considerations; and public transport timetable vagaries.

Depending on the destination there may be a number of alternative methods of travel available. Deciding which is the most efficient will require consideration of both cost and time constraints. For instance travelling by train allows you to work while on the train but may have added constraints in travelling to and from the railway stations.

Each method will have its own challenges. Planning road travel requires you to consider:

- The type and number of vehicles to use (if several people are travelling can they share a car or would a mini bus be most efficient?)
- The most appropriate route
- Whether any long term road works affect the journey
- Parking facilities
- The effect of a long journey on the driver

The choice of rail travel depends on:

- How near to the railway station the traveller lives
- How far from the railway station the destination is
- Travelling time
- Number of changes
- Frequency and convenience of service
- Amount of luggage and equipment to be carried
- Ease of travel between station and destination

The choice of air travel depends on:

- How near to the airport the traveller lives
- How far from the airport the destination is
- Frequency and convenience of service
- Travelling and check-in times
- Ease of travel between airport and destination

The choice of sea travel depends on:

- Length of crossing
- Frequency and convenience of ferries
- How near to the port the traveller lives
- How far from the port the destination is
- Ease of travel between port and destination

The final decision will depend on comparing the above and factoring in the overall cost and the traveller's personal preferences – if they are a bad sailor they won't thank you for booking them on a ferry from Heysham to Douglas in the Isle of Man in November, however much cheaper it might be than flying.

Also, consider the cost of the traveller's time. A saving of £50 by travelling by train instead of a flight may not be cost-effective because of the extra time the person spends travelling instead of working.

If they are staying overnight you will need to arrange accommodation, choosing this in relation to:

- Price
- Standard
- Convenience for the station, airport or port and the venue
- Car parking if travelling by road

If car hire is required you will need the following information:

- Driver's licence number
- Type of car required
- Length of hire
- Arrangements for return of vehicle
- Insurance details

Relieving colleagues of the need to worry about tickets, visas, hotel confirmations etc. will reduce the stress involved and allow them to concentrate on the purpose of the trip. You will also be responsible for ensuring that they have the necessary currency, traveller's cheques etc., dealing with any problems that arise during the trip and evaluating the suppliers used for future reference.

 When organising business travel and accommodation you will need the following skills:

- Communicating
- Problem solving
- Researching
- Negotiating
- Planning
- Organising
- Checking
- Recording
- Managing time
- Managing resources
- Evaluating

These skills are covered in chapter 1.

Planning the trip

Travel and accommodation requirements will be identified to you by the traveller or their line manager. They will specify where they need to be, by when and for how long. It may be a simple 'there and back' trip or a more complicated journey.

They may be travelling by car and merely require accommodation or travelling by public transport and require a full itinerary. You will need to arrange appropriate travel and accommodation in order to make arrangements that are within the budget. You will also need to identify any special requirements the traveller may have such as extra leg room on a plane, smoking room in the hotel, assisted travel if they have a disability or special dietary requirements.

When you have identified all of the requirements it is a good idea to prepare a draft itinerary. Where public transport is involved your arrangements are to some extent decided by the timetable. Where road travel is planned, allow for road works, congestion, or other problems that may cause delays.

Check the draft itinerary and schedule with the traveller before making any firm bookings to be sure it meets their requirements. They may have more experience of the actual journey than you. It may be that they overlooked some detail in giving you their requirements which they will realise when they see the itinerary. Checking before making the bookings will avoid possible cancellation charges. Consider using on-line sites such as:

- www.theaa.com or www.multimap.com for road travel

- www.nationalrail.co.uk or www.scotrail.co.uk for rail travel or
- www.cheapflights.com or www.expedia.co.uk for air travel

There are many more sites to choose from, your organisation may have their own contacts or travel agency that they regularly use.

All forms of transport will require payment in advance of travel so you will need to know what payment facilities your organisation uses. Many organisations nowadays operate credit card accounts as this allows greater flexibility for booking on-line. If you make your bookings through a travel agent you will probably need to open an account with them. This will also be true for hotels that you use regularly.

 What you need to know

How to access information on available
hotel rooms and their cost

> What websites would you use to look
> for bargain travel and accommodation?

Where to find flight times and prices

> If you were arranging for someone to
> catch a flight from Edinburgh to London
> leaving at 09.30, what time would they
> need to check in?

How to use a railway timetable

> Where would you look for information
> about long-term road-works?

How to arrange travel by road, rail, air
and sea

> What details must you have before you
> can start to arrange travel and
> accommodation for a colleague?

Organising the trip

Now that you have agreed the itinerary, the time has come to make bookings for travel and accommodation. How you do this will depend largely on organisational policy:

- You may have arrangements with certain hotel groups that give you a special rate. In this case, telephone the reservations department and give them the details of the number of rooms, number of nights, date of arrival and names of guests
- You may use on-line facilities to book travel and accommodation. You will need access to a credit card unless your organisation has an account with the supplier
- You may use a travel agent to make the arrangements for you. You will telephone them with the details and they will do the rest
- You may make bookings direct with the hotel or travel company by telephone or fax. You will still need the same information

However you make the bookings, you will need to get confirmation and a booking reference.

If foreign travel is involved you may need to obtain visas. These are usually obtained from the Embassy or Consulate of the country being visited. They may take a while to be issued so application well in advance of travel would be advisable. There may be medical requirements that your traveller will need to be aware of in order that they can arrange any necessary inoculations or medication. Again this may require some time to arrange. Foreign currency or traveller's cheques will need to be arranged, this can be done through a bank, travel agent or at the post office.

All of these will need to be obtained and sorted so that each traveller has all they need in chronological order (outward journey – hotel booking – meeting documents – homeward journey).

Next, arrange any meetings necessary during the trip. You will need to know who is attending. If all of the attendees are from your organisation, you may be arranging all of their travel; if some are from other organisations you may need to liaise with the person organising their travel in order to co-ordinate everybody's itinerary. You may have to supply:

- Room booking confirmations
- Agendas
- Minutes of previous meetings
- Directions

Check who is organising the room for the meeting. It may be you and nobody has told you! If it is you, think about refreshments, equipment, stationery, and other resources or materials that may be needed. You can now get together the paperwork required for the travel and accommodation plus any documentation necessary for meetings.

TRAVEL ITINERARY
Fred Cluskey - Sales Manager
12-15 September 2005

Date	Time	Item
Mon 12/09/05	0700	Train from Reading to Paddington arrive 0732
	0748	Train from Paddington to Gatwick arrive 0845
	0900	Check in Gatwick Airport
	1100	Departure to Paris
	1600	Arrival Paris
		Accommodation booked at Hotel Georges V
	2000	Dinner with M. Simenon, Chief Buyer
Tue 13/09/05	0830	Breakfast with Mme. Bardot, Designer
	1000	Meeting with clients at Rue St. Morgue

In order to prepare for their trip, the traveller will need the information as soon as possible. Provide the traveller with an itinerary and required documents in good time and confirm that they meet their requirements. Make sure that when you have collated their visa, currency, tickets, seat reservations, hotel bookings and meeting information you pass them on immediately. A business trip can be very stressful, especially for anyone inexperienced, and having all of the information well in advance will reduce the stress. Remember how you feel when you are arranging your holidays. If you have given the traveller all of the information in good time, they will be able to confirm that their requirements have been met. If any changes are needed there will still be time to make them. Last minute changes are much more difficult and often incur additional cost.

What you need to know

Whether your organisation holds meetings
on its own premises or hires rooms

> If you were asked to arrange a meeting
> for 25 members of staff to be held in
> Brighton, where would you arrange it?

The hotel groups your organisation uses
regularly

> What inoculations/medication would
> you need for a visit to India?

Which countries require visas

> What is the quickest and most cost
> effective way to travel from Hull to
> Bristol?

The payment facilities available to you
when booking accommodation and travel

> What currency is used in Argentina?

During and after the trip

In order to deal with any queries that may arise, you will
need to maintain accurate records of travel, accommodation
and meetings. Copies of all bookings made must be kept in
a 'live' file for ease of reference. When the trip has been
completed all records should be transferred to a 'dead' file.
Records should also be maintained of meetings booked and
feedback received on the accommodation, facilities, etc.

The list of problems that may arise in arranging travel and
accommodation is endless:

- Tickets may not be received; make sure you chase
  them up in time for replacements to be sent
- Trains and planes may be delayed; your traveller may
  need you to check whether connections will still be
  met and to re-schedule if not
- People travelling by car may be delayed by road-
  works or breakdowns, or may get lost in a strange

town; in the case of a breakdown you may have to arrange for recovery and a hire car
- The hotel may have made a mistake with your booking; you will need to speak to them to resolve the matter or arrange alternative accommodation
- The traveller's luggage may be mislaid at the airport; they will need you to solve this for them while they get on with the purpose of their visit. If the visit is for several days they may need you to arrange financial assistance

If the problem leads to a delay you will also have to inform anybody who is waiting for the traveller to arrive that they have been delayed.

When invoices and credit card statements are received these must be checked carefully against the bookings in the dead file. Any discrepancies should be reported to the supplier immediately. Your organisation's procedures must then be followed to ensure prompt payment. This will avoid any charges for late payment and also ensure a good relationship is maintained with the supplier. If you need a favour, such as a last minute change of arrangements, a good relationship will make this much easier.

Detailed records will need to be kept of any problems that arose during the trip. Feedback from the traveller on the standard of the accommodation will be useful when considering future bookings. Positive feedback is just as important if you are to evaluate any external services used.

For example, you will feel more confident in booking a hotel for future use if you have had good reports on it.

Some organisations will formalise this feedback by use of an evaluation report after each trip. Where this is not in place, informal feedback should be sought and recorded. When your traveller returns ask how it all went, would they stay in that hotel again, were the trains clean and tidy, did all the taxis arrive on time, was the meeting room set up the way they would have expected, did all the timings go to plan? The answers to these questions will help you when you have to book for the same person to go on another trip, you will know what sort of thing they are looking for. It will also be valuable information should you need to book a similar trip for someone else. People will be much more forthcoming with criticism; if you want to hear their good experiences you will have to ask.

 ## What you need to know

The records you need to keep on travel, accommodation and meetings

> How long do you keep information in a live file before you transfer it to a dead file?

How to obtain, analyse and record feedback from travellers

> What action do you take if a train ticket has not arrived by the morning of the trip?

Whether your organisation has roadside assistance cover

> What are the possible knock-on effects of a delayed train journey?

Websites that may be useful in assisting travellers lost in a strange town

> You are informed by a colleague whose trip to Istanbul you have arranged that their luggage has not arrived. What are you going to do about it?

Sometimes it may seem that everybody else is off on glamorous trips to exotic places while you're stuck in the office with the paperwork. Anybody who makes business trips regularly will tell you they are greatly over-rated. All they will see of the exotic location is the inside of a hotel room which will look exactly like the inside of every other hotel room. They will all rely heavily on your expertise in making the trip run as smoothly as possible. You are the one that can make their trip comfortable and problem-free. Who knows, they might bring you back a souvenir!

You will feel great job satisfaction from knowing that you have got your colleagues there and back safely

Are you ready for assessment?

To achieve this unit of a Level 2 Business & Administration qualification you will need to demonstrate that you are competent in the following:

- Confirm travel, accommodation and budget requirements
- Check the draft itinerary and schedule with the traveller
- Arrange any meetings necessary during the trip
- Book travel arrangements and accommodation as agreed
- Obtain and collate documents for travel, accommodation and meetings
- Maintain records of travel, accommodation and meetings
- Arrange credit and payment facilities
- Deal with problems that may arise
- Provide the traveller with an itinerary and required documents in good time
- Confirm with the traveller that itinerary and documents meet requirements
- Evaluate and maintain a record of external services used

(Remember that you will need the skills listed at the beginning of this chapter and that these are covered in chapter 1.)

Your Assessor will need you to produce evidence from a variety of sources. If you carry out the activities that follow they will provide some of the evidence for you.

Activity 1
Put together a copy of all the paperwork relating to one particular trip that you have organised.

Activity 2
Keep a work diary over the period of a month recording all of the travel and accommodation you have arranged and how successful they were.

Activity 3

You have arranged a trip for your Sales Manager, who lives in Reading, to visit Paris and Edinburgh. The itinerary is as follows:

Mon 12/09/05	0700	Train from Reading to Paddington arrive 0732
	0748	Train from Paddington to Gatwick arrive 0845
	0900	Check in Gatwick Airport
	1100	Departure to Paris
	1600	Arrival Paris
		Accommodation booked at Hotel Georges V
	2000	Dinner with M. Simenon, Chief Buyer
Tue 13/09/05	0830	Breakfast with Mme. Bardot, Designer
	1000	Meeting with clients at Rue St. Morgue
	2000	Dinner with Mr. Jenkins, Director of Paris office
Wed 14/09/05	0600	Train from Gare du Nord to Charles de Gaulle
	0800	Check in Charles de Gaulle Airport
	1000	Departure to Edinburgh
	1700	Arrival Edinburgh
		Accommodation booked at The Scotsman Hotel
Thu 15/09/05	0900	Meeting in Edinburgh office
	1500	Taxi to Edinburgh Airport
	1600	Check in Edinburgh Airport
	1700	Departure to Gatwick
	1830	Arrival Gatwick
	1930	Train from Gatwick to Paddington
	2027	Arrive Paddington
	2053	Train from Paddington to Reading
	2125	Arrive Reading

You are in your office at 09.30 on Monday 12/09/05 when you get a phone call from the Sales Manager telling you the flight to Paris has been delayed by four hours. What steps will you need to take and who will you need to inform?

Activity 4

True or false, organising business travel and accommodation efficiently reduces overall costs?

What is the main reason for controlling the budget for travel and accommodation?

Where would you obtain a visa for Thailand if your traveller needed one?

What would you need to check before passing an invoice from a national hotel group?

What will you have to do in ALL cases of delayed travel?

What one thing is absolutely essential if accurate evaluation is to be made of travel and accommodation?

Remember: While gathering evidence for this unit, evidence **may** be generated for units 110, 201, 202, 204, 209, 210, 211, 212, 213, 214, 215, 216, 219, 224 and 225.

CHAPTER 8
UNIT 206 Deal with visitors

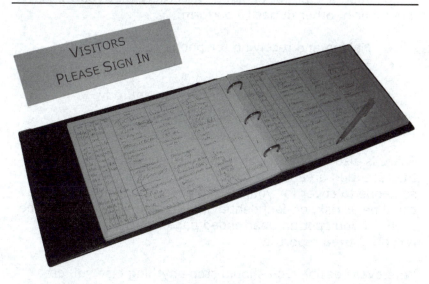

The way in which you deal with visitors on arrival is very important. First impressions are made within thirty seconds, and the first impression the visitor gets of your organisation could have a vital effect on the outcome of the visit. Making the visitor feel welcome, while appearing efficient, will create a positive impression which will last. The way you greet visitors will, of course, vary according to the circumstances. There are some situations in which a cheerful smile would not be appropriate, but a pleasant and friendly demeanour is always required.

The appearance of the reception area needs to be one which creates a favourable image of the organisation. It should be pleasantly decorated with sufficient comfortable seating and occasional tables with reading material. This may be an opportunity to place promotional leaflets or information that the visitor may find interesting. If possible, visitors should have the opportunity to be offered tea or coffee on arrival and access to washroom facilities is always welcome after a long journey.

When working on reception you will usually operate from behind a desk. This should be kept uncluttered and any files or documents kept out of sight. It is likely that you will have a number of other duties to perform:

- Making and receiving telephone calls
- Taking messages
- Maintaining the visitors' book
- Keeping the reception area clean and tidy
- Keeping leaflets etc. up to date
- Watering the plants

There is also the matter of security to consider. Don't leave the reception area unattended, if you need a break ask someone to cover for you. Don't leave valuables where they could be at risk, or confidential information where it could be seen. If you spot an unattended bag or package in the reception area report it.

Wherever possible you should stop anything else you are doing and greet visitors on their arrival. If you are taking a telephone call when a visitor arrives make eye contact with the visitor so that they know you are aware of them, then finish the telephone call before dealing with them; don't try to do both at once or you will do neither efficiently.

Visitors may be internal or external. Internal visitors are people who work for your organisation, external visitors may be customers, salesmen, delivery drivers, maintenance men or contractors. You will need to be able to identify each visitor and find out the purpose of their visit in order to meet their needs. Every visitor who passes through reception should be recorded in a visitors' book, even if they are internal and visit the premises regularly, as it is essential to know who is in the building in the event of an emergency. For the same reason they should sign out on leaving.

Colleagues may need to be advised that visitors have arrived, and there will be procedures in place for visitors to be collected or escorted to their destination. Remember if you are escorting them to get somebody to stand in for you on reception.

When dealing with visitors you will need the following skills:

- Interpersonal skills
- Presenting yourself
- Questioning
- Listening
- Negotiating
- Decision making
- Communicating
- Problem solving

These skills are covered in chapter 1.

Giving visitors the right impression

The major role of the receptionist is to make visitors feel welcome. Remember to smile. The impression you make on visitors is decided in less than 30 seconds. The whole organisation may be judged on how you deal with a visitor.

If you project a positive, friendly, polite and helpful image, that is how your organisation will be seen by others. It is important for you to be appropriately dressed, clean and tidy. Time spent on how you look is time well spent. People judge on appearance. What does how you look say about you? Positive body language, sitting or standing upright rather than slouching, making eye contact, not chewing gum, all of these will help to assure the visitor that they are visiting a professional organisation.

It is also true that your reception area should be kept clean and free of clutter, this creates the impression that your organisation is looking for. Treat each visitor as if they are the first one you have had today, even though they may be the hundredth.

What you need to know

Your organisation's dress code for reception (service reception in a garage will dress differently from a dental receptionist)

> Could you explain to someone starting work with your organisation as a receptionist what is and isn't acceptable dress?

The importance of positive body language

> How do you give the impression that you are actively listening to the visitor?

Why the reception area must be kept clean and tidy

> Do you know where to keep the keys, visitors' book etc. when they are not in use?

The difference between making eye contact and staring

> For how long is it appropriate to make unbroken eye contact?

Receiving visitors

It is important to identify visitors and the reason for their visit. Visitors may include the postman, couriers, delivery drivers, maintenance men and contractors. You will need to know how to deal with these as well as clients or customers. You will probably have a list of expected visitors; dealing with these should not be a problem.

You will need to know everything possible about your organisation. Not all visitors will have come to see someone specific. Many will just want information which you will be able to provide, such as the products or services your company supplies. Visitors who have an appointment will expect you to be able to contact the person they have come to see quickly and efficiently.

Don't give the impression that unexpected visitors are an intrusion into your day. You will need to question them to find out who they are and what their needs are. Some will already know the name of the person they want to see, others won't; this is where you can help them by using your knowledge of your organisation to get detailed information that will enable you to assist visitors.

Most organisations will have procedures for 'logging in' visitors into a visitors' book. Obviously this will only refer to visitors who are remaining in the building, not postmen, couriers, etc. This is to ensure that in an emergency you know who is in the building. Be sure that you always follow the organisation's security procedures. In many buildings, security requires that visitors' identities are checked. Where staff are required to carry identity passes, visitors will need to be issued with a visitor's badge. This may well detail health and safety information for the visitor's well-being. You must collect this when they leave and their departure must be noted in the visitors' book. If it becomes necessary to evacuate the building, take the visitors' book with you, it will be needed to check that the building is empty.

There may occasionally be visitors who are unpleasant and impolite. The best way to deal with these is to remain calm. The visitor may be annoyed about delays to their journey, or you may have had to inform them that you are unable to help them as much as they had hoped. Raising your voice will not help. If you are calm it will help to defuse the situation. Make sure you get all the facts, without them you cannot sort out the problem. If despite all of your best efforts the visitor is still behaving unreasonably, you may have to call for assistance. You may have a security or customer relations department to call on, always have their number at hand (you may never need to use it but it is as well to have it handy, just in case!) If you don't have a security department you will need to know what your organisational procedures are.

 ## What you need to know

How you are expected to address visitors.
(do you call them 'Sir/Madam' or is it OK
to call them 'mate/love'? Maybe you refer
to them by their first name.

> Do you know why it is OK to call
> visitors by their first name in some
> situations but unacceptable in others?

How to deal with post and couriers

> Do you know what types of post need
> to be signed for?

Your organisation's attitude to engaging
your visitor in small talk (do you discuss
their journey or last night's episode of
Eastenders or do you simply invite them
to take a seat?)

> Can you tell from a visitor's body
> language if they want to chat or not?

How to deal with deliveries

> Are deliveries accepted at reception or
> do they need to be re-directed?

How to deal with unexpected visitors
(the person they want to see may be
unavailable or simply unwilling to see
them)

> Do you know how to pass on the
> information to an unexpected visitor
> politely that they cannot be seen
> today?

How to deal with contractors

> Do contractors have to sign in?

How to question visitors to obtain
information in a pleasant and
professional manner

> Could you ask an unexpected visitor what
> they want and direct them to the right
> person to see them?

Whether visitors need to be issued
with visitors' badges

> Do visitors to your organisation need any
> form of identification – if so what is
> acceptable?

Where to find the visitors' book

> What information is needed in the visitors'
> book?

Go and look at the visitors' book in
your building. Could you tell from the
entries which visitors are currently in
the building?

> Do you know why vehicle registration
> numbers are recorded in the visitors' book?

Where the assembly point is in the
event of an evacuation

> If you were asked about Health and
> Safety by a visitor, would you know
> where to find the information?

How to deal with difficult visitors

> Have you had training on dealing with
> problems that you might encounter?

Who to call on for assistance if it is
required

> Do you know the telephone number of
> the security department?

Meeting visitors' needs

Above all, remember to be positive. Wherever possible don't
say 'no', offer an alternative. The objective is to make sure
visitors' needs are met. The organisation that 'goes the
extra mile' is the one that will still be in business in the
future. Visitors may also expect you to have information
such as local taxis, train times, etc. Using open ended
questions such as 'who is your appointment with?' or 'would

you prefer tea or coffee?' and listening to what the visitor says will help you establish what their needs may be. Listening to them improves the feeling of being welcomed. Give them your full attention, look at them, stop doing anything else and particularly stop talking to anyone else.

It may be policy that visitors have to be collected from the reception area. In this case you will need to let someone know they have arrived. Offer them coffee or tea, show them where the cloakrooms are, ask them to take a seat and advise them that someone will collect them shortly.

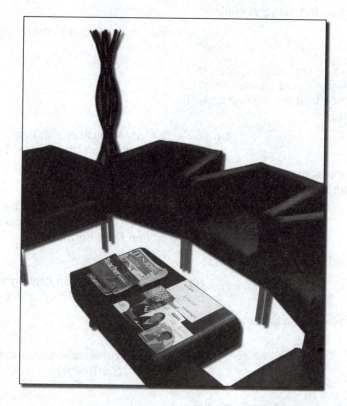

If policy is to direct visitors to the office they want, ring that office and let them know the visitor has arrived. You may avoid an embarrassing moment for your colleague who may be on the telephone with a competitor. Give clear directions, remembering that the visitor won't necessarily know the building as well as you do.

Alternatively, you may be required to escort them. Consider the visitors and don't walk too fast for them to keep up. Don't take the visitors on a tour of the building so that you can visit other departments on the way. If you have other calls to make, make them on the way back. Speak to the visitor rather than walking in silence, giving warning of any potential risks on the way, opening doors for them etc. When you reach your destination, introduce the visitor. If the person they have come to see is not there, you may leave the visitor with someone else, but do not leave them on their own.

If you cannot meet the visitor's needs exactly be prepared to offer an alternative. Try to be part of the solution rather than part of the problem. For instance, if a visitor has an appointment with the Human Resources Manager who has been called away unexpectedly, you may be able to suggest the visitor speaks to the Assistant HR Manager or makes another appointment. If you do not have the authority to meet a visitor's needs, you may be able to pass the request on. If there is no alternative, make sure you can explain the reason. Don't fall back on 'it's company policy.' The visitor is not interested in company policy, they are only interested in having their needs met.

 What you need to know

Who to ask if you don't have the authority

> What are the limits of your authority to meet a visitor's needs?

The reasons that you may be unable to meet the visitor's needs

> In what circumstances would you have to apologise to a visitor and explain that you cannot help them?

How to explain to the visitor that you cannot help them

Could you deal with a visitor that you were unable to meet the expectations of?

The alternatives that you can offer

Can you always offer a positive solution?

Where to find the extension number of everybody in the organisation

Do you know the extension number of the Human Resources Manager?

The location of every department in the organisation

If you were asked to go to the Marketing Department would you know where to find it?

Details of local transport

If the Managing Director asked you the time of the next train to London, would you be able to find out?

The location of cloakrooms

If a visitor needs to freshen up before their appointment, would you be able to direct them?

Availability of tea and coffee

If a visitor wanted a coffee, would you be able to make it for them or direct them to the coffee machine?

Whether visitors need to be collected from reception

Are external visitors and internal visitors treated differently in this respect?

In conclusion all visitors must be treated with the same courtesy. Remember you are the public face of the organisation. The way the visitor is received will make a lasting impression. Business can be lost before the meeting even takes place if the visitor is given a poor impression by the receptionist. Make sure you ask the correct questions to find out who the visitor is and the purpose of their visit. Know and follow your organisation's procedures for dealing with visitors and the wide range of circumstances that can arise when greeting them. Whether you inform someone of their arrival, direct them to the department they need or escort them act promptly, don't keep the visitor waiting unnecessarily.

Every visitor is a guest, treat them as such and you won't go far wrong

Are you ready for assessment?

To achieve this unit of a Level 2 Business & Administration qualification you will need to demonstrate that you are competent in the following:

- Help visitors feel welcome
- Present a positive image of yourself and your organisation
- Identify visitors and the reason for their visit
- Follow organisational and security procedures
- If appropriate, inform colleagues of the visitors' arrival
- Make sure visitors' needs are met

(Remember that you will need the skills listed at the beginning of this chapter and that these are covered in chapter 1.)

Your Assessor will need you to produce evidence from a variety of sources. If you carry out the activities that follow they will provide some of the evidence for you.

Activity 1
If the company you work for has an organisation chart, find a copy and highlight your position on it. If it doesn't, then create one.

Activity 2
If your company has an internal telephone directory, find a copy and highlight your extension on it. If it doesn't, then create one.

Activity 3
You are working as a receptionist in a doctor's surgery. The doctor is running behind with his appointments, so there are a number of patients in the waiting room. At 10.30am the patient due to see the doctor at 10.00am has still not been seen. The doctor indicates that she is ready to see the next patient and you call Amanda Patel, whose appointment was for 10.00am. Matthew Graham, who has just arrived for his 10.30am appointment, comes to the desk and protests loudly that he should be seen now as it is time for his appointment and he has urgent work to return to. How do you deal with this situation?

Activity 4

Which of the following would be appropriate if you were working on the reception desk at the Head Office of a traditional company?

1. Chewing gum
2. Tongue stud
3. Jeans and a crop top
4. Business suit
5. Skirt and blouse
6. Reading a novel

Activity 5

Write an account of approximately 250 words stating the role of the receptionist and why they should be friendly and efficient.

Activity 6

The Human Resources Manager is interviewing applicants for a Sales Manager's job. You are working on reception and the following visitors arrive unexpectedly asking to see him. For whom, if any, would you interrupt the Human Resources Manager?

1. A pensions salesman
2. The Company Chairman
3. His wife
4. The police looking for information on a member of staff
5. An Inland Revenue inspector
6. The local newspaper selling advertising space

Office Floor Plan

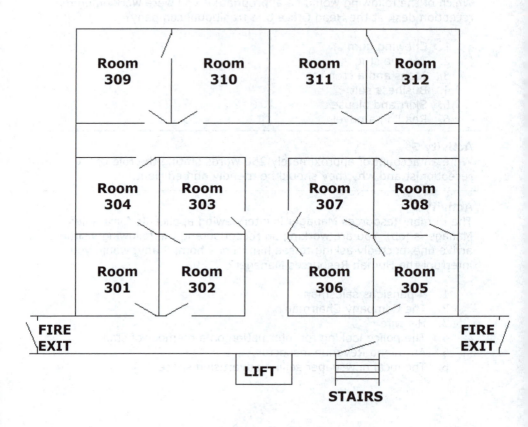

Activity 7

Above is a plan of the third floor of an office building

- If you were in room 308 with a visitor and a fire broke out in room 305 what route would you take to leave the building?
- If you were in room 309 with a visitor and a fire broke out in room 304 what route would you take to leave the building?
- If you were in room 310 and your visitor was in room 311 and a fire broke out in room 307 what route would you take to leave the building?
- What must you be sure to take with you when you leave the building?

Activity 8

Keep a work diary over the period of a month recording all of the visitors you deal with, their requirements and how you met them, indicating any security procedures involved.

Activity 9

If you have a job description as a receptionist, take a copy. If you don't, but there is such a job description in the company, ask if you may have a copy. If there is no job description for a receptionist, write one and ask your supervisor to check it.

Remember: While gathering evidence for this unit, evidence **may** be generated for units 110, 201, 202, 219 and 225.

CHAPTER 9
UNIT 207 – Process customer financial information

One of the most important departments in any organisation is the accounts department. The responsibility of the accounts department is to receive payments for goods and services provided, make payments for goods and services received and record the transactions so that the organisation knows where its money is coming from and going to.

Accounts departments are usually divided into sales ledger and purchase ledger departments. The sales ledger department is responsible for invoicing customers, receiving and banking payments and maintaining records of monies owed to the organisation. The purchase ledger department is responsible for receiving and checking invoices from customers, making payments and maintaining records of monies owed by the organisation. Both will need to open accounts for new customers or suppliers and amend the existing details for changes of address, telephone number etc. The day-to-day procedures of the sales ledger will be dealt with in detail in this chapter.

When you are working in an accounts department there are a number of terms that you will come into contact with that it will be helpful to understand. We will explain these briefly here:

- **Creditor** - This is someone the organisation owes money to
- **Debtor** - This is someone who owes money to the organisation
- **Credit** - This is an item of income to the organisation
- **Debit** - This is an item of expenditure by the organisation
- **Double entry book-keeping** - Every transaction is entered as both a credit and a debit, so the accounts will always balance
- **Ledger** - Literally a book in which transactions are recorded or a set of individual accounts
- **Nominal Ledger** - This is the record of all the credits and debits, showing where the money comes from and where it goes to. Nominal Ledger Accounts are usually given code numbers
- **Payment terms** - The agreed length of time between the invoice date and payment due date
- **Remittance advice** - This tells you which invoices a payment refers to
- **Allocate** - This is the process of matching invoices together with a payment
- **Period end** - This is the end of an accounting period. Depending on the organisation, this may be weekly, four weekly, every calendar month, quarterly or annually
- **Balance** - The amount outstanding on an account at any time. The total of all of the credit balances must equal the total of all of the debit balances. The accounts are then said to balance

This may be clearer if we follow a sales transaction and a purchase transaction through the book-keeping system.

Sales transaction

The organisation sells goods valued at £50.00 to Alfred Burke on September 2$^{nd.}$ Payment is received one month later.

2nd Sept	Credit Sales Account	£50.00
2nd Sept	Debit Alfred Burke Account	£50.00
2nd Oct	Credit Alfred Burke Account	£50.00
2nd Oct	Debit Bank Account	£50.00

Purchase transaction

The organisation purchases stationery valued at £27.43 from Wilson's on September 23rd. Payment is made one month later.

23rd Sept	Debit Stationery Account	£27.43
23rd Sept	Credit Wilson's Account	£27.43
23rd Oct	Debit Wilson's Account	£27.43
23rd Oct	Credit Bank Account	£27.43

In the above examples the Sales Account, Stationery Account and Bank Account are Nominal Ledger Accounts while Alfred Burke is a Sales Ledger Account and Wilson's is a Purchase Ledger Account.

If you are operating a computerised accounts system, you will only be making one of the pair of entries, the computer will automatically make the other. If you are operating a manual accounts system it is vital that you make both entries as failure to do so will mean the accounts do not balance. Understanding the principle of double entry book-keeping will help even if you are using a computer, as it will avoid you entering credits as debits and vice versa.

When processing customers' financial information you will need the following skills:

- Planning
- Organising
- Researching
- Checking
- Communicating
- Using technology
- Reading
- Recording
- Problem solving
- Using number
- Managing time

These skills are covered in chapter 1.

Sales ledger

Sales ledger starts with an invoice. The invoice may be raised in the sales department or the dispatch department, and a copy sent to the sales ledger department, or it may be part of the sales ledger department's responsibility to raise the invoice from information provided by the sales or dispatch department and send the original to the customer, keeping the accounts department copy. If another department raises the invoice all the information you need will already be completed; if you are raising the invoice you will need to know the sale price of the goods or services provided, any discounts offered to the customer, payment terms and rates of VAT.

Having either raised an invoice or received a copy of a sales invoice, you will then need to process it. The following details will need to be entered either into the computer or your manual invoice records:

- Customer name
- Customer account number
- Invoice date
- Purchase order number
- Nominal ledger code
- Details of goods or services provided

- Discount given (if any)
- Net price (the price before any VAT)
- VAT rate
- VAT amount
- Gross amount (net plus VAT)

Sometimes customers may return goods or have been overcharged. In this case a credit note will be raised. This is in effect a reverse invoice and is often printed in red to avoid confusion. Credit notes are processed in exactly the same way as invoices. When you have processed all the invoices and credit notes for the day they will need to be filed so that they can be found in case of query.

Many sales ledger departments, particularly if they send large numbers of invoices to the same customer, will send a monthly statement of account to each customer listing the invoices and credit notes outstanding.

Hopefully at some point you will receive payment from the customer. Payment may be made in a number of ways:

- **Cash** – The customer may come into the office and give the money to you
- **Cheque** – The customer may send a cheque in the post
- **Credit or debit card** – The customer may provide their credit or debit card details
- **BACS (Banks Automated Clearing System)** – Payment is made direct to the organisation's bank account
- **Direct Debits** – The customer may have an arrangement where the balance on their invoice or statement is paid on an agreed date

You will need to know which invoices (and credit notes) the payment refers to. The customer may send you a remittance advice, a copy of the invoices paid or a copy of the statement, or may write the invoice numbers on the back of the cheque. Separate the cash and cheques from the remittance advices, copy invoices etc. Where no separate advice has been received make a note of the customer name and the amount received.

Credit and debit card remittances, Direct Debits and BACS payments are transmitted to your organisation's bank account electronically. Cash and cheques must be physically taken to the bank and paid in. Details are entered onto a Deposit Slip which accompanies the cash and cheques.

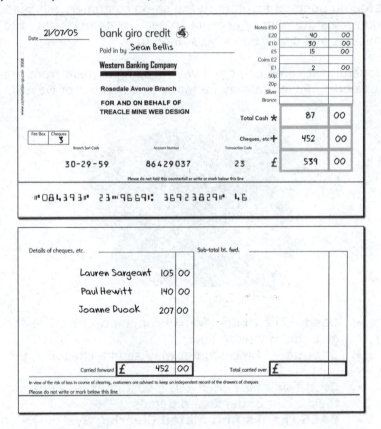

On the main part of the deposit slip:

- Complete the date
- Sign on the 'Paid in by' line

- Complete the number of cheques in the 'Cheques' box
- Enter the cash by denomination
- Enter the total cash
- Enter the total cheques
- Enter the total of cash and cheques

On the reverse list the cheques individually with the drawer's name and the amount. Deposit slips have counterfoils which are effectively your receipt from the bank for the money deposited. On the front of the counterfoil enter the date, the total cash, the total cheques and the total of cash and cheques. On the reverse of the counterfoil list the cheques individually. The completed deposit slip, cash and cheques must now be placed in the safe or a locked drawer until they are taken to the bank in accordance with your organisation's procedures.

You can now enter the payments into the accounts using the customer name, account number and amount paid. When you have entered all the payments you are then ready to allocate the payments against the outstanding invoices. Where you have remittance advices, copy invoices or copy statements allocation should be simple. Open the relevant customer account, identify the invoices that have been paid and indicate on the account those invoices and the payment.

Activity for Account Chez Bonné (CB2107)

A/C	CB2107	**Balance**	£270.00
Name	Chez Bonné	**Amount Paid**	£137.63
Credit Limit £500.00			

No	Date	Ref	Details	Amount (£)	O/S	Debit	Credit
8135	17/08/04	8507	1x Publication	17.63		17.63	
8588	17/09/04	100783	Sales Receipt	17.63			17.63
9291	21/10/04	8733	4x Registration	120.00		120.00	
9986	23/11/04	BACS	Sales Receipt	120.00			120.00
10319	07/12/04	9103	8x Publication	270.00	270.00	270.00	

The interesting part of allocation comes when you haven't received anything that tells you which invoices are being paid, all you have is a note that a payment has been received. In this case you open the relevant customer account and attempt to recognise invoices which add up to the amount paid. If you can, then allocate those to the payment. If you are unable to allocate a payment it remains on the account as unallocated. It may be your responsibility to contact the customer and ask for clarification, or you may simply be required to leave the payment as unallocated until you carry out the period end procedure.

At the period end a statement is produced for each customer account and sent to the customer showing outstanding invoices and balance owed. A list is created of customer balances showing any invoices not paid in accordance with the agreed payment terms and any unallocated payments. This list is given to the person responsible for credit control so that they can take the necessary action.

 ## What you need to know

Accounting terms you will come into contact with

> What is meant by 'allocating' a payment?

Who to seek advice and guidance from if a query exceeds your personal authority

> What are your organisation's payment terms?

How the Data Protection Act applies to the accounts department

> What methods of payment does your organisation accept?

The current rates of VAT

> What is meant by an unallocated payment?

Fixed payments

Some organisations, particularly utility companies such as electricity, gas, water and telephone suppliers, operate a system of fixed payments by Direct Debit on a periodic, usually monthly, basis.

The organisation will estimate the customer's annual spend and divide this by 12, producing an average monthly spend. The customer will then agree to pay this average amount monthly by Direct Debit, regardless of the actual amount consumed.

Invoices will be produced regularly for each customer, but these will show the actual amount spent and the payments received, leaving a balance. This balance may be a debit amount if the payments have not fully covered the consumption, or a credit amount if payments exceed consumption.

Usually, on an annual basis, the customer will be asked to make a payment to cover a debit balance, or a refund will be made to repay a credit balance. At this point the amount of the fixed payment for the next year will be adjusted.

The advantages of this system to the customer are that it:

- Enables them to level out their outgoings over the year and avoid peaks and troughs of consumption; for instance electricity and gas usage may be significantly greater in the winter than in the summer
- Avoids a large quarterly bill which they may find it difficult to meet

The advantages of this system to the organisation are that it:

- Provides a regular cash flow, avoiding peaks and troughs in their supply
- It improves customer loyalty, as customers are less likely to switch suppliers if they have a Direct Debit arrangement with their existing supplier

Your bank will supply you with details of Direct Debits received, and these will need to be processed to the customers' accounts.

Activity for Account T J Anderson				
A/C 5689615			**Balance**	
Name T J Anderson				
Direct Debit 36.00			**Date Payable** 15th Monthly	
Date	**Ref**	**Details**	**Amount (£)**	**Bal**
15/08/07	DD	Payment	36.00	-36.00
15/09/07	DD	Payment	36.00	-72.00
01/10/07	5566	Invoice	114.26	42.26
15/10/07	DD	Payment	36.00	6.26
15/11/07	DD	Payment	36.00	-29.74

The bank will also supply you with details of failed Direct Debits, and your organisation's procedures for dealing with these will have to be followed. There may be a standard letter which is sent in the first instance, and a sequence of follow-up procedures should no satisfactory response be received.

Sometimes the customer's response will be to complain that the fault lies with the organisation. They may have already had communication with the organisation agreeing that their Direct Debit would not be actioned, or they may be awaiting a recalculation of their fixed payment.

Your organisation may have a department for dealing with customer complaints, or the manager or supervisor may handle complaints. You need to know who deals with complaints in your organisation. It may be necessary to involve a supervisor or the customer care department, but you shouldn't deal with complaints yourself.

Once you have collected as much information as possible from the customer, give a clear explanation of the complaint to your colleague to help them to solve the problem. Never ask the customer to repeat themselves, as this is not effective customer service.

Handing the complaint over effectively and efficiently will not only help your colleague to resolve the matter, but it will also help the customer to feel confident that their complaint is being taken seriously and that they, and their custom, are valued.

What you need to know

How to process a Direct Debit payment

> Who in your organisation can authorise the processing of a refund in respect of overpayment?

How to raise a cheque

> Where will you find customers' payment terms?

How to handle a customer complaint

> Who in your organisation deals with customer complaints?

How to complete a standard letter

> Who in your organisation do you refer persistent non-payments to?

How to calculate average monthly spend

> Who do you pass queries on customers' accounts to?

Information handling

It is vital that all of your work is accurate and legible. Whether you are entering data into a computer or manually, check all of the input. If working manually, check the calculations that you make. It is a lot easier to correct mistakes if they are uncovered as soon as they are made rather than when attempting to balance the accounts.
In every accounts department there will be a need to file information in such a way that it can be readily accessed. Information may be in the form of paper files or electronically maintained.

Electronic filing systems will have their own in-built sorting and storing mechanisms. Your responsibility will lie in learning what they are, so that you can store information accurately in approved locations and find it again quickly. Most will include a facility to store the information in folders within the main directory. These should be used to group files together to speed up retrieval.

Paper records will have to be sorted manually. There are a number of different methods that can be used:

- **Alphabetical** – Filed in order from A–Z. Files starting with the same letter are filed in order of the second letter (Aa, Ab, Ac) and so on. People's names are filed by their surnames, and if there is more than one person with the same surname they are filed in first name order. Names starting with 'The' are filed by ignoring the 'The'. Names beginning with 'Mac' or 'Mc' come before 'Ma', 'Mb' etc
- **Numerical** – Files are given numbers and filed from 1 to infinity. This is useful for information which naturally lends itself to being filed this way (account numbers, sales invoices, for instance)
- **Alpha-numerical** – Files have a combination of letters and numbers. Examples include postal codes, National Insurance numbers and car registration numbers. These are usually large databases, as they hold more information than numerical systems and are more flexible than alphabetical systems. The order of filing depends on the sequence of the file name. If file names start with letters followed by numbers, they are filed in alphabetical order first, and numerical order within each letter
- **Chronological** – This is often used within one of the other methods. For instance, each customer's records are filed alphabetically, but the information within the file is stored chronologically, usually with the most recent at the front. This ensures that the most up–to-date information is easily accessible. However, it can be used based on dates of birth or start dates
- **Geographical** – This is a method of sorting by areas, for example: North West England, East Anglia, South West England; you can then sort them into counties, North West England to include Cheshire, Lancashire and Merseyside; then into towns such as Chester, Lancaster and Liverpool
- **By subject or category** – Some organisations need to sort their filing under topics rather than names. For instance, a shoe manufacturer may keep files under product names such as 'Ladies', 'Gentlemen' and 'Children's'

Whichever method is adopted, if the information is not stored accurately it will be extremely difficult to find. Be aware of

'American' dates. In the United Kingdom the 7th September 2008 is written 07.09.08, while in America it is written 09.07.08. If you are filing in chronological order this may cause confusion. Special care needs to be taken when filing numerically to avoid transposing numbers.

Wherever the information is stored, electronically or on paper, it is essential that you update the information as required. As soon as any new or amended information is received the existing record should be updated. For instance, addresses will change as people or businesses move, or names may change as people marry.

Paper files may be stored in locked cabinets. Electronic files may be password protected. If you are responsible for storing the files, you must be sure that only authorised people have access to them and that you follow agreed procedures and legislation for maintaining security and confidentiality. If somebody asks you to show them records that you are not sure they are allowed to see, always check before allowing them access.

Working in an accounts department gives you access to a great deal of information about both your own organisation and customers. Much of this information is confidential, either because it is subject to the Data Protection Act or because it is commercially sensitive. Keep anything you find out to yourself.

 What you need to know

Which method of storing information is in use in your organisation

> What passwords are in use in your organisation?

The principles of the Data Protection Act

> What does 'confidential' mean in your organisation?

Who has authority to change a password

> Who is authorised to access information?

Every organisation will have policies regarding the way their accounts are maintained. Depending on the organisation you are working in, there may be industry regulations or professional codes which must be complied with. It is essential that you know and understand what these are and how they affect your work.

As in any other job, your work will be subject to the Health and Safety at Work Act. This makes you responsible as an individual for taking reasonable care for your own health and safety, and that of others who may be affected by your actions, and co-operating with others.

The accounts department keep the wheels of the organisation turning by receiving money from customers and passing it on to suppliers

Are you ready for assessment?

To achieve this unit of a Level 2 Business & Administration
qualification you will need to demonstrate that you are
competent in the following:

- Make sure that all documents, entries and records are
  accurate and legible
- Receive payments from and make payments to
  customers
- Confirm that calculations and balances are accurate
- Recognise discrepancies in documents and take
  appropriate action
- Identify any balances outstanding over the time
  period stipulated with your employer, and take
  appropriate action
- Keep accurate records of transactions
- Comply with legal requirements, industry regulations,
  organisational policies and professional codes

(Remember that you will need the skills listed at the
beginning of this chapter and that these are covered in
chapter 1.)

Your Assessor will need you to produce evidence from a
variety of sources. If you carry out the activities that follow
they will provide some of the evidence for you.

Activity 1

On 4th November 2005 you receive a cheque from Peterson and Giles Ltd. for £1047.48 with no indication of which invoices or credit notes it refers to. From the customer account details below allocate the payment. List the invoices which are overdue following allocation.

Account No. 05682 Payment terms 30 days		Peterson and Giles Ltd	
Date	**Inv. No.**	**Amount (£)**	**Balance (£)**
03.09.05	1471	39.99	39.99
07.09.05	1612	393.47	433.46
08.09.05	CN36	-19.99	413.47
10.09.05	1711	236.41	649.88
12.09.05	1936	1.93	651.81
16.09.05	2131	1267.01	1918.82
17.09.05	CN43	-39.99	1878.83
21.09.05	2611	437.59	2316.42
25.09.05	2993	1361.32	3677.74
01.10.05	3714	23.46	3701.20
06.10.05	3949	112.22	3813.42
17.10.05	4172	42.22	3855.64
22.10.05	4963	137.46	3993.10

Activity 2

You have been responsible for dealing with fixed payments in your organisation for some time. You have been asked to move to the credit control department, and your present role is to be taken over by a new member of staff.

Write a procedure covering:

- Dealing with Direct Debit payments
- Dealing with failed Direct Debits
- Handling customer complaints.

Activity 3

You work in the sales ledger department of a wholesale supplier of hardware and garden supplies. The sales department send you the following purchase order.

Purchase order No. 1471		Peterson and Giles Ltd
100	Packs	4" nails
50	Packs	2" hexagonal nuts
4	Each	Wheelbarrows with 16" wheels
27	30ltr	Potting compost
2	Pairs	Size 11 waders

Using the price list below create an invoice.

PRICE LIST		
Item	Unit Price (£)	Quantity
½" nails	0.19	Per pack
1" nails	0.21	Per pack
2" nails	0.36	Per pack
4" nails	0.56	Per pack
6" nails	0.76	Per pack
½" hex nuts	0.26	Per pack
1" hex nuts	0.34	Per pack
2" hex nuts	0.56	Per pack
3" hex nuts	0.68	Per pack
4" hex nuts	0.89	Per pack
6" hex nuts	1.02	Per pack
½" screws	0.26	Per pack
1" screws	0.39	Per pack
2" screws	0.46	Per pack
4" screws	0.63	Per pack
6" screws	0.86	Per pack
Waders size 9	26.99	Per pair
Waders size 10	31.99	Per pair
Waders size 11	33.99	Per pair
Waders size 12	35.50	Per pair
Potting compost	1.99	10ltr
Potting compost	3.99	20ltr
Potting compost	4.56	30ltr
Wheelbarrows	19.99	12" wheel
Wheelbarrows	25.99	14" wheel
Wheelbarrows	31.99	16" wheel
Wheelbarrows	35.99	18" wheel
Carriage	20.00	Over £400 Free of charge

All prices subject to VAT at current rate

Activity 4

What do you understand by the following terms:

Credit	Debtor
Ledger	Double entry book-keeping
Allocate	Payment terms
Balance	Remittance advice

Activity 5

Research the principles of the Data Protection Act. Write a short report explaining how this applies to the sales ledger.

Remember: While gathering evidence for this unit, evidence **may** be generated for units 110, 201, 202, 203, 209, 212, 213, 215, 216, 219, 220, 224 and 225.

CHAPTER 10
UNIT 208 – Operate credit control procedures

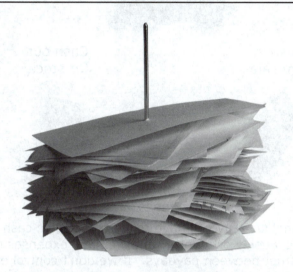

Every organisation involved in supplying goods and services will have customers. Apart from a few purely cash organisations, all will have credit customers who will receive the goods or services prior to paying for them. This includes non-commercial organisations such as Local Authorities, whose customers include householders and whose invoices cover Council Tax demands and Local Authority tenancy agreements. Careful monitoring of the total amount outstanding is important, as there will be a limit to the total credit the organisation can afford to extend without affecting its cash flow.

Cash flow is the movement of money through the organisation. Every organisation has to spend money on day-to-day running; wages, rent, rates, light and heat, stationery, postage and office equipment. Manufacturing business has to buy raw materials, a wholesale or retail business has to buy stock. The money to pay for all of these things comes from the sales of goods or services. A business may appear very successful in that its sales figures are very healthy; it may even be making an acceptable profit on paper, in other words the total of its sales is greater than the total of its expenses; but it can still go bankrupt if the cash flow is not controlled. If the money is not available to pay suppliers because its customers have not paid their invoices then the business can collapse.

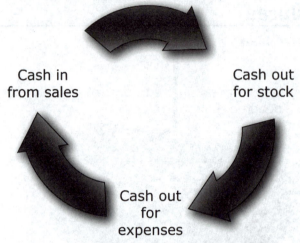

Cash in from sales

Cash out for stock

Cash out for expenses

On a personal level, we all have to watch our own cash flow. We get paid weekly or monthly and we have expenses that have to be met between paydays. If we don't control our cash flow and spend all our income as soon as we get it, we will have a problem meeting demands on our purse as the next payday approaches.

The purpose of credit control is to protect your cash flow by ensuring that monies owed to the organisation are received when they are due, which allows the organisation to pay its debts on time. Credit control starts with checking the credit worthiness of new customers before allowing them credit. There are three main sources of information used to establish the suitability of a potential new customer:

- **Credit agencies** - There are companies whose sole purpose is to supply information on other companies' credit records
- **Trade references** - These are companies who have supplied the potential new customer in the past and are willing to say that they are a good risk
- **Banks** - The potential customer's bank may be prepared to give an opinion as to the customer's ability to pay

Taking up references before allowing credit will reduce the risk of non-payment that your company is exposed to.

Once credit has been agreed, payment terms will need to be set. Payment terms state the agreed length of time between the invoice date and payment due date. These terms will appear on the invoice and may differ from customer to customer as major purchasers will negotiate longer payment terms in exchange for larger contracts.

When operating credit control procedures you will need the following skills:

- Organising
- Checking
- Communicating
- Using technology
- Reading
- Recording
- Using number
- Managing time

These skills are covered in chapter 1.

Analysing overdue payments

To monitor customers' performance against the agreed payment terms a list is created at the end of each accounting period. This shows customer balances and any payments not received in accordance with the agreed payment terms and any unallocated payments. This list is given to the person responsible for credit control so that they can take the necessary action.

One of the first the first actions to take on receipt of the list is a comparison with the previous list to look for reasons for non-payment. These may be:

- The customer is still waiting for part or all of the order
- There is a query on the invoice that is being dealt with
- The customer is waiting for a credit note
- Action is already being taken to recover the outstanding amount
- The customer is a member of a vulnerable group and subject to a vulnerable groups' tariff

In-line with corporate social responsibility, many utility companies will identify customers in vulnerable groups, such as the elderly, people with disabilities, large families and low-income families. Customers in these groups will be charged on a vulnerable groups' tariff, and failure to pay will be treated more sympathetically.

As at May 2006, the following table shows examples of some of the companies and their social tariffs.

Supplier	Social tariff	Value	Eligible groups	No.
British Gas	Rebate	£30 per fuel	All British Gas consumers on benefits in deprived areas (consumers must apply)	250,000
EDF (current)	Price freeze	Worth £40 for dual fuel	All people living in fuel-poor areas	77,000
Npower 'First step'	Discount	Transfer to cheapest tariff	People in arrears or 'struggling to pay their bills'	30,000
Powergen ACES	Price freeze	Worth £40 for dual fuel, plus CWP worth £20	Older people on Age Concern Energy Services package	180,000
Powergen Staywarm	Fixed price	'Peace of mind'	All older people, providing consumption is below a certain level	430,000

Scottish Power	Rebate	£30 for dual fuel	All ppm users on PSR	5,000
SSE energycare plus	Discount	Up to 20% discount	Severe fuel-poor households on benefits	30,000

Make notes against each of these accounts so that the information will be available when the next list is prepared.

The next action is to check the unallocated payments. Possibly invoices or payments may have been entered onto the wrong account creating two errors, an overdue amount on one account and an unallocated payment on another. The source documents need to be checked and any corrections made.

This will leave you with a list of unexplained overdue payments. Before taking any action to recover these, it is worth having a look at the individual account records for any payments received or credit notes actioned since the list was created. Also check for any payments received that have not yet been entered. You don't want to be chasing a customer for payment if the payment has already been received in the last few days. If a payment has been made you will need to make a note of the date and amount paid on the list.

 What you need to know

The purpose of credit control

What do you understand by the term 'cash flow'?

At what point credit control begins

What are trade references?

Possible reasons for non-payment

When does a payment become overdue?

Your organisation's payment terms

Why do you look at unallocated
payments when analysing overdue
payments?

The reason for taking up references

Why do you compare the current
overdue list with the previous list?

Recovering overdue payments

Starting from your list of unexplained overdue payments,
action will need to be taken to find out whether there is a
reason for non-payment. Each organisation will have its own
procedures and time-scales to follow; make sure you know
what these are.

It is particularly important that, if you work in an
organisation which has a vulnerable groups' policy, you
follow the organisation's guidelines for dealing with these
customers.

Many organisations will follow a procedure similar to the
following:
A standard letter will be written to each customer on the list
asking them to pay within seven days or give a reason for
non-payment.

Make a note on your list that a letter has been sent and the
date. As a result of the letter one of three things will
happen:

- Payment will be received. Note this on your list
- The customer will contact you to explain why they
  have not paid. There may be a number of reasons
  and you will need to deal with each one on its merits
  and record the information on your list
- No response. Seven days after the letter was sent,
  you will need to contact the customer by telephone

Before making telephone calls ensure you have all the
information to hand:

- The telephone number and name of contact
- Full details of the overdue payment. If possible
  copies of the invoices as this will give you all of the
  information
- The account information showing payments and
  allocations

```
Elliott and Company Ltd.
32 Weldon Road
Southampton
SO1 4FT
Tel 01256 22569

Johnson & Co
126 North Street
Southampton
SO5 P98

13th October 2008

Dear Sirs,

Re: Account No. 012569

According to our records the amount of £356.98 remains unpaid at the
above date and is overdue.  If there is a reason for non-payment we
would be glad to hear from you in order that we can deal with the
problem.

If there is no problem payment is requested within 7 days.

Yours faithfully

S Carter

S Carter
```

During the call remember to be polite and ask for payment
without demanding it. If they say:

- They have paid, it is not professional to indicate that
  you don't believe them
- They have posted a cheque that has not been
  received ask them to contact their bank as it may be
  necessary to stop the cheque and issue a new one
- They have not received the invoice, send a copy
- There is a reason for non-payment, take all the details
  so that you can pass these on to the appropriate
  department
- They will pay, take the details of when payment will
  be made and the name of the person you are
  speaking to

After the call record all of the details of the call; the date and
time of the call, the name of the person you spoke to and
what outcome was agreed. Make sure you pass on to the
relevant people any information the customer has given you
as to the reason for their non-payment. Follow up any offers

of payment to make sure they have actually been carried out and deal with any that haven't been.

Your organisation will have procedures for dealing with customers who fail to pay after you have exhausted the normal systems. A customer who offers to address an overdue payment and fails to do so will create a potential bad debt.

A bad debt is a debt which cannot be collected, and the final outcome will be that the organisation has to write it off, which will reduce the organisation's profit. Before this stage is reached there will be a number of steps open to the organisation: they can take the customer to court and use bailiffs to recover goods, but, at the end of the day, if the customer doesn't have the money it cannot be recovered.

What you need to know

How to follow up a customer's failure to meet agreement to pay

What information do you need to record during a telephone call?

Your organisation's procedures and time-scales for recovering overdue payments

What responses might you receive to a letter requesting payment?

How to ask for payment

What information do you need to have available before you make a telephone call requesting payment?

Whether your organisation has a vulnerable groups' policy

How are customers in vulnerable groups dealt with when their payments are overdue?

What is meant by bad debts

What is your organisation's policy on recovering bad debts?

Information handling

It is vital that all of your work is accurate and legible. Whether you are entering data into a computer or manually, check all of the input. If working manually, check the calculations that you make. It is a lot easier to correct mistakes if they are uncovered as soon as they are made, rather than when attempting to balance the accounts.

In every accounts department you are working in, there will be a need to file information in such a way that it can be readily accessed. Information may be in the form of paper files or electronically maintained.

Electronic filing systems will have their own in-built sorting and storing mechanisms. Your responsibility will lie in learning what they are so that you can store information accurately in approved locations and find it again quickly. Most will include a facility to store the information in folders within the main directory. These should be used to group files together to speed up retrieval.

Paper records will have to be sorted manually. There are a number of different methods that can be used:

- **Alphabetical** – Filed in order from A–Z. Files starting with the same letter are filed in order of the second letter (Aa, Ab, Ac) and so on. People's names are filed by their surnames, and if there is more than one person with the same surname they are filed in first name order. Names starting with 'The' are filed by ignoring the 'The'. Names beginning with 'Mac' or 'Mc' come before 'Ma', 'Mb' etc
- **Numerical** – Files are given numbers and filed from 1 to infinity. This is useful for information which naturally lends itself to being filed this way (account numbers, sales invoices, for instance)
- **Alpha-numerical** – Files have a combination of letters and numbers. Examples include postal codes, National Insurance numbers and car registration numbers. These are usually large databases as they hold more information than numerical systems and are more flexible than alphabetical systems. The order of filing depends on the sequence of the file name. If file names start with letters followed by

numbers, they are filed in alphabetical order first, and numerical order within each letter

- **Chronological** – This is often used within one of the other methods. For instance, each customer's records are filed alphabetically, but the information within the file is stored chronologically, usually with the most recent at the front. This ensures that the most up-to-date information is easily accessible. However, it can be used based on dates of birth or start dates
- **Geographical** – This is a method of sorting by areas, for example: North West England, East Anglia, South West England; you can then sort them into counties, North West England to include Cheshire, Lancashire and Merseyside; then into towns such as Chester, Lancaster and Liverpool
- **By subject or category** – Some organisations need to sort their filing under topics rather than names. For instance, a shoe manufacturer may keep files under product names such as 'Ladies', 'Gentlemen' and 'Children's'

Whichever method is adopted, if the information is not stored accurately it will be extremely difficult to find. Be aware of 'American' dates. In the United Kingdom the 7th September 2008 is written 07.09.08, while in America it is written 09.07.08. If you are filing in chronological order this may cause confusion. Special care needs to be taken when filing numerically to avoid transposing numbers.

Wherever the information is stored, electronically or on paper, it is essential that you update the information as required. As soon as any new or amended information is received the existing record should be updated. For instance, addresses will change as people or businesses move, or names may change as people marry.

Paper files may be stored in locked cabinets. Electronic files may be password protected. If you are responsible for storing the files, you must be sure that only authorised people have access to them and that you follow agreed procedures and legislation for maintaining security and confidentiality. If somebody asks you to show them records that you are not sure they are allowed to see, always check before allowing them access.

Working in an accounts department gives you access to a great deal of information about both your own organisation and customers. Much of this information is confidential, either because it is subject to the Data Protection Act or because it is commercially sensitive. Keep anything you find out to yourself.

What you need to know

Which method of storing information is in use in your organisation

What passwords are in use in your organisation?

The principles of the Data Protection Act

What does 'confidential' mean in your organisation?

Who has authority to change a password

Who is authorised to access information?

Every organisation will have policies regarding the way their accounts are maintained. Depending on the organisation you are working in, there may be industry regulations or professional codes which must be complied with. It is essential that you know and understand what these are and how they affect your work.

As in any other job, your work will be subject to the Health and Safety at Work Act. This makes you responsible as an individual for taking reasonable care for your own health and safety, and that of others who may be affected by your actions, and co-operating with others.

Successful credit control requires a continuous monitoring of customers' accounts and is not a job that can be carried out once a month. You will get to know the customers who will regularly fail to keep to their payment terms, and the ones who will always have a different excuse for doing so. You will also get to know the ones who will pay once you have called them and asked for payment, and not before. Your experience will enable you to limit the risk of non-payment to your organisation.

A sale is not complete until the money has been banked

Are you ready for assessment?

To achieve this unit of a Level 2 Business & Administration qualification you will need to demonstrate that you are competent in the following:

- Assess the nature of non-payment
- Identify bad and potentially bad debts accurately
- Take action to recover monies due
- Establish the reasons for non-payment
- Clarify discrepancies and request any outstanding amounts
- Obtain the customer's agreement to pay the amount owed
- Agree appropriate methods of payment with the customer and monitor compliance with these
- Identify continued non-payment and take appropriate action
- Take the nature and circumstances of the account holder into account when deciding what action to take
- Keep accurate and up-to-date records of all actions taken
- Comply with legal requirements, industry regulations, organisational policies and professional codes

(Remember that you will need the skills listed at the beginning of this chapter and that these are covered in chapter 1.)

Your Assessor will need you to produce evidence from a variety of sources. If you carry out the activities that follow they will provide some of the evidence for you.

Activity 1
You have been carrying out the role of credit control in your organisation for some time but the procedure has never been written down. A new employee is about to start working with you and you have been asked to write out a description of what you do to give to them on their first day. Write a detailed job analysis.

Activity 2
Research the available credit reference agencies. Find out what information they are able to provide on potential customers and at what cost.

Find out what credit information is held about you. Obviously, include as evidence the process you went through to obtain the information, not the actual information – as this is confidential to you.

Activity 3
Research corporate social responsibility. Find out which organisations operate a vulnerable groups' tariff and how these tariffs compare with tariffs available to the general public. Produce a report identifying where the vulnerable groups' tariff actually costs the consumer more than the cost to the general public.

Activity 4
Collect information on payment terms from as many sources as possible. These may include credit cards, store cards, credit agreements, rental agreements, suppliers to you organisation, bank accounts or mortgage agreements. Compare the different types of terms and conditions that are used.

Activity 5
Consider the current processes used for reducing the extent of non-payment in your organisation and suggest improvements that might be made.

Remember: While gathering evidence for this unit, evidence **may** be generated for units 110, 201, 202, 203, 207, 209, 212, 213, 215, 216, 219, 220, 224 and 225.

CHAPTER 11
UNIT 209 – Store, retrieve and archive information

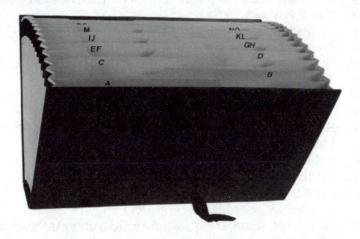

It has often been said that 'knowledge is power'. Information is a valuable commodity, so the way that it is stored, the ease with which it can be retrieved, and the effective archiving of it when it is no longer current are all important to the efficient operation of the business. Filing is one of the most important parts of any office procedures, but is often mistakenly seen as something that can be done by anybody, and without any training.

Though most organisations are aiming for a 'paper-free' office, for some of us there always seems to be a pile of papers waiting to be filed. These will require a variety of filing systems and equipment. Our computers also contain more and more files of information, and a system to enable us to find this information quickly saves a great deal of time. Much of this information, whether on paper or on computer, will need to be kept long after it ceases to be current. It is just as important that archived information is stored in a way that enables easy retrieval.

There are a surprising number of Acts of Parliament which refer to information retention and disposal:

- Occupiers' Liability Act 1957
- Employers' Liability (Compulsory Insurance) Act 1969
- Equal Pay Act 1970
- Taxes Management Act 1970
- Prescription and Limitations (Scotland) Act 1973
- Health and Safety at Work Act 1974
- Sex Discrimination Act 1975
- Race Relations Act 1976
- Limitation Act 1980
- Social Security Contributions and Benefits Act 1992
- Education Act 1994
- Value Added Tax Act 1994
- Disability Discrimination Act 1995
- Data Protection Act 1998

There are a large number of Statutory Instruments, each of which tells you how long you have to keep documents. Among those you are most likely to come across in your working day are:

- Employment records:
  - forms P11, three years
  - forms P38(S), three years
  - staff personal records, seven years after leaving
  - unsuccessful job applications, one year
  - payroll, 12 years
  - salary registers, five years
  - tax returns, permanently
  - expense accounts, seven years
  - works council minutes, permanently
  - wage records, five years
  - medical records, 12 years
  - accident books, 12 years

- Contracts and agreements:
  - contracts with customers, suppliers and agents, six years after expiry
  - rental and hire purchase agreements, six years after expiry
  - guarantees, six years after expiry
  - leases, 12 years after termination
  - licensing agreements, six years after expiry

- Accounts records:
    - limited companies must retain accounts records for six years from the end of the accounting period
    - businesses that are not limited companies must retain accounts records for five years from the 31st January following the tax year

- Transport records:
    - drivers' log books, five years after completion
    - vehicle mileage records, two years after vehicle disposed of
    - vehicle maintenance records, two years after vehicle disposed of
    - MOT test records, two years after vehicle disposed of
    - registration records, two years after vehicle disposed of

If the records you are responsible for are not listed above, check the relevant Act for information.

 When storing, retrieving and archiving information you will need the following skills:

- Communicating
- Problem solving
- Planning
- Organising
- Reading
- Writing
- Using number
- Using technology

These skills are covered in chapter 1.

Storage equipment

Whether files are to be stored on paper or electronically, there is a variety of equipment available. Paper files can be stored in:

- **Vertical filing cabinets** - These are the most common type of filing cabinets and are found in almost all offices. They have two, three or four drawers and files are kept in suspension files hung from runners within the cabinet
- **Lateral filing cabinets** - These are the same as vertical filing cabinets except the suspension files are hung from front to back rather than from side to side
- **Horizontal filing cabinets** - These have shallower drawers than vertical filing cabinets. The drawers may be narrow, to hold A4 paper, or wide enough to accommodate architects' plans
- **Filing trolleys** - These are filing cabinets on wheels which can be moved around the office as required
- **Box files** - These are boxes made of board, in which papers can be filed loosely held in position by a spring. The box files are then stored on shelves or in rotary filing cabinets. These are stands which can be rotated to give all round access to the files. Their main advantage is that they space-saving
- **Lever arch files** - Papers are hole-punched and placed over two split arch posts which are then closed to hold the papers in place. Papers can easily be inserted in any position in the file by opening the arch
- **Ring binders** - These are similar to lever arch files except that the rings are opened to place hole-punched papers into the file

Electronic files can be stored on:

- **A hard disk** - This is an integral part of the individual personal computer and has the advantage that it cannot be mislaid, however the disadvantage is that if the computer 'crashes' the information may be lost
- **A mainframe/file server** - This is a separate piece of hardware to which a number of PCs can be connected. The advantage is that all PCs have access to files, subject to password protection. The disadvantage is that if the server 'crashes' access to all files may be lost
- **An external hard disk** - This is a hard disk that can be connected to any PC
- **A memory card** - These can be inserted into a variety of peripheral equipment such as printers, digital cameras, palm pilots or laptop computers
- **A memory stick** - These are similar to a memory card but needs to be connected to a USB port in the back of a PC or on the side/back of a laptop
- **A zip disk** - These are portable storage devices which require a zip drive connected to the PC. They are mainly used for backing up systems on a regular basis
- **Floppy disks** - These are used for the everyday storing and transferring of data
- **Recordable CDs/DVDs** - These are used for data that needs to be stored as they are easy to label and file

More and more information is being stored electronically. Although it may seem an expensive option, modern electronic storage devices which hold an immense amount of information are relatively cheap, especially if the floor space saved is taken into consideration. The downside is that many people still require the 'comfort blanket' of being able to hold a piece of paper in their hands.

What you need to know

The types of storage equipment in use in
your organisation

> What is the difference between a hard
> disk and a floppy disk?

The types of files stored in each type of
equipment in your organisation

> Which type of electronic storage is best
> for transferring data?

The advantages and disadvantages of
each type of storage equipment

> What is the difference between vertical
> filing and lateral filing?

Process information

You may be required to research information and store it for
later use. The first step is to identify and collect the required
information. Information on almost every imaginable subject

can be accessed through the internet. Where this is not readily available, or the information you need cannot be found, more traditional methods have to be relied on. These may include directories, price lists, dictionaries, timetables and maps for example. Remember, however, that copyright exists in most published materials. You should check whether storing such items in an information system is permitted. Often the best solution is to have the information in its original form close to hand for reference.

Paper files may be stored in locked cabinets. Electronic files may be password protected. If you are responsible for storing the files, you must be sure that only authorised people have access to them and that you follow agreed procedures and legislation for maintaining security and confidentiality. If somebody asks you to show them records that you are not sure they are allowed to see, always check before allowing them access.

Whatever sort of organisation you work in, there will be some information which is not meant for everyone to see. This may include personnel records, security information, complaint records and customer information.

Some of this information may be marked 'confidential'. Make sure you know exactly what is meant by 'confidential' in your organisation. It may mean senior staff are allowed access, it may mean only the person who created the file is permitted to read it. Access to information about individuals is covered by the Data Protection Act and you must be very careful to comply with its requirements.

Electronic filing systems will have their own in-built sorting and storing mechanisms. Your responsibility will lie in learning what they are so that you can store information accurately in approved locations and find it again quickly. Most will include a facility to store the information in folders within the main directory. These should be used to group files together to speed up retrieval.

Paper records will have to be sorted manually. There are a number of different methods that can be used:

- **Alphabetical** - Filed in order from A–Z. Files starting with the same letter are filed in order of the second letter (Aa, Ab, Ac) and so on. People's names are filed by their surnames, and if more than one has the same surname by their first names. Names starting with 'The' are filed by ignoring the 'The'. Names beginning with 'Mac' or 'Mc' come before 'Ma', 'Mb' etc

- **Numerical** - Files are given numbers and filed from 1 to infinity. This is useful for information which naturally lends itself to being filed this way (purchase orders, sales invoices, for instance)
- **Alpha-numerical** - Files have a combination of letters and numbers. Examples include Postal Codes, National Insurance Numbers and Car Registration Numbers. These are usually large databases as they hold more information than numerical systems and are more flexible than alphabetical systems. The order of filing depends on the sequence of the file name. If file names start with letters followed by numbers, they are filed in alphabetical order first, and numerical order within each letter

The following table shows the effect of filing the same information in three different ways.

Alphabetical	Numerical	Alpha-numerical
Rachel Clark Flat 6 The Bends Weston-by-the-Sea Somerset WA2 9QR DOB 15.04.71 A/c No. 080521 Category Life Insurance	A/c No. 027493 Aaron Clarke 146 Brights Terrace Holdsworthy Middlesex HC1 9DA DOB 13.10.51 Category Pensions	HC1 9DA Aaron Clarke 146 Brights Terrace Holdsworthy Middlesex DOB 13.10.51 A/c No. 027493 Category Pensions
Aaron Clarke 146 Brights Terrace Holdsworthy Middlesex HC1 9DA DOB 13.10.51 A/c No. 027493 Category Pensions	A/c No. 080521 Rachel Clark Flat 6 The Bends Weston-by-the-Sea Somerset WA2 9QR DOB 15.04.71 Category Life Insurance	IM6 5QA Alan McPherson 27 Matthew Street Douglas Isle of Man DOB 06.10.59 A/c No. 643591 Category Mortgages
Alan McPherson 27 Matthew Street Douglas Isle of Man IM6 5QA DOB 06.10.59 A/c No. 643591 Category Mortgages	A/c No. 090354 Graham Wilcox 105 Planters Row West Chester Co. Durham WC9 8DR DOB 29.05.85 Category Savings	PD1 2PW Peter Mathews 33 William Street Poole Dorset DOB 06.08.49 A/c No. 361364 Category Savings

Peter Mathews 33 William Street Poole Dorset PD1 2PW DOB 06.08.49 A/c No. 361364 Category Savings	A/c No. 361364 Peter Mathews 33 William Street Poole Dorset PD1 2PW DOB 06.08.49 Category Savings	WA2 9QR Rachel Clark Flat 6 The Bends Weston-by-the-Sea Somerset A/c No. 080521 DOB 15.04.71 Category Life Insurance
Graham Wilcox 105 Planters Row West Chester Co. Durham WC9 8DR DOB 29.05.85 A/c No. 090354 Category Savings	A/c No. 643591 Alan McPherson 27 Matthew Street Douglas Isle of Man IM6 5QA DOB 06.10.59 Category Mortgages	WC9 8DR Graham Wilcox 105 Planters Row West Chester Co. Durham DOB 29.05.85 A/c No. 090354 Category Savings

- **Chronological** - This is often used within one of the other methods. For instance, each customer's records are filed alphabetically, but the information within the file is stored chronologically, usually with the latest at the front. This enables a picture of the activity to be gained. However, it can be used based on dates of birth or start dates
- **Geographical** - This is a method of sorting by areas, for example: North West England, East Anglia, South West England; you can then sort into Counties, North West England to include Cheshire, Lancashire and Merseyside; then into towns such as Chester, Lancaster and Liverpool
- **By subject or category** - Some organisations need to sort their filing under topics rather than names. For instance, a shoe manufacturer may keep files under product names such as Ladies, Gentlemen and Childrens

The following table shows the effect of filing the same information in these three different ways.

Chronological	Geographical	Subject or Category
DOB 29.05.85 Graham Wilcox 105 Planter Row West Chester Co. Durham WC9 8DR A/c No. 090354 Category Savings	NORTH Alan McPherson 27 Mathew Street Douglas Isle of Man IM6 5QA DOB 06.10.59 A/c No. 643591 Category Mortgage	Category Life Insurance Rachel Clark Flat 6 The Bends Weston-by-the-Sea Somerset WA2 9QR DOB 15.04.71 A/c No. 080521
DOB 15.04.71 Rachel Clark Flat 6 The Bends Weston-by-the-Sea Somerset WA2 9QR A/c No. 080521 Category Life Insurance	NORTH Graham Wilcox 105 Planter Row West Chester Co. Durham WC9 8DR DOB 29.05.85 A/c No. 090354 Category Savings	Category Mortgage Alan McPherson 27 Mathew Street Douglas Isle of Man IM6 5QA DOB 06.10.59 A/c No. 643591
DOB 06.10.59 Alan McPherson 27 Mathew Street Douglas Isle of Man IM6 5QA A/c No. 643591 Category Mortgage	SOUTH Rachel Clark Flat 6 The Bends Weston-by-the-Sea Somerset WA2 9QR DOB 15.04.71 A/c No. 080521 Category Life Insurance	Category Pensions Aaron Clarke 146 Brights Terace Holdsworthy Middlesex HC1 9DA DOB 13.10.51 A/c No. 027493
DOB 13.10.51 Aaron Clarke 146 Brights Terace Holdsworthy Middlesex HC1 9DA A/c No. 027493 Category Pensions	SOUTH Aaron Clarke 146 Brights Terace Holdsworthy Middlesex HC1 9DA DOB 13.1051 A/c No. 027493 Category Pensions	Category Savings Peter Matthews 33 William Street Poole Dorset PD1 2PW DOB 06.08.49 A/c No. 361364
DOB 06.08.49 Peter Matthews 33 William Street Poole Dorset PD1 2PW A/c No. 361364 Category Savings	SOUTH Peter Matthews 33 William Street Poole Dorset PD1 2PW 06.08.49 A/c No. 361364 Category Savings	Category Savings Graham Wilcox 105 Planter Row West Chester Co. Durham WC9 8DR DOB 29.05.85 A/c No. 090354

Whichever method is adopted if the information is not stored accurately it will be extremely difficult to find. Beware 'American' dates. In the United Kingdom the 7th September

2005 is written 07.09.05 while in America it is written 09.07.05. If you are filing in chronological order this may cause confusion. Special care needs to be taken when filing numerically to avoid transposing numbers.

Wherever the information is stored, electronically or on paper, it is essential that you update the information as required. As soon as any new or amended information is received the existing record should be updated. For instance, addresses will change as people or businesses move or names may change as people marry for example.

Apart from the inconvenience which out-of-date information can cause, it is an offence under the Data Protection Act to store personal information that is not up-to-date. When amending information held electronically saving the file will automatically update the previous version.

What you need to know

The types of information that your
organisation will need to access

How do you use a search engine?

The potential sources of information

Do you understand the law on
copyright?

The passwords needed to access files

Are you familiar with the principles of
The Data Protection Act?

Who has authority in your organisation to
access information

What does confidential mean within
your organisation?

Retrieve information

When you are asked to retrieve information from the system, to avoid error it is important to confirm the information required. You may be asked for particular information from within a file rather than the file itself. Make sure you understand exactly what you are being asked to provide before wasting your time and theirs. Your organisation may have internal rules covering access to information. It may be that an official form must be completed, or that only staff of a particular level of seniority can see certain files. It is essential that you comply with procedures and legislation for accessing information systems. There will certainly be procedures covering access to confidential information. Where this material relates to individuals, it is covered by the Data Protection Act. If you handle confidential files you must do so carefully.

- **Receiving confidential information** - Do not open post marked 'confidential' unless you have been told to do so. If you are given information over the telephone write it down and pass it on immediately. If you receive it accidentally return it immediately or pass it on to the person it was intended for
- **Working on confidential information** - Learn your passwords and security codes, do not write them down. Make sure no-one is looking over your shoulder if you are typing a confidential letter, and don't leave it on your desk. If you are printing or photocopying sensitive material stay at the machine until all the papers have been printed. Remember to destroy unusable copies and to remove the original
- **Sending confidential information** - Post confidential material in a marked envelope. It may be a good idea to send it Recorded Delivery. Except in unavoidable circumstances don't fax confidential information. If it is absolutely essential, telephone the recipient and make sure they will be by the fax machine to collect it. Don't send confidential information by e-mail. E-mails are not secure
- **Filing confidential information** - Make sure it is in the correct file, in the correct cabinet or protected by a password if filed electronically
- **Destroying confidential information** - Your organisation will have procedures for destroying sensitive material. It may be shredded or collected separately by professional security companies. It must never be simply thrown in the bin

- Remember not to talk about confidential information to anyone who doesn't have the right to know it, and to be careful that you cannot be overheard if you are discussing it with someone else.

If you are asked for a file, you should try to produce it as quickly as possible. You may need to copy information from a file rather than presenting the whole file. If your information system is up to date, it should be easy to locate and retrieve the required information. If you understand the way the filing system is set up this will make retrieval of information much easier. You may be asked to search for all the information you can find on a given subject. This may involve searching within your own information system and external sources such as the Internet.

In even the best-run organisations, from time-to-time you will identify and report problems with information systems. In paper-based and electronic systems the most common of these will be an inability to find the information or the information being out-of-date. First you must identify the cause and then suggest a solution.

- If the cause is mis-filing the solution may be further training or further practice
- It may be the problem is that filing is not up to date. The solution will depend on whether the cause is a resource issue or a time-management issue. If filing is done frequently it is not as daunting a prospect as it would be if it was done every month
- Problems also arise when files are removed and not returned. The solution is to install a system of recording who has the file and when it is returned

File Reference	Name	Date Taken	Date Returned
Williams and Son	Bill Perry	14.05.04	15.05.04
Bluebird Builders	Malcolm Watling	14.05.04	21.05.04
Aspect Training	Matthew Roberts	16.05.04	
Carter Regan	Brian Ash	17.05.04	

- Electronic systems may suffer hardware or software failure. These should be reported to the relevant department immediately the problem is discovered

Often you will be asked for particular information rather than the whole file. For instance, the accounts department may ask for a list of all invoices paid to a particular supplier in the last year. They do not want to be presented with a pile of invoices. What they want is a list. The sales department may want to know how many widgets have been sold in Wales this month. All they want is a number, not a list of all the customers in Wales. A customer may want a brochure which is stored electronically sent to them. You will need to find out whether they would prefer it electronically or printed off and posted. It is important to provide information in the agreed format and within agreed timescales. An author writing a book may be able to wait weeks for requested information, a journalist on a daily newspaper probably won't.

 What you need to know

Your organisation's internal rules regarding access to information

> If a letter is placed on your desk addressed to a colleague and marked 'confidential' what should you do with it?

Whether there is an official form used to request information in your organisation

> You are sending a confidential fax to the Managing Director. What is the first thing you should do?

How confidential documents are disposed of

> Name two issues that could cause filing not to be up-to-date

Who to report problems to when they
arise

Why may an author be prepared to
wait longer than a journalist for
information?

Archive information

If you don't cull your information system regularly it will fall
over under its own weight. This means reviewing the
contents and removing information that is no longer current.
The decision that has to be made when information is
considered no longer necessary to keep in the main system is
whether it can be disposed of entirely or whether it needs to
be archived. This decision will depend on legislation as well
as organisational requirements. Before disposing of any
information, confirm information to be archived. Your
information system should contain only sufficient records for
the day-to-day running of the organisation.

For example:

- Accounts departments will usually keep this year's
  and last year's records
- Human Resource departments will usually keep
  current personnel files
- Sales departments will usually keep information on
  'live' customers
- All departments will keep correspondence for an
  agreed length of time

Other records will either be destroyed or archived. Your
organisation will have its own requirements for archiving
information but these must also comply with the procedures
and legislation for archiving information. The length of time
many records must be retained is governed by bodies such
as the Inland Revenue and HM Customs and Excise.
Personal information is governed by the Data Protection Act,
which states that information must be kept no longer than
necessary.

Information that is to be archived should be stored using the
same system as the live files, using whichever method is
appropriate to the task. Remember the reason that you have
archived the information and not destroyed it is that

somebody may want access to it at a later date so archive information correctly and within agreed timescales. Simply storing everything without a system will not enable you to retrieve it on request. If the Inland Revenue request documents from five years ago you will be expected to be able to find them. It is also important that information which was considered confidential when it was live is still treated as such and stored separately.

You will need to maintain a record of archived information and where it has been stored. As with any other record system this must be kept up-to-date. Archive boxes should be kept in chronological order. It will be useful when the time comes to destroy files that no longer need to be archived as the record will identify where these can be found.

Remember to separate confidential information and destroy it using your organisation's procedures.

From time-to-time you may be asked to retrieve files which have been stored in the archives. If they have been stored using the same system as the live files and an accurate record kept, you will be able to retrieve archived records on request. Don't forget that it is just as important to record who has taken files from the archive as it was live files.

 What you need to know

How often files are archived/destroyed in your organisation

How long does the Inland Revenue require you to keep payroll records?

The period of time that files are archived before being destroyed

Why is archived information filed using the same method as live information?

What storage system is used to archive electronic files in your organisation

For what period of time are you required to keep VAT records?

Looking after an information system may not seem to be the most important job in the organisation but it is vital. There are a lot of decisions to be made and the success of the whole organisation may depend on access to reliable and up-to-date information. Only if the storage system is efficient will it be possible to find information quickly. This applies equally to archived information as there is legislation to be complied with, and failure to do so could have serious consequences.

Remember, everybody is grateful to the person who can lay their hands on exactly the right information when it is urgently required

Are you ready for assessment?

To achieve this unit of a Level 2 Business & Administration qualification you will need to demonstrate that you are competent in the following:

- Identify and collect required information
- Follow agreed procedures and legislation for maintaining security and confidentiality
- Store information accurately in approved locations
- Update information as required
- Confirm information for retrieval
- Comply with procedures and legislation for accessing an information system
- Locate and retrieve the required information
- Identify and report problems with information systems
- Provide information in the agreed format and within agreed timescales
- Confirm information to be archived
- Comply with procedures and legislation for archiving information
- Archive information correctly and within agreed timescales
- Maintain a record of archived information
- Retrieve archived records on request

(Remember that you will need the skills listed at the beginning of this chapter and that these are covered in chapter 1.)

Your Assessor will need you to produce evidence from a variety of sources. If you carry out the activities that follow they will provide some of the evidence for you.

Activity 1
Keep a work diary over the period of a month recording requests for information that you have met.

Activity 2
Which of the following is likely to contain confidential information?

- Personnel records
- Bank records
- Telephone directories
- Newspaper archives
- Patient records
- Disciplinary records

Activity 3
True or false, it is an offence under the Data Protection Act to retain out-of-date information on an individual?

True or false, Inland Revenue records must be retained for at least 25 years?

Activity 4
Write an account detailing how each of the following may be affected by an information system not being kept up to date.

- Stock replenishment
- Data Protection Act
- Submission of accounts to Companies House
- VAT return

Activity 5
If the organisation you work for has a form for requesting information, find a copy. If it doesn't, then create one.

Activity 6
You have been asked to provide a list of customers with an average spend in excess of £1,400 per month. Account records show annual expenditure. Which of the following would you include in your list?

A.	Allington Papers	£17,200.47
B.	Lytham Works	£134,479.60
C.	Bluebird Personnel	£14,567.98
D.	Matthews Printing	£5,879.56
E.	Douglas Aircraft	£345,801.98
F.	Jefferson Gardening	£3,591.92

Activity 7
Sort the following company names into alphabetical order.

7/11 Stores Ltd.
Peterson's of York
The West Group
Megasave Superstores
24 Hour Plumbing Co.
Harvard Engineering
Singh and Danse Theatrical Agents
Reid Rentals
McHenry Shoe Co.
St. Barnabas Hospital
Kingdom Plant Supplies
Mackintosh and Leverhulme
Langton's Ltd.
MacIntyre and Bridgetown
Saint and Sisters Co.
Patterson's Telephones
Barton Box Co.
West and Hammond Ltd.
Megasaver Hypermarkets
Read and Wright
Todfell and Son
Alveston Gardeners
Peter Benton Co. Ltd.
Halshall of Weston PLC
Parsons Stores
A & S Removals
Peter Ashton and Son Ltd.
AAA1 Taxis

Remember: While gathering evidence for this unit, evidence
may be generated for units 110, 201, 202, 212, 216, 220
and 225.

CHAPTER 12
UNIT 210 – Research and report information

All organisations depend on the effective management of information. This could be information on products, customers, competitors, sales, purchases, staff or legislation. The list is endless.

Information can be obtained from a wide variety of different sources and it is important to find out how to do research well and present your finding appropriately.

The reasons for storing information will also vary from organisation to organisation. There are, of course, some organisations whose main purpose is the storage and processing of information. Others will store information which they feel they will need regular access to, and research information that is only needed occasionally.

Once information has been sourced it needs to be organised, analysed and presented in a way that meets the requirements of the user. Research will usually provide quantitative or qualitative information. In robust research projects the employer may want you to find out both quantitative and qualitative information.

Quantitative research works best with large numbers of people. It provides data in numeric terms. Data is usually obtained by asking potential customers to complete a carefully planned questionnaire, either directly by telephone or face-to-face or indirectly by post or e-mail. Qualitative research is used to explore less easily defined objectives, such as opinions. It is usually carried out with small groups of people to investigate their views or behaviour.

There are five main research methods. The first four involve you doing the research and are known as primary research methods:

- **Observation** - where the researcher observes practices and activities, without joining in, to identify what's happening and why. Observation is usually a qualitative method of research but last century there were mass observations designed to provide policy makers with quantitative data
- **Experiment** - when a test or tests are specially designed to see what happens under controlled conditions. This type of research is commonly used in areas such as the pharmaceutical industry
- **Interviews** - which can be planned and carried out face-to-face, over the phone or via a video facility. A small series of in-depth interviews will provide qualitative information while a big series of small interviews can provide quantitative information
- **Questionnaires** - which are usually designed to collect information from a variety of sources. The most sophisticated questionnaires are designed to collect and analyse data using a computer program. Initially, this costs more to design and implement but relatively little to analyse

The last is a secondary research method:

- **Desk research** - where you find out as much as you can from existing sources. This can be as simple as getting information about train or plane times for a colleague to a complex activity where you may have to go to many different sources to gather lots of bits of information

- Try not to overlook trends which your research uncovers. For instance, if you had researched the sale of word processors and discovered a 50% increase in the last two years, you might have deduced that there was no future in typewriter ribbons, carbon paper or correcting fluid.

When researching and reporting information you will use the following skills:

- Planning
- Researching
- Organising
- Reading
- Writing
- Using number
- Communicating
- Using technology
- Presenting information

These skills are covered in chapter 1.

Research information

When you are asked to research information there are a number of things that you need to know before you can start. Obviously you will need to know what information is wanted but also how much, by when, in what format, from what sources and in what depth.

It may be necessary to liaise with other departments to obtain information which they may hold in databases, or to go to internal or public libraries to research information in reference books, magazines, newspapers and brochures. You may find the necessary information on the computer, either the organisation's own systems or the internet.

Once you know exactly what information is needed, you can consider all the possible sources and decide which ones you are going to use. Think about the following:

- What information you are going to need
- What information do you already have

- What past research might provide information
- What information is available within the organisation
- What information is available on the internet or other external sources
- When is the information required by

You will have been told the purpose of the research you are going to undertake. This may be a relatively simple task such as listing all the outstanding invoices more than three months overdue, or a major research project such as gathering information on the comparative advantages and disadvantages of computerising the accounts system.

The first place to look is at information you may already have. In a relatively simple task there is a good chance that you already have most, if not all of the information that you are looking for. This may be held in a database or spreadsheet program for instance. To list all the outstanding invoices over three months overdue only requires you to sort those invoices out from all the others. However, a major research project will involve much more time and much wider research.

In a simple task it is possible that the information asked for is a regular requirement. Reference to the previous time that the information was provided will often mean that all that is needed is an up-date. In a major project it may be that research has been carried out in the past which may be a good starting point.

Having looked at past research you will then need to look at information within the organisation that may be relevant. Obviously if the task is wholly internal then all of the information will be found within the organisation. In a major project you will need to gather information from both inside and outside. Talk to everybody you can think of who may have helpful knowledge. You may be surprised at how much your colleagues already know. You could find that someone has experience from a previous job of carrying out the very project that you are researching.

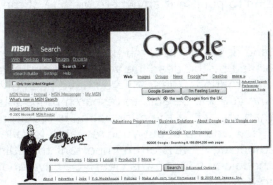

Once you have exhausted internal sources you will have to broaden your horizons. The obvious first port of call is the internet, which holds information about everything under the sun and has the advantage of being free. You can greatly speed up your research by the use of 'search engines'. Their purpose is to help you to find websites that contain the information you are looking for. Among the best known are 'google', 'msn' and 'askjeeves'. Whichever search engine you choose the words you use to describe the information you are looking for will greatly affect the number of results you get. If you can't find what you are looking for on the internet there are a number of other sources:

- Telephone directories
- Trade directories
- Suppliers
- Libraries
- Catalogues
- Reference books
- Magazines
- Newspapers
- Leaflets
- Brochures

These will be of varying relevance depending on what the research is that you are carrying out.

In all searches for information bear in mind the questions of copyright and confidentiality. Any published work is likely to be subject to copyright, whereby the work belongs to those that wrote it and you will need to check carefully whether you are entitled to use it. Any personal data will be subject to the Data Protection Act. Most commercial information will be confidential and you would certainly need the approval of the organisation to publish it anywhere outside of the organisation.

The breadth and depth of research that you can carry out will be partly informed by the deadline you have been given to produce the information. Clearly if you have been given a distant deadline you will be able to research more sources of information than you will if the information is required at short notice. How you go about your research is called 'research methodology'. It is often important to outline your research methodology so that it is clear you have understood what is required.

At this stage you are only gathering information, not necessarily being selective about it. It is a good idea, if you have time, to take on board all current information which appears to be relevant rather than choosing the most important and discarding the rest. Sometimes it is the detail which appears to be fairly unimportant which can prove to be the critical factor in the long run.
You will need a method of recording the information in some form that will allow you to retrieve it easily and organise it once you have gathered all that you can. You may find it useful to either print off all of the internet-based information so that you have everything in hard copy, or, if you have the facility, scan in the paper-based information to the computer so you have everything electronically.

Whichever way you choose to record the information it will be useful to keep a record of the sources used. These can be put together at the end of a report in alphabetical order, often referred to as a bibliography. You may be asked to justify any conclusions that you have drawn from the information, or similar information may be required in the future, and it will be easier to refer to your previous search than to go through the whole process again to find it. Records may be kept on paper or electronically, but either way will need to be cross-referenced so that they can be found again.

What you need to know

The type of information your organisation has available

Do you know how to use search engines?

Previous research carried out by your organisation

What sources of information are available to you?

The difference between quantitative and qualitative research

What are the five main research methods?

The difference between primary and secondary research

What is meant by research methodology?

The deadline to complete the search for information

Why should you record the sources of information used?

Exactly what information is required

What would you find in a bibliography?

Report information

When you have gathered all the information you need, you will have to organise it into a suitable format. Remember to match the information that you produce to the request that you were given in the first place. If all that is required is a list of outstanding invoices, deliver a list not a pile of invoices. If the information is numeric, you may choose to present it in the form of a spreadsheet.

	This year	Last year	Inc/dec
Sales	15552	20353	-4801
Maintenance	205	584	-379
Telephone	315	263	52
Stationery	504	72	432
Total expenses	1024	919	105
Sales - Expenses	14528	19434	-4906

If you are asked for a summary of customer contact you could supply it in the form of a memo.

MEMO

To: Sales Manager
From: William Weston
Date: 15th August 2005

Subject: Preston Works – Customer contact summary

01.04.05	Request for catalogue
02.04.05	Catalogue sent
05.04.05	Telephone call to make appointment for rep
06.04.05	Visit by rep
14.04.05	Order received by telephone – order number 2546448
17.04.05	Order despatched by post
18.04.05	Invoice raised – invoice number 886654
19.05.05	Payment received

If the project is a complex one, you will probably need to write a report. In this case the first thing to do is to write an outline structure for the report, for instance: introduction, methodology, findings, conclusion and recommendations. Having written the outline, sort the information under these headings. You will then be able to organise the information within each heading to produce a report that delivers the information in a logical order. Remember, if your project has included desk research, put your sources at the back of your report in a bibliography.

At this stage it may be a good idea to produce a draft report. A report is normally structured as follows; title, introduction, methodology, main body where you report your findings, conclusion, recommendations, acknowledgements, appendices and bibliography. In a draft report you would complete the title, introduction and methodology, and in the main body list an outline of the facts you discovered.

TITLE: DRAFT REPORT ON THE ADVANTAGES AND DISADVANTAGES OF COMPUTERISING THE ACCOUNTS SYSTEM

INTRODUCTION: This report is to consider the advantages and disadvantages of computerising the accounts system taking into account the cost of purchasing software, training needs, the requirement to operate parallel running and the timescales involved.

MAIN BODY: Information on:
- Available software
- Cost
- Training needs analysis of staff
- Case study from a similar organisation

Show the draft to the person you are preparing the report for. Agree with them what the final report is likely to contain before completing the detailed information in the main body, drawing your conclusion, making your recommendations and compiling the acknowledgements, appendices and bibliography.

Having confirmed that the outline of the report meets these requirements, you will then be in a position to produce a final copy. In this copy the report will contain:

- **The Title**
- **The Introduction** - in this section you give the background to the report and an overview of what the report contains
- **The Methodology** - in this section you report what methods you used to collect information, for example internet research and telephone interviews
- **The Main Body** - in this section you report all your findings. Display all the information that you have gathered in a logical form so that the reader is led towards the conclusion
- **The Conclusion** - in this section you will have analysed your findings and stated what your research has led you to, and how. Be careful to draw your conclusion from the information that you have

included in the report, not from any previously held opinions of your own

- **Recommendations** - in this section you should state any action that you feel should be taken as a result of the conclusions
- **Acknowledgements** - if you have received help from others in compiling the report acknowledge their contribution in this section
- **Bibliography** - source material should be referred to. This should be listed alphabetically by author and the date of publication given
- **Appendices** - there may be information which you have referred to in the main body which is too detailed to be given in full without distracting from the purpose of the report. In that case it may be useful to give the whole of the information in an appendix

When you have completed the report it is essential that you proof read it before printing and distributing copies. Most word processing packages contain spell checking and grammar checking facilities. Use these first to correct the more glaring errors, but do not rely on them entirely.

The dictionary usually defaults to use American spelling and grammar, so will accept 'color' and reject 'colour', for instance. However, this can be set to use the English (UK) dictionary in the Spell Check options menu.

When the automatic checking is complete, read the document carefully to look for missed errors, and also for correct use of paragraphs, headings, subheadings, style and formatting. Be particularly careful to proof read numbers, dates, times and amounts. Check for errors between similar words such as 'affect' and 'effect' or 'less' and 'fewer'.

If the information is to be provided to a group of people you may choose to present it as a slide show. In this case you would transfer the main points, probably the title, the conclusion and the recommendations onto slides and show it to the group, talking them through the full information and providing hand outs for them to consider.

When you have presented your report you will find that you are left with the information that you gathered. You will need to review the information and decide whether it is worth keeping for future reference. If you decide to keep it make sure that you review it from time-to-time and throw away anything that has become out of date. Out of date information is less useful than a blank sheet of paper.

What you need to know

How to structure a report

Why is it important to agree aims, objectives and deadlines?

The different formats that can be used to present information

Why should you match the information produced to the request received?

How to organise information

How would you record the sources of information?

There are as many ways of researching and reporting information as there are organisations. The important thing is to ensure that you look in as many places as possible when researching the information, select the most relevant information, organise it in a way that meets the requirements of the user and present it in the most user-friendly way.

Research is only as useful the information is current; out of date information is worse than no information at all

Are you ready for assessment?

To achieve this unit of a Level 2 Business & Administration qualification you will need to demonstrate that you are competent in the following:

- Confirm aims and objectives and deadlines for the information search
- Confirm relevant sources of information
- Search for and obtain information to meet deadlines
- Record the information
- Maintain a record of sources used
- Organise the information in a way that will help analysis
- If necessary, get feedback on what you have found
- Present information in the most appropriate format, accurately and on time

(Remember that you will need the skills listed at the beginning of this chapter and that these are covered in chapter 1.)

Your Assessor will need you to produce evidence from a variety of sources. If you carry out some of the activities that follow they will provide some of the evidence for you.

Activity 1
Your sales manager is planning a trip to China, India, Malaysia and Singapore. You have been asked to research relevant information on these countries, for instance currency, whether visas are needed or inoculations are required – whatever you think will be useful. Produce the information in the format you think best meets the needs of your manager.

Activity 2
Your office manager is considering the purchase of a new printer. She has asked you to find out what is available and compare features, prices and performance. Do the research and write a report giving your recommendations.

Activity 3

Whatever sort of organisation you work in, there will be a certain amount of waste produced. This may include paper, printer cartridges, cardboard, drinks cans, disposable cups from the water dispenser. Research the cost of disposing of the waste and the possibility of re-cycling some or all of it; perhaps selling the paper or having the printer cartridges re-filled. Calculate the savings that could be made over the course of a year.

Activity 4

You want to send a parcel weighing 2kg to the United States of America. Find out what alternative methods are available, the costs of each and the delivery times. Compare the costs and times and state which method would be most cost effective and why.

Activity 5

Imagine you own the following shares:

1000	shares in Sainsbury's		500	shares in Barclays Bank
200	shares in House of Fraser		100	shares in Aviva
400	shares in Severn Trent Water		1000	shares in BP

Over the period of a month record the value of each holding once a week. At the end of the month produce a graph which shows how the value of each has increased or decreased, and the change in the total value.

Analyse your findings and record what you intend to do with each block of shares.

Remember: While gathering evidence for this unit, evidence **may** be generated for units 110, 201, 202, 209, 212, 213, 214, 216, 217, 219, 220, 224 and 225.

CHAPTER 13
UNIT 211 – Organise and support meetings

All businesses get involved in meetings. Some have a wide variety of meetings while others, like small businesses, may only participate in a few meetings.

Meetings can be formal or informal, but if they are to have any significant effect they will need to be recorded. A meeting that is not organised before it happens, structured while it is happening and the main points of agreement recorded and followed up after it has happened, is only a discussion.

Before a meeting can be held it is necessary to decide what sort of meeting it is going to be and what the purpose is. There are all sorts of reasons to hold meetings, for instance:

- **Annual General Meetings** - All companies with shareholders are obliged to hold a meeting at least once a year where all shareholders are invited to attend. Their purpose is to give shareholders the opportunity to question directors and vote on resolutions

- **Extraordinary General Meetings** - Additional meetings can be called if the holders of at least 10% of the shares require them. Their purpose is to discuss issues that have arisen since the last Annual General Meeting that can't wait until the next, e.g. dismissal of CEO or Management
- **Board meetings** - The directors of the company meet regularly to discuss the general running of the organisation
- **Management meetings** - The managers meet to discuss the day-to-day running of the organisation. The purpose of the meeting is to decide how the strategy agreed by the Board is to be implemented
- **Team meetings** - These may include the sales team, the production team, the customer service team, the design team or the accounts team each discussing the issues that affect them directly. At these meetings team leaders will 'cascade' information from the management
- **Staff meetings** - These are held less often than team meetings. Their purpose is to inform all of the staff simultaneously of major issues that will affect everybody
- **Committee meetings** - These range from official public committees such as Parish Councils to things like Social Club committees or the Health and Safety committee within the organisation

It is not always necessary for all the participants in a meeting to be in the same place. Modern technology allows for video-conferencing, where people can see and hear each other via cameras and microphones, and teleconferencing where any number of people can be connected by telephone simultaneously. These can save travelling time and costs, especially if some of the participants are from overseas. These should be arranged with care as some people find the technology intimidating and the lack of physical interaction can reduce the effectiveness of the meeting.

Meetings require organising, to ensure that all attendees know the time, place and purpose of the meeting. As far in advance of the meeting as possible send out invitations to attend. This will give time for people to diarise the meeting and advise whether or not they are able to attend. They can also advise if they have any special requirements so that you have plenty of time to make the necessary arrangements.

At this time also send a map showing the location of the meeting, car parks, the nearest railway station together with directions to the venue.

A week before the meeting send an agenda and copies of any meeting papers to those who indicated they would be attending.

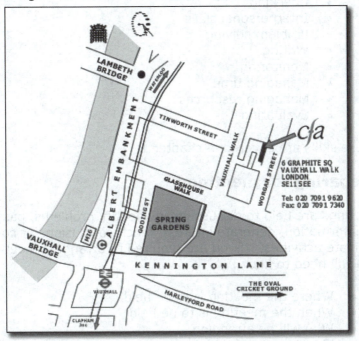

The agenda of a meeting sets out in a logical order what is to be discussed at the meeting.

Ask people to confirm their attendance and make a note of replies so that you can prepare the apologies for absence.

Meetings also require recording, so that attendees and others can be sure what future actions were agreed, who is to carry them out, and to what timescales. The record of the meeting is known as the minutes, which must then be circulated to all those who were present and those who sent their apologies.

When organising and supporting meetings you will use the following skills:

- Negotiating
- Planning
- Organising
- Communicating
- Checking
- Interpersonal skills
- Problem solving
- Writing
- Monitoring
- Managing time
- Managing resources
- Evaluating

These skills are covered in chapter 1.

Preparing for meetings

Meetings are held to discuss ideas, identify problems, pass on information, generate interest, reach conclusions or co-ordinate activities. If you are required to arrange a meeting you will need to know:

- Where the meeting is to be held
- When the meeting is to be held
- Who will be attending
- The purpose of the meeting
- What resources are required
- Whether any catering arrangements need to be made
- Any special requirements for attendees

The decision on the venue will depend on factors such as:

- The purpose of the meeting
- The number of attendees
- The seniority of the attendees
- The geographic location of the attendees
- Whether your organisation has in-house facilities for such a meeting
- Potential disruption to the business

Selecting a venue within your own premises or nearby has the advantage of saving travelling time and cost for people based on the premises, as well as the convenience of being able to refer to any information held on the premises. Having decided on the venue you will need to book the meeting room, any necessary equipment and catering requirements. If the venue is outside of the organisation obtain quotes from suitable suppliers and, if possible, contact other people who have used the venue previously. This will give you an idea of the standards you can expect. It is important to ensure that the standard of hospitality and catering is appropriate. Make sure it is clear exactly what the venue is providing. Is equipment and catering included or does that need to be organised separately? Stay in regular contact with the venue so that you can be aware of any potential problems that may arise and inform them of any changes in the number of attendees.

The layout of the room will depend on the purpose of the meeting. There are three common layouts for meeting rooms:

- **Classroom** - This is where a speaker stands in front of an audience seated round a number of tables. This layout is useful if people are to take part in 'workshops'
- **Boardroom** - This is where the whole group sit round a table. If people attending are to discuss ideas, reach conclusions or co-ordinate activities this layout may be most appropriate
- **Theatre** - This is where a speaker stands in front of an audience seated in rows of seats. This layout may prove more suitable if information is to be passed on

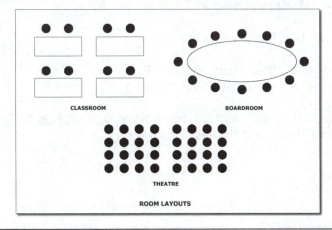

CLASSROOM   BOARDROOM

THEATRE

ROOM LAYOUTS

Where a screen or flipchart is being used it is essential that everyone can see it. If you are arranging a meeting for a large number of people consider whether microphones are necessary to enable everybody to hear what is being said, but remember not to place speakers where people will be deafened by the sound.

Other equipment you may need to have available includes:

- A laptop, to allow a PowerPoint presentation to be shown
- A multi-media projector
- Whiteboards and dry-wipe markers, for brainstorming sessions
- An easel, to put the flip chart on

Don't forget the small stuff; pencils, paper and maybe a dish of sweets to keep the voice box lubricated.

Laptops and multi-media projectors have virtually replaced the use of overhead projectors in recent times. The opportunities to include sound, animation and video clips, as well as the ease with which the presenter can move from one slide to the next by remote control make overhead projectors obsolete.

Having organised the venue you will need to prepare and agree an agenda and collate meeting papers. In a regular formal meeting the first three items of the agenda are usually:

- Apologies for absence
- The minutes of the last meeting
- Matters arising

The last two items are always:

- Any other business (A.O.B.)
- The date of the next meeting

The actual business of the meeting is sandwiched between the first three and the last two items.

Social Club Meeting held on 19th May 2004
West Hotel, Pendleton. 2.30pm.

Agenda

1. Apologies

2. Minutes of the last meeting

3. Matters arising

4. Chair's report

5. Treasurer's report

6. Recruitment of Chair discussions

7. A.O.B.

8. Date of the next meeting

Copies of any documents the people attending will need in advance of the meeting will have to be produced and sent to them with the agenda, as this will give them time to read and consider them. If they are to discuss the content of the papers they will need to receive them well before the meeting in order to prepare.

The person chairing the meeting (the Chair) will need to know before the meeting what the desired outcomes are, so ask the attendees to also let you know if there are any major issues that they wish to discuss. In many cases the Chair will have been involved in the initial planning of the meeting and will be well aware of its purpose, but there will be occasions when they will need to be briefed on the particular stances or viewpoints of the attendees.

Also ask people to let you know if they have any special requirements. These may include dietary, mobility, hearing or vision impairment, travel and accommodation. If you are told that anybody has a particular need, liaise with the venue organiser to ensure that it can be met. You will also need to ensure that all Health and Safety and security requirements have been taken into consideration.

What you need to know

The differences between various types of meetings

> What five items are on every agenda?

The Chair's needs prior to the meeting

> Why do you need replies from attendees confirming their attendance?

The types of equipment that may be needed for a meeting

> What are the advantages of holding a meeting on your own premises?

Before arranging a meeting you need to know where it will be, when it will take place, who will attend and the purpose of the meeting

> What would be the best room layout for a social club committee meeting?

What attendees will need prior to a meeting

> How would you arrange a venue for a national sales conference?

On the day of the meeting

- Arrive well before the start time of the meeting. This will allow you to check that all the arrangements are in place
- Check that the catering is organised for the times that the agenda states it will be available
- Check that all of the equipment is in place and that it works
- If the meeting is not on your premises:
  - make sure you know where the toilets are
  - whether there is a fire alarm test arranged that day
  - where the fire exits are
  - where the assembly point is
  - where lunch is going to be served
  - if there are facilities for smokers
  - if there is disabled access
  - who is responsible for first aid and how to raise the alarm if you need to

Make sure that you have spare copies of the papers you sent prior to the meeting available for those who have lost them, forgotten them or claim never to have received them. There may be other items for discussion at the meeting, which were not included on the agenda. If this happens, make sure you have sufficient copies of relevant papers for the meeting, because these have not been circulated in advance. These should be collated into the order in which they will be discussed and placed in position on the tables. Sorting the papers into order will enable people to follow the agenda more easily and reduce the distraction that searching through piles of paper causes. Make sure everyone has a full set of papers.

When people start to arrive make sure someone is on hand to greet them, sign them in and give them a delegate's badge if necessary, tell them where the cloakroom is, where refreshments can be found, the location of the meeting room and answer any questions they may have.

The level of recording of the meeting will depend on the type of meeting. The more formal the meeting, the more detailed the notes that must be kept. Notes of all meetings, however, must be accurate as they may be used later in a variety of circumstances. The most formal meetings will require minutes to be taken and signed by the Chair as a true record. There are various ways in which minutes can be taken including:

- **Verbatim** - Everything is recorded word for word
- **Narrative** - A summary of the meeting including discussions and conclusions. Formal resolutions are recorded verbatim
- **Resolution** - A resolution is a motion which has been voted on and passed. Details of the proposer and seconder are recorded with a verbatim recording of the resolution

Minutes are a written record of what took place at a meeting, and whichever form is used they must contain everything of importance. They must be written in a neutral fashion and always in the past tense. For instance, if Mr. McTavish says, "I am pleased to report that sales are up by 25% this year compared to last", the minutes would record, 'Mr. McTavish reported that sales in the current year were 25% up compared to the previous year'. The words 'I' and 'we' are not used in minute taking.

While taking the minutes:

- It is better to write too much than too little
- Record what is said and agreed in the order that it happens, not necessarily in the order the items appeared on the agenda
- Try to persuade the Chair to stick to the agenda
- If you are uncertain what someone has said, ask them to repeat it and read it back to them before you record it to check that you have it right
- Where someone refers to something that has been discussed at a previous meeting, cross-refer this in the minutes
- Record names and times of late arrivals and early departures
- If formal resolutions are being voted on, record the names of the proposer and seconder
- If asked, record details of any opposing view to the majority
- Make sure all agreed actions state who is responsible for carrying them out and the target date
- If necessary record the agreed date, time and place of the next meeting

- Include a list of all attendees
- Ensure that all attendees and those whose apologies for absence were noted receive a copy

Minutes of Social Club Meeting held on 19th May 2004 West Hotel, Pendleton. 2.30pm.

Those present

Bill Banstow   Chair
Mike Willis   Secretary
Pete Axty   Treasurer
Carol Carter
Brian Williams
Kevin Bissle
Janet Hewitt

Apologies for absence were received from: Michael Ford

Late Arrivals were Kevin Bissle and Janet Hewitt

Minutes of the last meeting were approved.

The Chair reported that discussion with management started with regard to the possibility of using the staff canteen for future events.

The Treasurer reported that there were 7 subscriptions still outstanding. It was agreed that letters be written to the appropriate members advising them that if payment was not received by 6th June their membership would be terminated.

Kevin Bissle proposed that Bill Banstow should remain Chair for a the next 12 month period. Seconded by Janet Hewitt.

Bill Banstow accepted the extension of his period as chair.

A.O.B.

Carol Carter suggested that a staff outing to the seaside in August could be arranged.

It was agreed that she would look into the costings of such an event.

The next meeting will be on 16th June 2004 at 2.30pm at the West Hotel, Pendleton.

As well as taking minutes it will probably be your responsibility to:

- Make sure everybody knows where the toilets are
- What to do in case of a fire alarm
- Where and when refreshments are available

If it is a formal meeting you may need to:

- Advise the Chair on legal issues or matters of convention
- You may have to arrange for the photocopying of papers during the meeting
- Deal with failures of power, equipment or caterers

If the meeting is not being held on your own premises you will need to have checked who to contact in any given set of circumstances. If the fire alarm should sound you will need to guide everyone to a place of safety.

Less formal meetings will still require that notes be taken of the actions agreed action. The item discussed, the outcome or action required and the name of the person or persons responsible for carrying out the action are recorded. The discussions are not recorded.

ITEM No.	ACTION REQUIRED	BY WHOM	BY WHEN
1	New office furniture to be ordered	Bill Welch	30.04.06
2	Year end procedures to be completed	Everybody	28.05.06
3	Office junior to be recruited	Karin Begum	28.05.06
4	Invoicing to be brought up to date	Mark Lennon	28.05.06
5	Filing to be brought up to date	Rachel Starr	30.06.06
6	Quarterly newsletter to be produced	Pete Biggs Samantha Wilson	13.10.06

What you need to know

Which type of minutes are required

> Why is it necessary to record late arrivals and early departures?

Who to send copies of the minutes to

> What duties other than recording the minutes might you have during the meeting?

What to include in and what to exclude from the minutes

> What is meant by the terms 'proposer' and 'seconder'?

The importance of recording who is responsible for carrying out agreed actions and by when

> In what circumstances would you record an opposing view to a majority decision?

After the meeting

When you have typed-up the minutes take them to the Chair and ask their approval of the content. Make any amendments that are necessary to ensure that the minutes are an accurate record of the meeting and agreed action points. Distribute the minutes to the attendees and those who submitted apologies for absence as soon as possible and before the agreed deadline. Some organisations have particular ways of highlighting action points to be completed before the next meeting as it is important to ensure everyone understands who's doing what and by when. Don't forget to keep a copy for the file. Check through the action points to see if there were any papers to be forwarded following the meeting and make sure these are enclosed. You may also need to send copies of papers distributed at the meeting to those who submitted their apologies.

Minutes of Social Club Meeting held on 19th May 2004 West Hotel, Pendleton. 2.30pm.

1.0 Those present

Bill Banstow   Chair
Mike Willis   Secretary
Pete Axty   Treasurer
Carol Carter
Brian Williams
Kevin Bissle
Janet Hewitt

1.1 Apologies for absence were received from: Michael Ford

1.2 Late Arrivals were Kevin Bissle and Janet Hewitt

1.3 Minutes of the last meeting were approved

2.0 The Chairman reported that discussions with management had started with regard to the possibility of using the staff canteen for future events

3.0 The Treasurer reported that there were seven subscriptions still outstanding. It was agreed that letters be written to the appropriate members advising them that if payment was not received by 6th June their membership would be terminated

4.0 Kevin Bissle proposed that Bill Banstow should remain Chair for the next 12-month period. Seconded by Janet Hewitt

4.1 Bill Banstow accepted the extension of his period as Chair

5.0 A.O.B.

5.1 Carol Carter suggested that a staff outing to the seaside in August could be arranged

5.2 It was agreed that she would look into the costings of such an event

6.0 The next meeting will be on 16th June 2004 at 2.30pm at the West Hotel, Pendleton.

You may receive requests to alter the contents of the minutes after you have distributed them. These must always be referred to the Chair. If they agree that the amendment will produce a more accurate record of the meeting, you will need to produce an amended set of minutes and circulate those. If the Chair is unwilling to have the minutes amended, you will need to advise the attendee accordingly and they will have to raise the matter at the next meeting.

You may need to diarise the action points so that you can contact the person responsible for taking the actions and check what progress has been made. Where there appears to be a potential problem, you may need to report this to the Chair or ask if there is any assistance that you can give to help achieve the desired result.

What you need to know

Whose approval of the minutes is necessary before they are distributed?

Why is it essential to keep a file copy of the minutes?

The actions to take if you are asked to amend minutes after they have been distributed?

What might you have to send to people who submitted their apologies?

Whose responsibility it is to follow up action points between meetings?

Why is accuracy vital in minute taking?

Whether any documents will need to be distributed to enable action points to be completed?

When should you distribute minutes of meetings?

The efficient organisation and accurate recording of meetings is essential to the effective running of a business. Meetings do not just happen, they require a great deal of work before, during and after the event. You will need to know and be able to spell the names of everybody at the meeting, as well as having at least a passing knowledge of the business being discussed. You must be able to concentrate throughout the meeting, remaining alert and be organised so that you can record what is happening without missing anything.

To be a successful meetings organiser requires the organisational ability of a general and the patience of a saint

Are you ready for assessment?

To achieve this unit of a Level 2 Business & Administration qualification you will need to demonstrate that you are competent in the following:

- Agree the meeting brief
- Organise and confirm the venue, equipment and catering requirements
- Prepare and agree an agenda and meeting papers
- Invite attendees and confirm attendance
- Make sure attendees' needs are met
- Collate and despatch papers for the meeting within agreed timescales
- Produce spare copies of meeting papers
- Arrange the equipment and layout of the room
- Make sure attendees have a full set of papers
- Take accurate notes of the meeting including attendance
- Provide information, advice and support when required
- Produce a record of the meeting
- Seek approval and amend the meeting record as necessary
- Circulate the meeting record to agreed timescales

(Remember that you will need the skills listed at the beginning of this chapter and that these are covered in chapter 1.)

Your Assessor will need you to produce evidence from a variety of sources. If you carry out the activities that follow they will provide some of the evidence for you.

Activity 1

You have been appointed the secretary of your organisation's Social Club. They are holding a committee meeting next Wednesday to discuss future events. Produce an agenda for the meeting and the notice you would send to the committee.

Activity 2

The following action points were recorded at the above Social Club meeting.

Bill Grates is to organise the firework display for November 5th.
Sharon Sloane is to make arrangements for the visit of Father Christmas to the local hospice on Christmas Eve.
Michael Fisher is to purchase the masks for the Halloween Ball.
Victoria Ashman has agreed to hire the Father Christmas outfit for the staff Christmas party.
Brian Graham has offered to arrange the transport home for people attending the New Year's Eve party.
Matthew Christian is going to buy the prizes for the Christmas Party raffle.

As secretary it is your responsibility to follow up the action points. Diarise the actions that you need to take.

Activity 3

Minutes must not be written in the first person and must always be in the past tense. Re-write the following statements to make them acceptable as minutes.

Bill Rich said, "I will have that report ready by Wednesday".
Anthony Banks feels that Wednesday will be too late.
The sales figures were produced yesterday.
It is essential that the work is carried out today.
Tomorrow is the deadline for completing the agreed action.
We have all agreed that the deadline needs to be extended.
Point six on the agenda will be carried forward to the next meeting.
Our prices have not increased over the last twelve months.
Rachel Matthews said, "I will be on holiday when the next meeting is held".
The Treasurer intends to resign at the next meeting.

Activity 4

You have been asked to organise a sales meeting to be held at work. Identify who should be invited to attend, the most suitable location, how long the meeting should last and the agenda items. Calculate the cost of refreshments and list the resources that will be required. Locate a suitable external venue and get quotes for holding the meeting there. Compare the costs of holding the meeting internally and externally.

Activity 5
You have been asked to arrange an all day meeting for 40 people with lunch and coffee/tea included. The purpose is to inform them of a new product that your organisation is about to launch onto the market. Research local venues for the meeting, obtain quotes and suggested room layouts. Two of the attendees are in wheelchairs and one is a vegetarian. Take their needs into account.

Activity 6
Attend a meeting (this could be a team meeting at work, a social club meeting, a meeting at college) and take notes of what is said. Produce minutes from your notes. Ask someone else who attended the meeting to review the minutes and check that you have included all the important points (if there are official minutes produced you could check yours against them).

Remember: While gathering evidence for this unit, evidence **may** be generated for units 110, 201, 202, 209, 210, 212, 213, 214, 216, 219, 220, 221, 222, 224 and 225.

CHAPTER 14
UNIT 212 – Use IT systems 2

We all need to work with Information Technology (IT) as part of our job role whatever that role may be. Even if we have chosen a career that does not directly involve working at a computer keyboard, we cannot avoid it; at the bank, at the shops, even in the home. The microwave is controlled by a computer and so is the central heating.

Computers may be as small as your hand or big enough to fill a room. In this chapter we will be looking at personal computers and peripherals such as monitors, keyboards, mice, external drives, digital cameras, web cameras, scanners, speakers, printers and modems, as well as methods of storing information. We will also look at linking personal computers together in networks, dealing with common problems that may arise, protecting your computer with passwords and anti-virus protection and health and safety issues surrounding personal computers (PCs).

All computers have certain things in common. They are, basically, calculating machines. Whatever their output, whether they be producing documents, controlling the traffic lights or operating a life support machine in a hospital, they achieve all of these by manipulating numbers.

The 'brain' of the computer is the central processing unit or CPU. This device, hardly bigger than a postage stamp:

- Reads instructions
- Performs calculations
- Makes decisions
- Stores and retrieves information
- Moves information from one part of the computer to another

The computer's CPU dictates how quickly the computer works and which functions it can carry out. In a desk top computer it is located in a box commonly known as a base unit. (This is the big box either under your monitor or under your desk which has the slots where you put your disks.)

The parts of the computer outside of the base unit are used to communicate with the CPU. They include 'input' devices which give instructions to the CPU and 'output' devices which receive information from the CPU. Input devices include:

- **Keyboard** - Used to type text and issue commands
- **Mouse** - A pointing device used to select words or objects on the screen
- **Scanner** - Used to copy photographs or images into the computer
- **Digital camera** - Transfers images directly from the camera to the computer
- **Webcam** - Transfers live moving images directly to the computer

Output devices include:

- **Monitor** - This is the screen that displays text and images
- **Printer** - Prints hard copies of text and images
- **Speakers** - Allow sound to be transmitted by the computer

Other peripherals include networking devices, which allow computers to communicate with each other. Probably the most common of these is the modem. The modem converts digital information from the computer into an analogue signal that can travel over the telephone system, and back again. Modems can be internal, situated in the base unit, or external, sitting on your desk. The advantages of external modems are:

- Visible status lights, which help to find the cause if you have a problem
- Easy transfer to another computer
- They can be more easily re-set without switching off the computer
- They don't take up space inside the computer

Integrated Systems Digital Network (ISDN) is a system which enables data and voice communication to be carried out at up to twice the speed of standard modems. Asymmetric Digital Subscriber Line (ADSL) is a high speed Broadband connection which operates at much greater speeds.

Another type of networking device is the network hub/router which connects PCs to one another, allowing them to share resources and files. The computers are connected to the network hub/router via cables and network cards. Some hub/routers are wireless access points which eliminate the need for cables.

Computers can use more storage space than is available on the hard drive in the base unit. Hard drives contain hard disks, stacked vertically inside the drive, on which data is stored. To add storage space there are a number of options available:

- **Floppy disks** - These are used in disk drives which may be part of the base unit or may be separate peripherals
- **CD ROMs** - These hold much more data than floppy disks. They are also used in disk drives
- **DAT tape** - These are cassette tapes which can record up to 8GB, or more than ten CD ROMs. They are commonly used to backup data using an external DAT tape drive
- **ZIP disks** - These hold more than a floppy disk but less than a CD ROM and have the advantage of being more robust. Reading Zip disk requires an additional peripheral called a Zip drive
- **DVD disks** - These are similar to CD ROMs but hold considerably more data – typically 4.7Gb
- **Universal serial bus (USB) storage devices** - These include pen drives and MP3 players. They are connected to the computer through a USB port

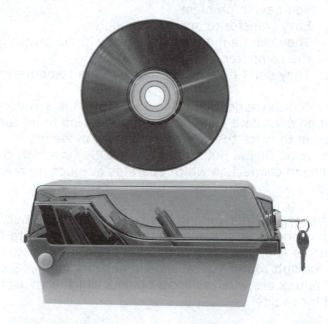

The information stored by your computer needs protection from people who are not authorised to access it. This is usually achieved by the use of passwords. In some situations you will select your own password, in others the password will be selected by a network administrator. Either way, it is advisable to change the password regularly, especially if someone leaves who knows it.

The other risk to your computer will come from viruses. These are programs that enter your computer without your knowledge and are designed to damage or delete files. Viruses infect your computer through the Internet, via e-mails or through software. There are a number of anti-virus programs which can be purchased which will check files for viruses before you open them. They can usually only detect viruses which existed before the anti-virus program was written, so need regular updating.

Many problems can be avoided if you perform regular maintenance on your computer software and hardware. There are a number of simple steps you can take:

- **Scan your hard disk** - This usually cleans up any disk errors
- **Defragment your hard drive** - Files get spread out over the hard disk, or 'fragmented'. This means the hard disk has to work harder to find the information
- **Back-up your hard disk** - This gives you a chance to retrieve any lost data if major problems occur with the computer
- **Clean the keyboard** - Hold the keyboard upside down and gently shake it to remove accumulated dust. Use a cotton bud to clean between the keys
- **Clean the mouse** – With a roller-ball mouse, turn the mouse upside down and open the twist lock. Take out the ball and carefully put it to one side. Clean the rollers and the ball then put the ball back and close the twist lock

As well as risks to your computer, you need to be aware of risks *from* using computers. Computers can be a major cause of health and safety problems: headaches, eye-strain, neck problems, repetitive strain injury and stress. Of course, it is not the computer itself that causes the problems, it is the use of the computer. To avoid some of these there are steps that you can take:

- Sit on an adjustable chair with your back supported. Your arms should be horizontal when on the keyboard and the monitor should be immediately in front of your eyes
- Make sure the screen is the right distance from your eyes to enable you to focus easily. If necessary change the zoom facility

- Consider using a wrist rest to prevent repetitive strain injury and a foot rest to improve your posture and reduce the risk of back, shoulder and neck strain
- Adjust the screen brightness to reduce glare
- Clean the screen regularly to prevent the need to squint
- Take regular short breaks

The Display Screen Equipment (DSE) Regulations apply to all who regularly use visual display units (VDUs) in their work, and relate to workstations as well as the equipment. They require employers to:

- Assess all workstations for health and safety risks and lower the risks as much as possible
- Plan work activities to incorporate rest breaks at regular intervals
- Arrange and pay for eye tests and pay for spectacles or lenses if these are prescribed specifically for VDU work
- Provide health and safety training for DSE users and re-train if the workstation is changed or modified
- Provide DSE users with information on all aspects of health and safety which apply to them and measures being taken to reduce risks to their health

All of the above applies equally to laptops, personal digital assistants or hand-held computers.

When using IT systems you will need the following skills:

- Organising
- Planning
- Using technology

These skills are covered in chapter 1.

There are a number of operating systems available. The most commonly used is Windows XP so the examples used in this chapter relate to Windows XP. Whether you use this system or another the principles are the same.

Setting up hardware

Before installing any hardware it is advisable to switch off your computer.

If you are starting from a base unit the first piece of hardware to connect is the monitor. Cables connect the monitor to the PCs video port and to mains electricity. Most monitors plug into a 15-hole port. Turn the computer on and it should detect the new hardware. The computer will give you directions for installing drivers for the monitor if they are required.

You will now need a keyboard and probably a mouse. These plug into the base unit using connectors which may look identical so take care to plug the right connector into the right socket. Many computers colour code the connectors, purple for the keyboard and green for the mouse. When you turn the PC on it should automatically recognise the new hardware. Some keyboards or mice require drivers. If so follow the on screen instructions.

Next you will want to install a printer. The printer will connect to the base unit using a parallel port, a 25 pin connection or a USB port. Make sure you connect the printer cable to the correct port and to the mains electricity. Check whether the printer has ink cartridges or toner cartridges already installed. If not install them, following the manufacturer's instructions. Turn on the computer, select 'My computer' from the desktop, select 'Printers', double click the 'Add Printer' icon. Follow the instructions to run the wizard. Print out a test sheet of paper to check that the printer is operating satisfactorily.

If you are going to use the computer to connect to the Internet you will want to install a modem. Modems are connected to a serial port in the base unit. These are usually 9-pin connectors. Plug one end of a serial cable into the modem and the other into a serial port in the base unit. Connect the modem to the mains electricity using an AC adapter then plug one end of a phone line into the phone jack and the other end into the back of the modem. Turn on the modem and the computer and Windows will launch an installation wizard.

If you need to import images from hard copies into your computer you will need to install a scanner. Scanners need to be on a flat surface. They can be connected to the base unit through a parallel port, a USB port or via a SCSI (small computer system interface) connection. If you are connecting through a parallel port you will probably have to disconnect the printer. If you want to connect both the scanner and printer at the same time you will need to connect the printer to the scanner with a cable, then connect the scanner to the base unit. Connect the scanner to the mains electricity and turn on both the computer and the scanner. Windows will know that new hardware has been added and you can follow the on screen instructions.

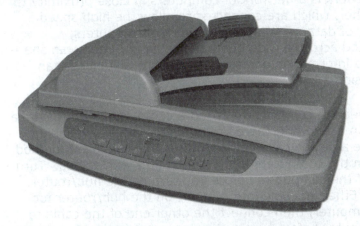

You may decide to install a digital camera so that you can import photographs that you have taken. Cameras connect through a USB cable; the computer will recognise that you are adding a digital camera.

The next step up from a digital camera is a WebCam which enables you to video-conference, put live images onto your website or send a movie clip to another computer. First you must install the software that came with the WebCam, then shut down the computer. Connect the WebCam to the base unit using a USB cable. When you turn on the computer Windows will detect the new hardware and launch a wizard. Follow the on screen instructions.

Networks

Computers may be connected in a Local Area Network (LAN) or a Wide Area Network (WAN). Often called an Intranet, a LAN network is a network of computers in close proximity to each other, which are connected to allow the high speed transfer of data. A WAN is a network of computers, connected across a wide geographical area. Users can share files and information across much greater distances than when using a LAN.

If you need to connect two or more computers, and maybe a printer in a network, there are two alternatives available; both use a device called a hub/router. The simplest method is to join the computers to the hub/router with cables. Turn off all of the computers before you turn on the hub/router. Plug an Ethernet cable into the port on the hub/router for each computer, then connect the other end of the cable to the computer before turning the computer back on. On each computer from the 'Control Panel' double click 'Network' then click 'File and Print Sharing'. Select the boxes that enable you to share files and a printer then click 'OK' twice. New drivers will be installed and the computer will ask if you want to restart. Click 'Yes'.

Alternatively, you can buy a wireless access point and plug it into the uplink part of the network. Choose which computer is to be the primary and put the CD supplied into that computer. Run the installation software. Install a wireless network device on each computer. Use the software installed with the network device to test the strength of the wireless connection. You may need to move the base station or the computer until you get the best reception possible.

If you encounter any problems setting up hardware there are a number of ways of obtaining help. Your organisation may have an IT department, the manual supplied with the hardware will give helpline details, or you can always use the 'Help' facility in the operating package.

What you need to know

The function of a modem

What is meant by the term 'networking'?

The function of a scanner

What is a CPU?

The function of a WebCam

Why do you use passwords?

The function of a Network hub/router

Why is it advisable to turn off the computer before attaching any peripherals?

Accessing data

Data is held in files in the software program in which it was first created. So a text document will be found in Word, a spreadsheet in Excel and a database in Access, for instance. To access data you must open the file that it is in, to open the file you must open the program. This can be done by clicking:

- 'Start'
- 'Programs'
- The name of the program that you want

Programs that you will be using regularly can be set up on the desktop so that you can open them with a double click rather than going through the above process. To do this click 'Start', click 'Programs', find the program that you want to put onto the desktop, left click, hold and drag to the desktop. An icon will appear which represents the program. When you want to open the program put your cursor on the icon and double click, the program will open.

To open a file:

- Select 'File' from the toolbar
- Click 'Open'
- From the 'Look in' drop-down menu browse to the correct location of the file
- Click on the name of the file
- Click 'Open'

The 'Look in' drop-down menu will display the names of folders and storage devices containing files, such as '3½" Floppy', 'Local disk', 'CD Drive' or 'Removable disk'.

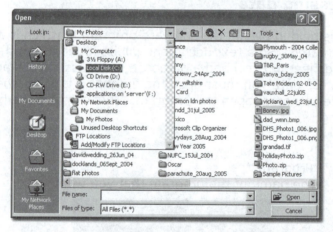

If you are opening a file on a networked computer, click on 'Start' and select 'My Network Places'. A list of all the shared folders on the network will appear. Double click on the folder containing the file that you want to open.

Protecting data

You may encounter problems with programs which are caused either by faults in the initial program, by incompatibility between two programs or by security problems. The solution to this may be a software patch.

A software patch is a software update, usually available from the manufacturer, which improves or corrects a problem with a currently installed software component or application.

Many large operating systems' authors release security patches monthly. These can be downloaded from the Internet, or automatically downloaded by activating 'Automatic Updates'. Automatic Updates allow patches to automatically install themselves while you use the Internet. To turn on Automatic Updates:

- Right click on 'My Computer' on the 'Start' menu
- Click on 'Properties'
- Click on the 'Automatic Updates' tab
- Click on the 'Automatic (Recommended)' box
- Click 'OK'

When downloading new software from the Internet, care must be taken to minimise the risk of getting a computer virus.

The best way to protect your system is to ensure you have an up-to-date virus scanning program which will automatically detect any potential virus in the software you are downloading. You should check that your operating system is kept current, allow automatic updates and ensure that you have installed all the latest security patches. Most importantly, only download software from safe and trustworthy websites, to minimise the possibility of a virus infecting your system.

Care should be taken before downloading patches that the solution will not be worse than the problem.

From time-to-time you will want to change the password that allows you to log-on to your computer. To do this:

- Click 'Start'
- Click 'Settings'
- Click 'Control Panel'
- Double click 'User Accounts'
- Click on the account that you want to change the password on
- Click 'Reset Password'
- Type a new password in the 'type a new password' box
- Type the new password again in the 'type the new password to confirm' box
- Type something that will remind you what the password is in the 'type a word or phrase to use as a password hint' box
- Click 'Change Password'

Alternatively:

- Press 'Ctrl', 'Alt' and 'Delete' keys all at once
- Click 'Change Password'
- Enter the current password
- Enter your new password
- Confirm your new password
- Click 'OK'
- Click 'Cancel'

You will want to choose a password that cannot be guessed easily. It is best to avoid using names, dates or words that appear in the dictionary as these can be 'hacked' (somebody remotely breaks into your system). You may wonder what can be used. A couple of suggestions are:

- Choose a word such as 'tyrefitter'. Then instead of typing 'tyrefitter' type the character one to the right of each letter on the keyboard (yutrgoyyrt)
- Choose two four letter words and a two digit number, for instance 'blue47wall'

Either of these is easy to remember and almost impossible to guess. Be careful when choosing the hint that it doesn't mean anything to anyone else. For instance, 'tyrefitter' may be your Uncle Fred's occupation so the hint would be 'Uncle Fred'.

You may want to lock your workstation so that no-one else can use it while you are away from your desk. You can only do this on Windows XP Professional, not Windows XP Home Edition. To do this:

- Press 'Ctrl', 'Alt' and 'Delete' keys all at once
- From the Windows Security dialog box click 'Lock Computer'
- The 'Computer Locked' window appears

To unlock the computer again:

- Press 'Ctrl', 'Alt' and 'Delete' keys all at once
- The 'Unlock Computer' dialog box opens
- Type your logon password in the 'Password' box
- Click 'OK'

In case you are likely to forget to lock your workstation every time you leave it you may want to use a screen saver that is password protected. This means that as soon as the screen saver appears because the computer has not been used for a period of time, no-one can get into the program that you were using without a password. This is done by:

- Clicking 'Start'
- Click 'Settings'
- Click 'Control Panel'
- The 'Windows Control Panel' opens
- Double click 'Display'
- The 'Display Properties' dialog box opens

- Click the 'Screen Saver' tab
- Click the 'Password Protected' option

To unlock the computer again:

- Press any key
- Enter the username and password that you use to log on

You may share your computer and want to protect your files and folders from being opened. You can 'encrypt' them so that if anyone else opens them they appear as nonsense. To do this:

- Select the 'File' menu
- Click 'Open'
- Right click the file or folder
- Click 'Properties'. The 'Properties' dialog box opens
- Select the 'General' tab
- Click 'Advanced'. The 'Advanced Attributes' dialog box opens
- Click the 'Encrypt contents to secure data' box
- Click 'OK'
- Click 'OK'
- Choose 'Apply changes to this folder only'
- Click 'OK'

If you install anti-virus software and keep its virus database up-to-date you should avoid problems with viruses. You will still need to be careful about what programs you install and what files you open from the Internet. Never open files sent to you by e-mail from people you don't know, even if they appear to be harmless. Be careful if you receive an e-mail from someone you do know with an attachment which looks suspicious. Check with the sender before you open the attachment as some viruses spread by sending e-mails to everybody in the affected computer's address book. If you are in doubt about the contents of the e-mail, then delete it.

From time-to-time you should scan your computer for viruses. The precise process for this will depend on the anti-virus software that you have running on your computer. On Norton AntiVirus 2002 the process is:

- Click 'Start'
- Click 'Programs'

- Click 'Norton AntiVirus'
- Click 'Norton AntiVirus 2002'
- Click 'Scan for Viruses'
- Click 'Scan My Computer'. This may take over an hour
- Click 'Finished'

The other essential maintenance to undertake is to 'back up' your hard disk to a removable drive, a network or the Internet. This is simply done:

- Click 'Start'
- Click 'Programs'
- Click 'Accessories'
- Click 'System Tools'
- Click 'Backup'. A wizard opens
- Follow the on screen instructions

 What you need to know

How to scan for viruses

What is a virus?

How to backup your hard disk

Why do you encrypt files?

How to encrypt files

Why should you not open e-mail attachments from unknown senders?

When to lock your work station

How do you choose a password that cannot be easily guessed?

How to open a file

How do you set up a desktop?

Take one step at a time, don't forget you can always get help from the IT department, the on screen 'Help' menu and the manuals that accompany the hardware or software you are installing and using.

When you have mastered the basics you will be able to go on to use a whole range of programs with confidence

Are you ready for assessment?

To achieve this unit of a Level 2 Business & Administration qualification you will need to demonstrate that you are competent in the following:

- Connect up a computer with other hardware and storage media safely
- Link a computer to other hardware safely
- Access files on a LAN or a WAN
- Set password levels on software and data
- Make backups of operating system data, where necessary
- Download software patches to fix any security flaws
- Take action to keep risks to a minimum, when downloading software
- Take action to avoid risks from receiving and opening attachments from e-mails

(Remember that you will need the skills listed at the beginning of this chapter and that these are covered in chapter 1.)

This unit is a generic unit. The skills used to demonstrate your abilities in this unit are very specific to your organisation and as such your supervisor, team leader or manager should supervise you carrying out tasks common to your organisation.

This may involve activities such as:

- Setting up a printer
- Installing a webcam
- Locating and opening files on a LAN or a WAN
- Troubleshooting problems such as why a printer doesn't seem to operate correctly
- Password protecting your PC when you are away from your desk

- Making backups of operating system data
- Downloading software patches to fix security problems

There are many other resources to assist you with this such as software help menus (F1), manuals and textbooks.

Remember: While gathering evidence for this unit, evidence **may** be generated for units 110, 201, 202, 213, 214, 215, 216, 217, 218 and 225

CHAPTER 15
UNIT 213 – Use IT to exchange information 2

One of the most exciting recent developments in the office environment has been the Internet. This is a world wide system that stores data and is accessible by anybody with a computer, a modem and an Internet Service Provider (ISP). It is used to access an enormous amount of diverse information via the World Wide Web (www) and to send and receive e-mails (email).

The advantages of e-mail for the administrator are:

- Instant communication with people anywhere in the world, providing they have an e-mail address
- The ability to access e-mail at any time and any place
- Fast and efficient distribution of mail shots with no postage costs
- Reduced costs of paper, photocopying and postage
- An electronic record of all correspondence, incoming and outgoing
- The ability to attach documents, photographs, spreadsheets, databases and much more

Users can connect to other users wherever they may be. An office worker can connect from a laptop anywhere in the world to their computer back in the office and have access to all the files held there.

The World Wide Web gives you access to massive amounts of information to facilitate any research project that you may be involved in. In addition to facts that can be found on web pages it is possible to join Forums and discuss issues with other people all over the world who may have views or knowledge that you can share. It is also possible to complete many forms and returns 'on line' for instance you can:

- Submit VAT returns and PAYE returns
- Place orders for goods and services
- Make bookings for travel, accommodation and training courses
- Place employment vacancies

Search engines such as Google, MSN and AskJeeves give you access to all of the information available on line. Once found, this information can be e-mailed to any other computer as an attachment.

Receivers of attachments need to take great care as a number of viruses have been spread across the network in this way. These are spread maliciously throughout the Internet and use many methods to corrupt data and 'attack' your computer. Protection against viruses can be purchased and downloaded, but there is a continuing risk as new viruses are being developed all the time and the protection software is always catching up.

There is also an on-going problem with unsolicited e-mails (SPAM), the Internet equivalent of junk mail. In the same way as you simply throw your junk mail in the bin, you can divert SPAM to a separate folder which will be emptied automatically.

When using IT to exchange information you will use the following skills:

- Planning
- Organising
- Researching
- Communicating
- Using technology
- Recording
- Reading
- Writing
- Problem solving

These skills are covered in chapter 1.

Basic e-mail facilities

Sending e-mails. E-mail can be sent to anyone anywhere in the world as long as they have an e-mail address. To send an e-mail, open your e-mail software (usually MS Outlook or MS Outlook Express or a web-based program such as MSN Hotmail) and click on 'New'. A template will appear.

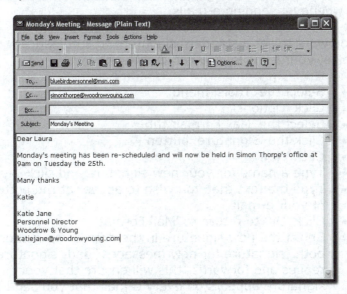

- The cursor will be flashing in the 'To' field. Input the recipient's e-mail address (there can be more than one recipient). An e-mail address looks like bluebirdpersonnel@msn.com, for instance

- Tab to the 'Carbon copy' or 'Cc:' field. Input the e-mail address of anybody that you want to receive a copy of the e-mail (there can be more than one)
- Tab to the 'Bcc' field. Input the e-mail address of anybody that you want to receive a copy of the e-mail without other recipients being aware that they have had a copy (there can be more than one). This is called a Blind Copy
- Tab to the 'Subject:' field. Input the subject of the message
- Move the cursor to the message field and type your message
- If necessary, indicate whether the message is of high importance (!) or low importance (⏬)

Click on the 'copy message to sent folder' box (in MS Outlook this can be found in the 'Options' menu and the message will be copied to your sent folder. Check the content of the message for accuracy and when you are satisfied click 'Send'. The message will be sent to all the addresses you specified. It is possible to add a 'signature' to your e-mails containing your contact details and possibly a legal disclaimer. Your organisation may have a signature template that you must use whenever sending e-mails.

If you want to set a standard signature to automatically send on all of your e-mails, you can create one by:

- Select the 'Tools' menu
- Click 'Options'
- Select the 'Mail Format' tab
- Click the 'Signature' button
- Click 'New'
- Type a name for your new signature and click 'Next'
- Type the text that you wish to appear at the bottom of your e-mail
- Click 'OK' to return to 'Mail Format'
- Select the new signature in the drop-down menus for both "signature for new messages" and "signature for replies and forwards" this will ensure that your signature appears on every e-mail that you send out or reply to
- Click 'OK' to return to 'Options'
- Click 'OK'

Setting priority to messages

When sending important e-mails, you can set the priority of a message to indicate its importance to the recipient. To set the priority of a message:

- Select the 'Options' menu
- Click on 'Importance'
- In the drop-down menu located next to 'Importance' select 'High', 'Normal' or 'Low'
- Click 'Close'

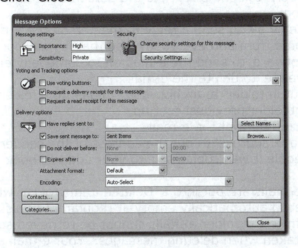

You can also set the priority of your message to high or low using the short-cut buttons in the message toolbar. The red flag will set the priority as high, and the arrow pointing downwards will set the priority as low.

From the 'Options' menu, you can also set a number of other options to your e-mail before you send it. These include setting a level of sensitivity, adding a hyperlink and requesting a delivery receipt. Most e-mail software will also provide you with additional tools and resources such as the option of flagging e-mails in your inbox to highlight their importance, saving copies of your messages and sending file attachments with your e-mails.

Receiving e-mails

E-mail can be received from anyone anywhere in the world as long as they have an e-mail address. To receive an e-mail open your e-mail program and go to your 'inbox'. The e-mails received will be listed in chronological order. Click on a name in the 'from' column and the e-mail will open. After reading the message you will have a number of options. You can click on:

- 'Reply' to send a reply to the person the e-mail came from
- 'Reply all' to send a reply to the person the e-mail came from and everybody else that it was copied to
- 'Forward' to send the e-mail on to somebody else
- 'Delete' to delete the e-mail
- 'Put in folder' to archive the e-mail into a folder or subfolder previously set up
- 'Print' to print the e-mail
- 'Save address' to put the address of the sender or the people it was copied to into your address book

Deleted e-mails are put into a 'Deleted items folder' which can be set to automatically empty at regular intervals. Once emptied from the folder e-mails cannot be retrieved so care must be taken when deleting messages. Your e-mail account will have limited capacity, however, so messages cannot be saved indefinitely.

There is an option on most e-mail servers to send and receive instant messages. The recipient must be added to the sender's list of instant contacts. When the sender wants to send an instant message, they click on the icon next to the contact and can see whether the contact is online. If they are, an instant message can be sent and a reply received. If the contact is offline, an e-mail can be sent as normal.

What you need to know

How to access your e-mails

Which e-mail ISP system does your organisation use?

When it is necessary to keep a copy of a sent e-mail

Can you explain the difference between 'cc' and 'bcc'?

Whether you need to print off and file received e-mails

What symbol is present in all e-mail addresses?

Advanced e-mail facilities

The names of people that you regularly correspond with by e-mail will have been saved in your address book. Using address books to send e-mails to individuals means that you do not have to type the complete e-mail address to select that person as a recipient and that more than one recipient can be identified.

Setting up groups of e-mail addresses can save a lot of time when sending e-mails to members of specific departments or grades. If you have numerous recipients that you regularly send the same e-mail to, you can set them up as a group:

- From the 'Inbox' screen click on 'Contacts'. This will bring up your address book
- Click on 'Actions' and then 'New Distribution List'. Give the group a name and then select members from your existing contacts list

- When you have completed a group click on 'Save and Close' and the name of the group will be added into your address book. When you want to send an e-mail to all the members, simply click on the group name in the address book

An e-mail message can have any file attached to it. This is a convenient way of sending large amounts of information to any number of recipients. When sending attachments, complete the e-mail message as usual then click on 'attach' then 'file'. You can then either enter the name of the file or use the 'browse' facility to find the file. If you are sending more than one file click on 'OK and attach another' until all the files are attached then click on 'OK'. You will be taken back to the message screen. Check that the files attached are correct then send the message as usual.

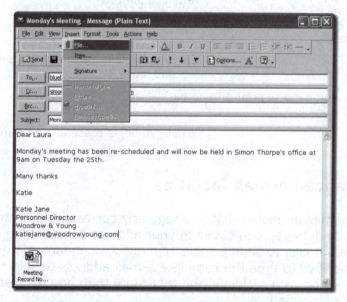

Consider that there is a limit to the amount of data you can store on your computer or company's system. This applies to your e-mails too. While e-mails can have small file sizes, their attachments can be very large. Compressing files and archiving e-mails drastically reduces the amount of storage memory that you use.

A file can be compressed or 'zipped' to reduce its size. This can save up to 80% of hard disk space, drastically reduce e-mail transmission time, save space in your inbox and enable you to send files as attachments that would otherwise be blocked for security reasons. Compressing and de-compressing file attachments to send or receive zipped files requires downloaded or purchased software that facilitates this.

If you receive an e-mail message with attachments read the message first then:

- Double click on the attachment and a screen will appear asking if you want to Open or Save the file
- Click on 'Open' to see the document in the appropriate software package
- To save the document without viewing it first, click on 'Save to Disk'. You will then be shown a screen which enables you to select a location for the file

Remember to take great care before opening any attachment that comes from an unknown source. Viruses which can attack computer systems and wipe out files are often hidden in attachments. Once you have opened the attachment it is often too late.

One of the great disadvantages of electronic mail is that advertisers can flood e-mail addresses with unwanted mail or 'SPAM'. Your ISP will almost certainly have a filter on the incoming mail to divert obvious 'SPAM' into a 'junk e-mail' folder, but some will inevitably get through to your 'inbox'.

If you receive an e-mail from an unrecognised sender, or with a subject that alerts your suspicion, check with a supervisor before opening it as junk e-mail can carry viruses which can damage your software.

Mail that is diverted to the junk e-mail folder will be automatically deleted after a set time. It is a good idea to look in this folder regularly to check that no genuine messages have been inadvertently diverted. If there is a message in this folder that belongs in the inbox click on 'not junk' and the message will be sent to your inbox.

The best way to maintain your e-mail inbox is to create folders and subfolders. Folders allow you to organise your messages and make them easier to find in future. You can create as many or as few folders as you require, and they can be easily accessed from in your e-mail inbox. To create a new folder:

- Select the 'Go' menu
- Click 'Folder List'
- Right click on the folder in which you wish to create a new folder (for main folders click on your inbox)
- Select 'New Folder'
- Type a name for your new folder
- Click 'OK'

Once you have created new folders, you can organise your e-mails. To move e-mails into your folders:

- Highlight the e-mail that you wish to move
- Select 'Edit' from the toolbar
- Click 'Move to Folder'
- Select the folder that you wish to move the e-mail into
- Click 'OK'

Another option for keeping your inbox organised is to archive your e-mails. This allows you to keep the number of e-mails in your inbox to a minimum, but keeps them stored on your computer in case you need to refer back to them at a later date.

A good option for archiving your e-mails is to set up 'AutoArchiving', which means your e-mails will automatically be moved from your inbox after a certain period of time. To set up 'AutoArchive' in your e-mail account:

- Select the 'Tools' menu
- Click 'Options'
- Select the 'Other' tab
- Click on the 'AutoArchive' button
- Select how often you want the archiving to take place, how old e-mails should be when they are archived and the name and location of the file you want the e-mails archived to
- Click 'OK' to return to the 'Options' screen
- Click 'OK' to return to your e-mail

It is also possible to archive your e-mails manually at any time. This option provides more control over the process and allows you to archive different folders to different archive files. To archive folders manually:

- Highlight the folder that you wish to archive
- Select the 'File' menu
- Click on 'Archive'
- Select a date next to 'Archive Items Older Than'
- Click on the 'Browse' and select which file you want to archive your e-mails to
- Click 'OK'

Once your e-mails have been archived they are stored indefinitely on your computer. To retrieve e-mails which have been archived:

- Select the 'File' menu
- Highlight 'Open' and click 'Outlook Data File'
- In the 'File Name' box type the name of the file that you want to open
- Click 'OK'

After you have finished using your archive folder, close it to ensure it does not slow down Outlook. To close the archived folder:

- Right-click on the folder name
- Select 'Close Folder'

When receiving and archiving e-mails, you will need to be aware of confidentiality and legislation. The storing of information is regulated by the Data Protection Act 1998, the main points of which are:

- All companies who hold information on people must be registered with the Information Commissioner
- Any information held on computer must have been obtained legally
- Data must only be used for the purpose for which it was originally obtained
- Data must be relevant, accurate, up to date and not excessive
- Data must not be kept longer than necessary
- People must have access to the information held about them
- Precautions must be taken to avoid access being available to people without permission

This includes people's signatures that they add to the end of e-mails, attached documents and contacts that you may be able to store in your e-mail software's contact database.

These guidelines must also be taken into consideration when using a company's internal network. Information must be held securely, kept up to date and not for longer than necessary.

In addition to legislation, your company may also have guidelines regarding appropriate materials. The Internet contains a whole host of useful and valuable material. With e-mail it makes it very easy to share this information.

Your company may have already decided what is and is not appropriate material. If not, it is up to you to judge whether the material you are accessing or forwarding is acceptable, not only in your office, but to those that you are sending it to.

What you need to know

How to add names to your e-mail address book

What e-mail group addresses does your organisation already have in place?

The value of setting up e-mail address groups

Does your organisation already have
file compression and de-compression
software?

The dangers of opening attachments
before they have been checked

Why should you open only e-mails from
recognised senders?

How to recognise 'SPAM' e-mails

Does your organisation automatically
filter 'SPAM' and junk e-mails?

What to do if junk e-mails appear in your
in-box

Why should you regularly check your
junk mail folder?

The potential effects of a computer virus

If you suspect that an e-mail contains a
virus, to whom should it be reported?

Using suitable search engines effectively

There are a large number of 'search engines' available on the
Internet. Their purpose is to enable you to find websites that
contain the information you are looking for. Among the best
known are 'Google', 'MSN' and 'AskJeeves'. Whichever
search engine you choose the words you use to describe the
information you are looking for will greatly affect the number
of results you get. The more words you use the narrower the
search. Search engines also have techniques for narrowing
the search.

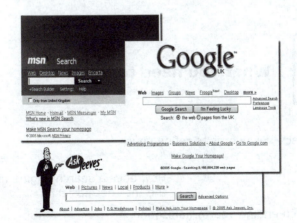

For instance:

- A search in MSN for car hire will produce 20,176,472 results
- Car hire in Portsmouth will produce 150,374 results
- Car hire in Portsmouth NOT van will produce 108,758 results
- Car hire in Portsmouth AND van will produce 34,235 results
- "Car hire in Portsmouth" will reduce the results to 173

Different search engines will have different features. Some will allow the use of wild cards, where a symbol, usually *, can be used in place of letters; some will allow Boolean notation where 'AND' or 'NOT' can be used to widen or narrow the search.

For a more detailed search, you may want to use a meta-search engine. In these you submit keywords in the search box, and your search is transmitted simultaneously to several individual search engines and their databases of Web pages. In a few seconds, you get back results from all the search engines queried. Meta-search engines do not own a database of Web pages; they send your search terms to the databases maintained by search engine companies.

Having found the information you are looking for you can then send it to other people by attaching the web page to an e-mail. If you are likely to need the information again you can 'bookmark' the page or add it to your 'favourites' so that you can return to it at a later date.

 What you need to know

How to select 'key' words to refine your search

How does a search engine make using the Internet easier?

Which search engine your organisation favours

What difference does using speech marks make in a search?

The advantages of book marking favourite websites

If you were asked to find a flight from London to Vancouver, would you know where to look?

The World Wide Web has opened up almost all of the World's information to anybody who has access to a telephone line and a computer. Information can be shared instantly at the press of a button. As with all major advances, however, there are risks attached. If you have access to every other user in the world, they have access to you. You can be flooded with unwanted information, or receive viruses that can wipe out your work. Used with care it is certainly one of the greatest inventions of all time.

Advances in IT have made it possible to send and receive information over vast distances in an instant

Are you ready for assessment?

To achieve this unit of a Level 2 Business & Administration qualification you will need to demonstrate that you are competent in the following:

- Use more advanced facilities, e.g. add a signature or set the priority of messages
- Send messages to groups of people using groups set up in an address book
- Send and receive instant messages with and without attachments
- Compress messages on sending and un-compress messages received
- Archive e-mails where necessary, such as by using folders and subfolders
- Choose a search engine that is appropriate for the information that is needed
- Carry out searches efficiently, such as by using meta-search engines, wild cards, 'AND' or 'NOT' (Boolean notation)

(Remember that you will need the skills listed at the beginning of this chapter and that these are covered in chapter 1.)

Your Assessor will need you to produce evidence from a variety of sources. If you carry out the activities that follow they will provide some of the evidence for you.

Activity 1

Find out who your Internet Service Provider is.

What command will send a received e-mail message on to another recipient?

What is the term for a collection of e-mail addresses in your contacts list?

When opening an attachment to an e-mail what options are you given if you click on 'download file'?

Activity 2

Over the period of a month archive the e-mails you have sent and received. Set up and use folders and subfolders for e-mails:

- To which you have added a signature
- In which you have set a priority
- You have sent to a group
- Which you have compressed on sending and un-compressed on receiving

Activity 3

Keep a copy of e-mail addresses and the groups you set up and the contacts you have sent instant messages to or received instant messages from.

Activity 4

Search the Internet for train times from Bury to Bristol Parkway, on Wednesday next arriving before 3.00pm. Find three trains which meet the requirements and available fares, single and return, returning the following day, leaving before 10.00am.

Activity 5

You have been asked to find information about Isambard Kingdom Brunel on the Internet using meta-search engines, wild cards and Boolean notation. Search for the necessary information to write a 250-word synopsis of his life and career.

Remember: While gathering evidence for this unit, evidence **may** be generated for units 110, 201, 202, 212 and 225

CHAPTER 16
UNIT 214 – Word processing software 2

Improvements in word processing software over the last few years have revolutionised the production of documents. Modern software can be used to create, edit and produce documents including letters, memos, newsletters, reports, envelopes and labels to a much higher standard than was previously possible.

While technology has expanded upon the skill of the typist, it now involves much more than typing letters. Although the skill of 'touch-typing' is still very useful, a wider knowledge of the various functions of the keyboard is now necessary. The arrow keys and the 'Home' and 'End' keys allow you to move around the screen easily. There are a range of commands available from the keyboard:

- Text commands
- Format commands
- Editing commands
- Print commands

Using available software, a wide range of simple but effective modifications can be made. Text can be amended, moved, enhanced, deleted and then saved. Numerous different typefaces are available such as *Monotype Corsiva* or Comic Sans MS each of which can be changed to include colour, shadowing, **emboldening**, *italics* and underlining for emphasis and impact.

Other features available include:

- **Word count** - As well as counting the number of words in a document it will count pages, characters, paragraphs and lines
- **Pagination** - This numbers the pages
- **Headers and Footers** - Repeats text at the top (header) or bottom (footer) of each page
- **Footnotes** - Numbers and positions footnotes where they are required
- **Split screens** - Lets you work on two documents at once
- **Spell check** - Uses the internal dictionary to check your spelling and suggest corrections
- **Thesaurus** - Provides you with a list of synonyms (words which have the same or similar meaning)
- **Hyperlink** – Allows you to link a certain section of text or graphic to another part of the document, a separate document, or to a website

It is advisable to become familiar with those you use regularly. Set up directories and save documents according to their type. Learning to use the full power of word processing software will enable you to produce documents more quickly, more accurately and to a higher standard of presentation.

When using word processing software you will use the following skills:

- Presentation
- Checking
- Communicating
- Planning
- Reading
- Organising
- Using technology

These skills are covered in chapter 1.

Basic word processing

When you start a new document you will create a new file. In word processing terms a file may be a single document, or a collection of connected documents. The common feature is that a file has a single file name. Click on the file menu, then on 'new'. Input the text and click on 'save'. At this point the program will name the file for you, probably 'Document 1' or something similar.

To name the file click on 'File' then 'Save As' and give the file a name which enables you to find it again at a later date. Your organisation may have a system for naming files such as the originator's initials followed by the date, for example.

Once you have named the file you can save it into a folder which contains related_files or into a directory which may also contain other folders on related subjects.

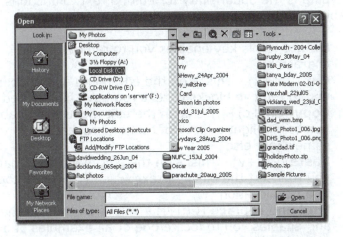

The important thing is to follow the system your organisation has in place to enable files to be easily found or, if no such system is in place, to create one which can be readily understood.

- When you want to find a file again click on 'open' and a list of file names will appear. Click on the file name and the file will open
- You may want to print a hard copy of the file. To do this click 'file' and 'print' or the 'print' icon. You will be given a number of options including changing the number of copies required

- If you want to send the file to another computer, you will need to know the recipient is using the same software as you. If they are not, their computer will not be able to read the file. You may have to convert the file to a format that can be read by them, alternatively many word processors can automatically convert documents received in other formats

Other formats that may be used include Rich Text Format (RTF) and Hypertext Markup Language (HTML). If you send an HTML or RTF message to someone whose mail program doesn't understand these formats, they will receive a plain text version. A plain text file can contain only unformatted text. A Word document saved in plain text format will lose all formatting, pictures, objects or tables; in fact everything except the text itself.

Probably the greatest advantage that word processing has over typing is the opportunity for editing text. Functions available include:

- **Delete** - This key enables you to remove single characters
- **Cut** (Ctrl+x) - This is on the edit menu and enables you to remove blocks of text you have highlighted
- **Copy** (Ctrl+c) - This is on the edit menu and enables you to highlight a block of text and repeat it somewhere else
- **Paste** (Ctrl+v) - This is on the edit menu and enables you to insert the block of text which you cut or copied to a new location
- **Find and replace** (Ctrl+f) - This is on the edit menu and enables you to locate one or all examples of a word or phrase and replace them with an alternative
- **Inserting special characters and symbols** - This is on the insert menu and enables you to use a wide range of non-Arabic letters and other signs
- **Mail merge** - This is on the tools menu and enables you to combine addresses from a database with the text in letters, mailing labels and envelope templates
- **Track changes** (Ctrl+Shift+e) - This is on the tools menu and enables you to indicate on a document where changes have been made for reviewing purposes

When you have completed a document, it is essential to check your work. Most word processing packages contain facilities for checking text such as spell checking and grammar checking. Use these first to correct the more glaring errors, but do not rely on them. They may not be able to distinguish between words which are spelt correctly but misused in context, such as 'there' and 'their'. Also, they tend to use American spelling and grammar, so will accept 'color' and reject 'colour', for instance. This setting can be altered, however, to the language of your choice by clicking options when using the spell checker. When the automatic checking is complete, read the document carefully to look for any missed errors, and also for correct use of paragraphs, breaks, headings and subheadings, style and formatting.

What you need to know

How to open an existing document

> What word processing application does your organisation use?

How to identify 'Americanised' spelling

> Can you find and use the edit menu?

How to save a document

> Could you set up a mail merge for a marketing mail shot?

Whether a document requires the use of the mail merge facility

> Do you know how the word processor indicates a spelling or grammatical error?

How to use the word count option

> Does your organisation have a standard format for naming documents? If so, what is it?

How to print a document

> Do you know how to create a new document?

Which menu contains the print command?

Which command on the edit menu would delete a block of text from a document?

More advanced word processing

At any stage during the production of a document, formatting text may be necessary. There are various options available in the format menu. It is possible to format:

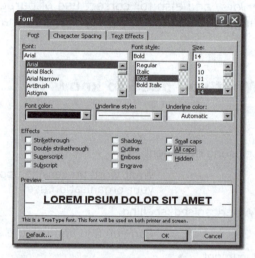

- **Characters** - By selecting 'font' you can change the *STYLE*, colour and size of letters, **embolden** them, *italicise* them, underline them, change the s p a c i n g , or add various text effects
- **Paragraphs** - You can align text using the centre or justify options, or by selecting 'bullets and numbering' add bullet points or numbers. You can make other amendments by selecting borders and shading, or by altering the line spacing, tabs and indents
- **Pages** - You can change the size, orientation and margins of pages, or add page numbers, headers and footers or the date and time. You can insert page breaks to indicate where a new page should begin, or columns to divide the page vertically

- Sections - As you will see from the examples above it is not necessary for the whole of a document to be in the same format. By highlighting individual sections of a document you can apply different formats.

If you use a format for part of the document and want to use it again later, you can select 'styles and formatting' and the software will show you what formats you have used previously in the document.

When combining information, you may want to introduce information from outside of the document. This may be from other files in the same software, from other software, through a scanner or digital camera, or from the Internet. This can be done from the insert menu using:

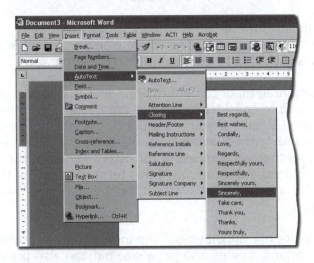

- **File** - Any file already held on your hard drive or on a disc can be imported. If your computer is Internet enabled you can import pages from the World Wide Web
- **Picture** - Any picture already held on your hard drive or on a disc can be imported. You can also import pictures from other software on your computer, or through a connected scanner or digital camera, or from the Internet. There is a facility to create charts, diagrams or drawings
- **Autotext** - This inserts a selection of common phrases such as 'yours sincerely' or 'Dear Sir or Madam'

- **Object** - This enables you to insert items from other software installed on your computer such as graphs and charts from spreadsheet programs
- **Hyperlink** - This enables you to take shortcuts to other parts of the document, other files or even to a web address such as http://www.cfa.uk.com. By clicking on the, usually highlighted, text, your web browser will open to the specified web page

As well as inserting external data into word processing documents, it is possible to combine information from other programs. For instance, pictures and images can be imported into presentation software, text can be imported into an image file or information from a database can be added to a website. You can insert pictures, charts and other information, using the 'Insert' menu.

The possibilities are endless when you start to import material into documents. The whole world of published material is available to you, subject to copyright laws.

Having gathered all of the information into the document, you will need to consider laying out the document in the appropriate format. If you are producing a letter or fax, you can use a pre-formed layout from the tools menu or create a template so that you can use a consistent layout in the future. Your organisation may have templates set-up for various documents such as letters, fax headers and memos for example.

This template not only lays-out the information with the correct margins, guides and page size but can also preselect font style, size and colour. This is important if your company has a standardised approach to how documents look.

If you want to create a new file using a template:

- Select the 'File' menu
- Click 'New' to display the new document task pane
- In the 'Templates' section, click the 'On My Computer' button to open the templates dialogue box
- Select the template you want to use
- Click 'OK'

To change a template:

- Select the 'Tools' menu
- Click 'Templates and Add-ins'
- Click the 'Attach' button
- Select the template you wish to use
- Select 'Automatically Update Document Styles' if you want to replace the styles in your current document
- Click 'Open'

There maybe text that would be more easily read in the form of a table, this can be created using the table menu.

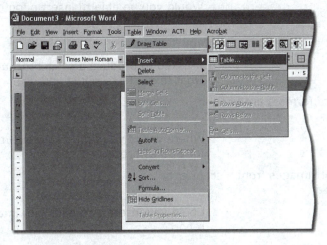

From this menu you can:

- Insert a table, specifying the number of columns and the number of rows
- Insert or delete columns, rows or cells
- Amend the height or width of cells
- Sort alphabetically
- Convert text to tables
- Add borders and shading

If you are producing a lengthy or complex document you may need to give each page a header and footer, or page number. You may also want to number paragraphs and include an index or table of contents to help the reader find their way around the document.

What you need to know

How to format characters

> Could you produce a newsletter with two columns?

What formats are suitable for different documents

> Would you be able to insert a footer with automatic page numbering?

When to use colour and highlighting

> If asked to produce a sales brochure, what text effects would you use?

Why standard formats are used in organisations

> Where would you find a suitable image for a sales brochure?

How to import images from a scanner or digital camera

> Could you insert a spreadsheet into a report?

What types of files can be imported into a word processed document

> How would you insert the phrase 'to whom it may concern' into a document?

When it is necessary to include a hyperlink in a document

> When is it necessary to use tables in a document?

How to create, edit and format tables

> How would you add an additional column to an existing table?

When to use appropriate templates

> If you were asked to produce a letter in the standard format, where would you find the template?

Techniques for inserting tables and using borders and shading

In which menu would you find options for 'borders and shading'?

Which menu allows you to alter the size, font and colour of text

What does a series of horizontal cells in a table form?

Using the keyboard effectively

There are a variety of Short cut key functions available on the keyboard to reduce the number of keystrokes necessary. The most common shortcut commands make use of the Control (Ctrl) button while pressing another key at the same time.

These include:

- Ctrl+b switches the bold function on and off
- Ctrl+c copies selected text or images into your clipboard
- Ctrl+x cuts selected text
- Ctrl+v pastes into the document the last selected text that was cut or copied
- Ctrl+i switches the italics on and off
- Ctrl+o takes you to your file directory
- Ctrl+p opens your print menu
- Ctrl+s saves the document that you are working on

Learn to use as many of these as possible. Different packages and different keyboards will have different functions available. You can also set up short cuts thereby improving efficiency.

For instance, to set up your word processing program as an icon on the desktop, so that you can access the program with one double-click rather than going through a series of menus:

- Left click on 'Start'
- Left click on 'Programs'
- Find the word processing program, left click and drag it onto the desk top

Another short cut is to customise your toolbars. For instance, if you use cut and paste often it would be easier to

---

have these functions on the toolbar so that you do not have to go into the edit menu every time you want to use them.

- Go to a blank area of your toolbar and right click
- Make sure your standard toolbar is switched on
- Left click on the toolbar arrow at the right of your standard toolbar
- Click on 'add or remove buttons'
- Highlight the standard toolbar on the drop-down menu
- Left click 'cut' and 'paste'
- Left click 'reset toolbar'

An advanced shortcut is to set up 'macros'. If you repeat a task regularly, you can automate the task so that a single command will carry out the whole task. For instance, if you always produce one copy of a letter on headed paper and a second on plain paper, you can set up a macro to produce the two copies on one command.

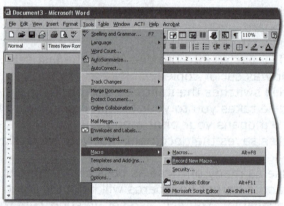

- Select the 'Tools' menu
- Highlight 'Macro' and click on 'Record New Macro'
- Click on keyboard
- Press the 'Ctrl' key and 'q' simultaneously
- Click on 'assign'
- Click 'close' this opens a small toolbar on the screen
- From that point on you are recording everything you do until you tell it to stop. Carry out the complete function that you wish to assign to the macro (set up print functions etc)
- Press the stop button in the new toolbar
  From then on use your shortcut by 'playing' the macro from the tools menu whenever you want to use the function it is set up to do

What you need to know

Why it is important to improve efficiency

> Can you set up a macro to print out a
> document on a variety of paper types?

How to use short cuts and macros

> When would it be necessary to add a
> short cut to your desktop?

Which icons you need to have on your
toolbars

> If asked, would you be able to show
> someone how to change the toolbars?

The functions available on the keyboard
to reduce key strokes

> Which two keys do you depress to
> switch on the 'bold' function?

Early word processors were just glorified electric typewriters
with a screen. Word processing software has advanced over
recent decades and the technology is still developing rapidly.
New and exciting word processing packages and features are
coming on to the market all the time but the results achieved
are only as good as the skills of the person operating them.
Keeping up to date with current trends in software is a
continuous challenge, but an exciting one.

Good use of the features of word processors will improve the quality and impact of your documents and letters

Are you ready for assessment?

To achieve this unit of a Level 2 Business & Administration qualification you will need to demonstrate that you are competent in the following:

- Use appropriate techniques to handle, organise and save files
- Link information in the same type of software
- Add information from one type of software to information produced using different software, such as a spreadsheet graph to a word processing document, text to an image file, picture to a presentation slide or simple information from a database onto a website
- Use a wide range of editing techniques appropriately, such as size and sort, inserting special characters and symbols and mail merge
- Format information in-line with an organisational house style
- Format word processing documents to make them look professional, using a wide range of tools and techniques for tabs; columns (such as adding columns to whole document and part of a page); styles (such as apply an existing style to a word, line or paragraph); pages (such as headers and footers or inserting page breaks); and files (such as change format of word processing documents to RTF or HTML)
- Use appropriate tools and techniques for creating, editing and formatting professional looking tables, such as insert tables; create, add and delete columns; modify column width and row height; and add borders and shading
- Select, change and use appropriate templates
- Use proofreading techniques to check that text looks professional

- Checking line, paragraph and page breaks fall in appropriate places, and check that headings, subheadings and other formatting techniques are used appropriately
- Set up short cuts

(Remember that you will need the skills listed at the beginning of this chapter and that these are covered in chapter 1.)

Your Assessor will need you to produce evidence from a variety of sources. If you carry out the activities that follow they will provide some of the evidence for you.

Activity 1
Import a graph from an existing spreadsheet program into a word processing document, and write a short report explaining the content of the graph. The graph can be from any existing file or, alternatively, if you are collecting evidence for Unit 215, the spreadsheet created in Activity 1 in that Unit may be used.

Activity 2
Keep a work diary over a period of a month recording which word processing functions you have learnt to use.

Activity 3
Produce a list of macros and short cuts you have created

Activity 4
Produce a sales brochure for a new lawnmower using appropriate file handling techniques and including relevant pictures and images.

Activity 5

Type up the following verbatim record of a discussion, correcting any errors and using suitable enhancements to improve the layout.

Assessor 'Ok Brian, thinking about the candidates that you have used for your evidence for the A1 portfolio can you tell me about the assessment methods you have used and why you chose them'
Candidate 'The assessment methods used was observation, oral questions and ask them to write personal written accounts and written questions it depends on the ones that I am seeing would dependon the type I would use, like the candidate I was today is at work and obsertation is the best way I use oral questions to backup some of the observation that I see that aren't quite there also the knowledge side of it.
Assessor 'Obviously authentic if you have seen them do it
Candidate 'That's right yes, obviously the witness testimony has got to be the managers here who you have seen and you can talk to them if its in writing. Written accounts the candidates obviously you have got to see the writing to be sure that it is their own, and you can encourage them to get someone to help you'.

Remember: While gathering evidence for this unit, evidence **may** be generated for units 110, 201, 202, 209, 210, 212, 221, 222, 223, 224 and 225.

CHAPTER 17
UNIT 215 – Spreadsheet software 2

Spreadsheets existed long before spreadsheet software. Originally they were simply sheets of paper divided into columns and rows by hand. Figures were entered into the columns and rows and calculations carried out using mental arithmetic or abacuses. The main drawbacks to this were if you made an error in entering or calculating it was difficult to make corrections; and when the data altered there was no alternative, a completely new spreadsheet had to be written out.

This gave no opportunity to use the spreadsheet as a 'model' to predict the result of variations. Spreadsheet software is designed to record data and perform calculations. It can be used for such tasks as:

- **Budgeting** - for example budgeting for wages. Before the year begins you input the number of staff you expect to employ, the number of hours you expect them to work and the hourly rates. The spreadsheet calculates the total planned cost of wages. As the year progresses you input the actual number of staff employed, the actual number of hours they work and the hourly rates. The spreadsheet calculates the total actual cost of wages and compares this to the plan. You are then able to adjust the number of staff, the number of hours and the hourly rates accordingly

- **Calculating costs** - for example the cost of producing items for sale. Fixed costs are entered at the beginning of the year and variable costs are entered as they occur. The spreadsheet calculates the total cost of production
- **Comparing costs** - for example if a number of employees are entitled to claim expenses, these can be entered on a spreadsheet as they are claimed, the spreadsheet will total the expenses for each employee enabling you to compare them
- **Management accounts** - income and expenses are entered and the spreadsheet calculates profit or loss. If previous months or years are also input the spreadsheet will calculate increase or decrease against the previous period. If planned income and expenses are entered the spreadsheet will calculate increase or decrease against plan

The calculations can be shown as plain data, in a table or in the form of graphs or charts. There are a number of different styles available including:

Column	Bar	Line	Pie
XY	Area	Doughnut	Radar
Surface	Bubble	Stock	Cylinder
Cone	Pyramid		

Spreadsheets are usually protected by passwords which need to be changed each time somebody who knows the password leaves the organisation. Passwords also protect the spreadsheet from malicious corruption from people who may want to alter the information held.

When using spreadsheet software you will use the following skills:

- Planning
- Communicating
- Using number
- Organising
- Using technology
- Checking

These skills are covered in chapter 1.

There are a number of spreadsheet packages available. The most commonly used is Microsoft Excel so the examples used in this chapter relate to Microsoft Excel. Whether you use this system, or another, the principles are the same.

Entering data

When using spreadsheet software you will be working in 'workbooks' which consist of a number of 'worksheets'. A worksheet consists of a grid of 'cells' made up of columns and rows. Columns are vertical and rows are horizontal. Cells are named by referring to the column and row that each cell is found in (for instance the cell that is in the third

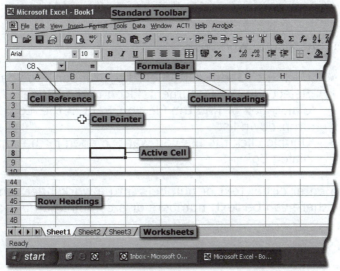

column from the left and the eighth row from the top is cell C8). You may be used to the term 'cursor' to mean the position pointer that is used when using word processing software, in spreadsheet software this position pointer is called a cell pointer and is a white cross shape.

The cell in which the cell pointer is positioned is called the active cell. There is always at least one active cell at all times. The active cell can be identified by its black border. It is possible for more than one cell to be active. A range of connected cells can be active at the same time, for instance the range A12:C14 includes the cells A12, A13, A14, B12, B13, B14, C12, C13 and C14.

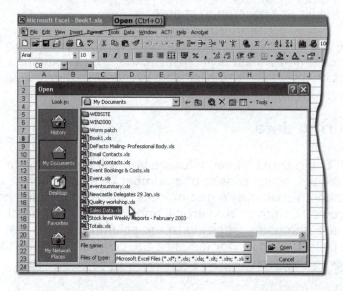

To open an existing workbook:

- Click the 'Open' button on the 'Standard' toolbar
- Select the 'My Documents' icon in the 'Open' dialog box or find the file you want in the 'Look In' drop-down list
- Double click the file you want to open in the 'Open' dialog box

You can enter either text or numbers into a worksheet. In any cell there can be text, numbers or a combination of both.

To enter data:

- Put the cell pointer in the cell that you wish to add data to
- Type the data required in that cell
- Press 'Enter' (on the right of the keyboard) if you wish to enter data in columns or 'Tab' (on the left) if you wish to enter data in rows
- The cell pointer automatically moves to the next cell down or the next cell to the right
- Repeat until you have entered all the required data.

If you type text into a cell, when you enter text that starts with the same letter into another cell, the software will assume that you are going to type the same word. The word will automatically be entered; if you do not want to use it keep typing and the new word will be typed in.

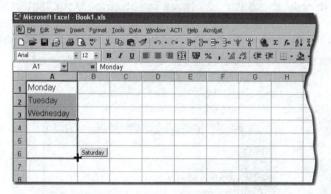

You may want to enter a series of data, for instance Monday, Tuesday, Wednesday, etc. If you type Monday into cell A1, Tuesday into cell B1, Wednesday into cell C1 you can then click and drag the cell pointer over cells A1:C1 move the cell pointer to the lower right corner of the range until it changes to a thin black cross and continue to drag over D1:G1, release the mouse and Thursday, Friday, Saturday will automatically be entered. This also works for numbers and months of the year.

It is possible to copy data from one worksheet to another. Highlight the data to be copied in the original worksheet, copy the data, open the worksheet you wish to copy the data to, place the cell pointer over the cell to be used as the top-left cell for the new data and paste.

A number of short cuts are available, using the right-click function. These include:

- Cut
- Copy
- Paste
- Insert
- Delete
- Clear Contents
- Insert Comment
- Format Cells

You will need to save your work regularly so that you don't lose your data in the event of a power failure or computer crash. To do this, click on the 'Save' icon on the 'Standard' toolbar. If you have saved your work regularly when you re-start your computer after a disaster such as this you will have lost only the data you have input since your last save. There is nothing more annoying than to input data for four hours only to lose it all because you have neglected to save.

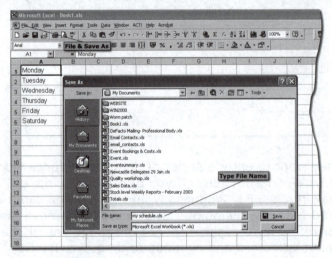

When you have entered all the data that you require:

- Open the 'File' menu and select 'Save As'
- Click the 'My Documents' icon or find the folder you want to save the file in from the 'Save In' drop-down list
- Type the file name in the 'File Name' field
- Click 'Save'

What you need to know

Your organisation's file naming systems

> Do you know the difference between a workbook and a worksheet?

How to open an existing workbook

> What is a horizontal series of cells called?

Methods of inserting a series of data

> Where would you find cell Y93?

How to select a range of cells

> Why is it important to save worksheets regularly?

Formulas and functions

A great advantage of using electronic spreadsheets is that you can add, delete or amend entries and the spreadsheet will automatically re-calculate the results. This works using formulas and functions. A formula calculates a value from the values in other cells. A function is an abbreviated formula that performs a specific operation on a group of values. For instance the SUM function automatically adds entries in a range.

The way the formula is affected when it is copied into another cell depends on the way cells in the formula are referred to. There are three types of cell references:

- **Relative cell references -** when a formula is copied from one cell to another, the cell references in the formula change to reflect the new location
- **Absolute cell references** - when a formula is copied from one cell to another, the cell references in the formula remain the same
- **Mixed cell references** - a single cell entry in a formula that contains both a relative and an absolute cell reference

In all of the instructions that follow we will be using relative cell references only.

One way to use a formula is to type it directly into the cell. Any cells can be included in the formula, they do not need to be next to each other. Different arithmetical operations can be combined in the same formula, for instance you can enter B2+B3-B5.

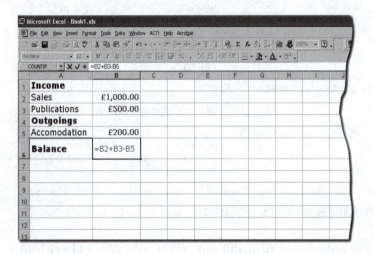

To enter a formula into a cell:

- Put the cell pointer into the cell where you want the result of the formula to appear (the resultant cell) and click
- Type = followed by the cells you want to calculate, for instance B2+B3-B5
- Press 'Enter'

There are more than 250 functions available which can be used to perform calculations for you. To find the function you are looking for:

- Click the 'down arrow' next to the 'AutoSum' button on the 'Standard' toolbar
- From the list that appears select 'More Functions'
- Either type a description of what you want to do (for instance, 'I want to find the highest number') in the 'Search for a function' text box and click the 'Go' button or

- Scroll through the list in the 'Select a function' box and click 'OK' when you find the one you want, for instance 'Financial', 'Statistical' or 'Lookup & Reference'

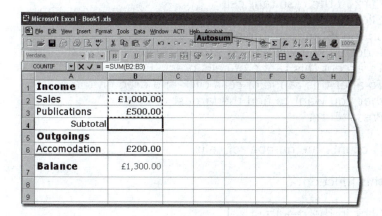

The following functions, which can be found by clicking the 'down arrow' next to the 'AutoSum' button, are among the most useful.

AutoSum (SUM) adds numbers in a range of cells.

To use this function:

- Click in the resultant cell
- Click the 'AutoSum' button on the 'Standard' toolbar
- A dotted line will appear around a range of cells
- To accept this range of cells press 'Enter'
- To alter this range of cells click and drag on the cells that you want to calculate
- Press 'Enter'

(AVERAGE) works out the average of a number of cells.

To use this function:

- Click in the resultant cell
- Click the 'down arrow' next to the 'AutoSum' button on the 'Standard' toolbar and select 'Average'
- A dotted line will appear around a range of cells
- To accept this range of cells press 'Enter'
- To alter this range of cells click and drag on the cells that you want to find the average of
- Press 'Enter'

(MAX) finds the largest of a number of cells.

To use this function:

- Click in the resultant cell
- Click the 'down arrow' next to the 'AutoSum' button on the 'Standard' toolbar and select 'Max'
- A dotted line will appear around a range of cells
- To accept this range of cells press 'Enter'
- To alter this range of cells click and drag on the cells that you want to find the largest of
- Press 'Enter'

(COUNT) counts the number of cells.

To use this function:

- Click in the resultant cell
- Click the 'down arrow' next to the 'AutoSum' button on the 'Standard' toolbar and select 'Count'
- A dotted line will appear around a range of cells
- To accept this range of cells press 'Enter'
- To alter this range of cells click and drag on the cells that you want to find the number of
- Press 'Enter'

(MIN) finds the smallest of a number of cells.

Note: This function recognises negative numbers, so -46 will be smaller than 0.

To use this function:

- Click in the resultant cell
- Click the 'down arrow' next to the 'AutoSum' button on the 'Standard' toolbar and select 'Min'

A dotted line will appear around a range of cells.

- To accept this range of cells press 'Enter'
- To alter this range of cells click and drag on the cells that you want to find the smallest of
- Press 'Enter'

After you have entered a function or a formula you may want to alter it.

There are three ways of doing this, click in the cell that you want to alter then:

- Press 'F2', edit the formula in the cell or
- Put your cell pointer onto the 'Formula' bar and edit the formula or
- Click the 'Insert Function' button on the 'Formula' bar, the 'Function Arguments' dialog box will open. Change the function in the dialog box and click 'OK'

A formula or a function can be copied from one cell to another by:

- Click the cell that you want to copy
- Click the 'Copy' button on the 'Standard' toolbar
- Click the cell into which you want to paste the function or formula
- Press 'Enter'

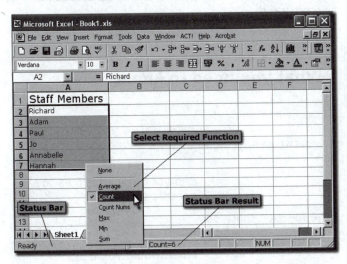

Remember the formula will change after copying, for instance if the formula in cell A11 is =AVERAGE(A1:A10) and

you copy it to cell D11, the formula in D11 will become
=AVERAGE(D1:D10).

AutoCalculate will carry out any of the functions described
above and display the answer in the 'Status' bar rather than
in a cell. To use AutoCalculate:

- Select the cells that you want to calculate
- Right click the 'Status' bar and select the required
  option (e.g. Count)

From time to time you will see symbols appearing in cells.
These are used to indicate where errors have occurred. You
will need to recognise which symbol indicates which error in
order to correct them.

If you see the following symbols in a cell this is what each
means:

- '####' means the cell is not wide enough to contain
  the information
- '#DIV/O!' means the formula is trying to divide a
  number by 0 or by an empty cell
- '#NAME?' means the formula contains an incorrectly
  spelled cell or function name
- '#VALUE!' means the formula contains text
- '#REF!' means the formula contains reference to a cell
  that isn't valid

What you need to know

The difference between a formula
and a function

Can you copy a formula to
another cell?

How to find the function that you
want to use

When would you use
AutoCalculate?

What the following symbols mean

'#####'
'#DIV/0!'
'#NAME?'
'#VALUE!'
'#REF!'

What would you use the following functions for?

'AutoSum'
'AVERAGE'
'MAX'
'COUNT'

Editing and formatting worksheets

One of the major advantages of an electronic spreadsheet is the ease with which you can correct any errors or omissions. You can insert a cell, column or row; delete entries; change values or find and replace data.

To insert a cell:

- Click on the worksheet where you want to insert a cell
- Select 'Cells' from the 'Insert' menu
- A dialog box will open. Select what you want to happen to the existing cells, for instance 'Shift cells Right' and click 'OK'
- The existing cells in the row shift to the right and a new cell is inserted

To delete a cell:

- Select the cell or cells you want to delete
- Select 'Delete' from the 'Edit' menu
- A dialog box will open. Select what you want to happen to the existing cells, for instance 'Shift cells Left' and click 'OK'
- The existing cells in the row shift to the left and the unwanted cells disappear

To insert rows and columns:

- Click on the cell above which you want to add a row or to the right of were you want to add a column
- Select 'Rows' or 'Columns' from the 'Insert' menu
- A new row or column is inserted

To delete rows and columns:

- Right click on the row header or column header
- Select 'Delete' from the short-cut menu that appears
- The row or column is deleted

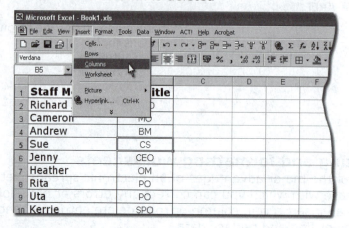

There will be times when you want to change the values in a cell. There are three ways to do this:

either:

- Click the cell that you want to change
- Type the correct data into the cell
- Press 'Enter'

or:

- Click the cell that you want to change
- Press 'F2'
- Using the 'Backspace' key delete the incorrect content and type in the correct content
- Press 'Enter'

or:

- Double click the cell that you want to change
- Using the 'Backspace' or 'Delete' key delete the incorrect content and type in the correct content
- Press 'Enter'

There will be times when you want to find specific information in a large spreadsheet more quickly than by scanning through until you come across it.

This can be done by:

- Selecting 'Find' in the 'Edit' menu
- A dialog box will open. Type the data you want to find in the 'Find what' text box
- Click the 'Find next' button
- The first cell containing the data will be indicated. If you want to find further examples continue to click 'Find Next' until you find the one you are looking for
- Alternatively click 'Find All' and all examples will be listed in a text box
- Click 'Close'

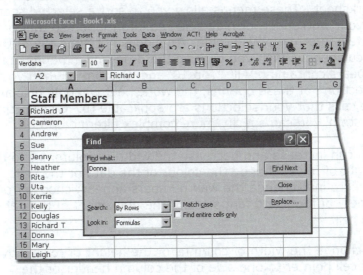

You may find that you have to change the same data in a number of cells throughout the worksheet. For instance, you may want to replace all references to 2007 with 2008. This can be done by:

- Selecting 'Replace' from the 'Edit' menu
- A dialog box will open. Type the data you would like to replace in the 'Find what' text box
- Press the 'Tab' key
- Type the new data into the 'Replace with' textbox
- Click 'Replace All'
- A dialog box will open telling you how many replacements have been made. Click 'OK'
- Click 'Close'

You can also format the worksheet to make its appearance more interesting or the information easier to read. If there is more data than can conveniently appear on one page you will need to insert page breaks. This is done by selecting 'View' from the toolbar, selecting 'Page Break Preview' and then clicking and dragging.

Alternatively, you can hide some of the information so that only the most significant data appears on the screen. This is done by selecting the 'Data' menu, selecting 'Filters', then 'Autofilter'.

Drop-down menus will appear in the top row of your worksheet. These menus allow you to sort a selected section of your worksheet, or hide selected information so that only certain information is visible. This does not alter any of the calculations. When you click on the drop-down menus, a list appears containing 'All', 'Top 10' and 'Custom'. When you select one of these options, the worksheet will only display the cells that your selections are applicable to. By selecting 'Custom' you can specify more complex filtering criteria.

You can increase and decrease the width of columns and the height of rows; change the colour of the data or the cell background; change the way numbers appear; choose from a variety of fonts and font sizes or the placement of the data in the cell.

To change the width of columns or the height of rows move the cell pointer to one side of the column header or the bottom edge of the row header. Click and drag the edge to the desired width or height.

To change the appearance of the data or cell background:

- Select the cells that you want to change
- Select 'Cells' from the 'Format' toolbar
- Select 'Font', 'Border' or 'Patterns' to make the desired changes
- Click 'OK'

Numbers can appear in a variety of ways. They can be simple numbers, decimals, currency or dates for instance.

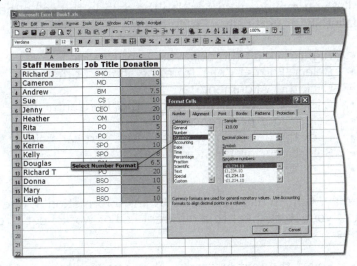

To format numbers:

- Select the cells you want to format
- Right click and select 'Format Cells' from the short-cut menu
- A dialog box opens. Click the 'Number' tab
- Select the 'Category' you require
- Click 'OK'

The most common formats for numbers are:

- **General** - for instance 143809
- **Number** - for instance 143,809.00
- **Currency** - for instance £143,809.00
- **Accounting** - for instance £143,809.00
- **Percentage** - for instance 14380900.00%

To add emphasis or to differentiate between different types of data you may want to change the font and font size. This is done by:

- Selecting the cells you want to change
- Click the font field down arrow in the 'Standard' toolbar
- Select the font that you want to use
- Click the 'font size' field down arrow
- Select the font size you want to use

Finally, you may want to position the data in the cell either horizontally or vertically. To do this:

- Right click on the cells you want to align
- Select 'Format Cells' from the short-cut menu
- Click the 'Alignment' tab
- Click the down arrow next to the 'Horizontal' field
- Select your preference
- Click the down arrow next to the 'Vertical' field
- Select your preference
- Click 'OK'

You may want to use hyperlinks to link information in one part of your worksheet to a different cell or worksheet. To do this:

- Select the text or graphic that you wish to make into a hyperlink
- Select 'Hyperlink' from the 'Insert' menu
- Under the 'Link To' column, select 'Place in this Document'
- Select the worksheet and cell number that you want the hyperlink to link to
- Click 'OK'

You can also insert pictures or diagrams into your worksheet from other documents and files. To insert a picture:

- Select 'Insert' from the toolbar
- Highlight 'Picture' and click on 'From File'
- Select the file that you want to insert
- Click 'Insert'

To insert a diagram into a worksheet:

- Select 'Diagram' from the 'Insert' menu

- Select the diagram that you want to insert
- Click 'OK'

Similarly, you can export part or all of your worksheet into other programs and files, such as a word processing or a presentation program.

What you need to know

How to insert rows, cells and columns

How do you delete a row from a worksheet?

The three ways to change the value in a cell

How would you find all the references to similar data in a worksheet?

How to replace data

How many different ways are there to format numbers?

The procedure for changing the width and height of columns and rows

If you want to change the alignment of data in a cell, what process would you use?

Presenting data

When you have completed the editing and formatting of your worksheets you will want to print off the results. There are a number of ways of enhancing the presentation of the data including the addition of charts which allow the reader to see the data presented graphically; headers and footers which allow you to title the report and include the date and time; choose between landscape and portrait; number the pages and add or remove the gridlines for clarity.

Before starting to print you will need to use 'Print Preview' so that you can decide which of the above enhancements you wish to make.

Open the worksheet that you want to print then:

- Click the 'Print Preview' button on the 'Standard' toolbar
- The worksheet will be displayed. Click the 'Zoom' button to make the worksheet on the screen larger
- Click 'Margins' and drag the margins to set the print area
- Click 'Close'
- Select the cells you want to print
- Select 'Print Area' from the 'File' menu
- Select 'Set Print Area'
- If the print area you have selected covers more than one page click the 'Print Preview' button
- Select 'Setup'
- Select 'Fit to 1 page(s) wide by 1 tall'
- Select 'Landscape' or 'Portrait'
- Click on the 'Header/Footer' tab
- Click the down arrow next to the 'Header' field
- Scroll through the header options and select one
- Click the down arrow next to the 'Footer' field
- Scroll through the footer options and select one
- Click on the 'Sheet' tab
- Click the 'Gridlines' checkbox
- Click 'OK'

You can create a selection of charts to help people understand the significance of the data.

To create a chart:

- Select the cells you want to include
- Click the 'Chart Wizard' button on the 'Standard' toolbar
- Select the chosen 'Chart Type'
- Select the chosen 'Chart Sub-type'
- Click 'Next'
- Select 'Rows' or 'Columns' in the 'Series in' area
- Type the name of the chart in the 'Chart title' field
- Type values for the x-axis and y-axis in the 'Category (X) axis' and the 'Category (Y) axis' fields
- Click 'Next'
- Click the 'As Object in' option
- Click 'Finish'

To change the chart type:

- Right click on the plot area and select 'Chart Type' from the short-cut menu
- Select the new 'Chart Type'
- Select the new 'Chart Sub-type'
- Click 'OK'

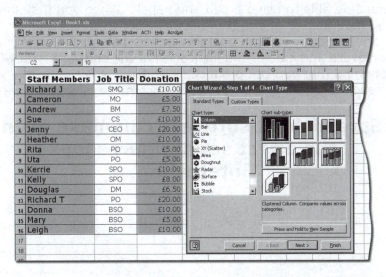

You can also move the chart in the spreadsheet by placing the cell pointer in the chart and clicking and dragging the chart to the desired position. If you want to change the size of the chart, click on the chart then place the cell pointer on one of the eight points marked on the border of the chart until it changes into a small arrow. Click and drag the chart border until it is the desired size.

When you are completely satisfied with the look of the worksheet and any chart that you have decided to use you are ready to print.

To do this:

- Select 'Print' from the 'File' menu
- Click the down arrow next to the 'Printer Name' field to choose the printer that you are going to use
- In the 'Print range' area click 'Page(s) From and To' and type the pages you want to include or click 'All'
- In the 'Number of Copies' field type the number of copies that you want
- Select 'Collate' if appropriate
- Select from 'Selection', 'Active Sheet(s)' and 'Entire workbook'
- Click 'OK'

Remember the purpose of spreadsheet software is to enable you to perform calculations much more quickly than you would be able to using a pen and paper. When you first start you may think that you could actually achieve your ends more efficiently using a pen and an Accounts pad; but, if you persevere and master the intricacies of the software, you will soon find that you can produce spreadsheets not only in a fraction of the time, but also in a much more interesting way.

Spreadsheet software can make even the driest set of figures look interesting

Are you ready for assessment?

To achieve this unit of a Level 2 Business & Administration qualification you will need to demonstrate that you are competent in the following:

- Use appropriate techniques to handle, organise and save files
- Link information in the same type of software
- Add information from one type of software to information produced using different software, such as a spreadsheet graph to a word processing document, text to an image file, picture to a presentation slide, or simple information from a database onto a website
- Insert data into multiple cells at once
- Use a wide range of editing techniques appropriately in more complex spreadsheets: using 'absolute' and 'relative' cell references, adding data and text to a chart or changing the type of chart
- Format more complex spreadsheets using a range of appropriate tools and techniques for cells (such as colour, shading and borders); charts (such as change chart type, move and resize chart); and pages (such as headers and footers and adjust page set up for printing)
- Check that page breaks fall in appropriate places and formatting is appropriate
- Check the accuracy of results and correct errors in formulas
- Use appropriate functions and formulas in more complex spreadsheets, such as mathematical, statistical, financial and relational
- Use appropriate tools and techniques for analysing more complex data such as filters
- Use appropriate methods to present more complex data, such as the range of graphs and charts provided by the software
- Set up short cuts

(Remember that you will need the skills listed at the beginning of this chapter and that these are covered in chapter 1.)

Your Assessor will need you to produce evidence from a variety of sources. If you carry out the activities that follow they will provide some of the evidence for you.

Activity 1
Create a spreadsheet containing at least 10 columns and least 20 rows. This can be based on any set of information of your choosing, for instance sales figures for each department over tenweeks; daily temperatures of different cities over a period of time; your own expenditure over a period of time; hours worked over a period of time; use your imagination and see what you can come up with. Try to use a mixture of mathematical, statistical, financial and relational formulas. Save the file as "Activity 1" in a folder named "Admin assessments".

Activity 2
Open the file "Activity 1" and check that the formatting is appropriate.

Carry out the following calculations:

- Find the average
- Find the total number
- Find the highest number
- Find the lowest number

Check the accuracy of the results and resolve any errors in the formulas.

Then carry out the following:

- Change the colour of selected cells
- Add shading and borders to selected cells
- Filter any insignificant information

Activity 3
Having completed the above task present the information as a variety of charts, each having titles on the 'x' and 'y' axes:

A column chart   An XY (scatter) chart
A bar chart   An area chart
A line chart   A doughnut chart
A pie chart   A radar chart

Activity 4

Compare the results and write a report showing each type of chart and explaining the circumstances in which you would use each to present this information and why. The report should contain headers and footers on each page and be appropriately formatted.

Activity 5

What do you understand by the following spreadsheet software terms:

AutoFill	Axis
Cell	Chart
Column	Data range
Dialog box	Drop-down list
Field	Format
Formula	Function
Mixed cell reference	Objects
Row	Sort
Wizard	Worksheet

Remember: While gathering evidence for this unit, evidence **may** be generated for units 110, 201, 202, 207, 208, 209, 210, 212, 213 and 225.

CHAPTER 18
UNIT 216 – Database software 2

A database is an information storage system which may be held on a computer or in paper-based form. Computer databases include National Insurance records, vehicle records, criminal records and library records.

Paper-based databases include telephone directories and trade directories, for instance, although these are usually produced from computer databases these days. Databases are widely used to hold data on people. In fact there is data held on all of us on an amazing variety of databases throughout the country. Every time you use a credit or debit card to make a purchase, or visit the doctor or dentist, or fill in a form, information is added to or amended in a database.

Organisations hold data on customers that will record not only their names, addresses, telephone numbers and e-mail addresses but also their purchase history, their payment history and even personal information such as family details, vehicle ownership, dates of birth or even financial information. Different types of organisation will hold different details. An insurance company will hold different information from a retail store because they will use the information for different purposes.

The advantage of a computer database is that the information can be retrieved much more easily than it can from a paper-based system. Paper-based systems do not allow you to find all customers who have purchased a mobile phone in the last six months without searching through all the records and making a list. A computer database will provide you with a list instantly.

Database software is designed to organise and collate the related information, for instance addresses and telephone numbers or sales figures. A database program allows data to be organised in various ways depending on the type of information stored.

These 'Relational Databases' store different types of data in separate tables in the same database. For example, a table can hold personal details about a customer including their name, address and telephone number. Another table in the database can include all of the sales made by the company. This data can then be interrogated to produce reports detailing, for example, how many washing machines have been bought by people who live in Halifax?

The features of a computer database are:

- **Form** - the interface screen where data is entered
- **Table** – where information on a particular topic is stored
- **Record** –information regarding a single item in your database. E.g. The details of one employee
- **Field** - a category for single pieces of data in a record. E.g. First name, postcode, stock number, unit price etc.
- **Data** - the information entered in a field
- **File** - a complete database

When entering and retrieving information, you will need to be aware of confidentiality and legislation. The use of databases is regulated by the Data Protection Act 1998, the main points of which are:

- All companies who hold data on people must be registered with the Information Commissioner
- Any information held on computer must have been obtained legally

- Data must only be used for the purpose for which it was originally obtained
- Data must be relevant, accurate, up-to-date and not excessive
- Data must not be kept longer than necessary
- People must have access to the information held about them
- Precautions must be taken to avoid access being available to people without permission

There are organisations whose sole purpose is to collect information from various sources, collate it and sell it on to other organisations, usually for the purpose of marketing. This enables the organisation to target their marketing at the customers most likely to make purchases. As with all databases these will need to be updated regularly, to delete any out of date records or input any new information.

Databases are usually protected by passwords which need to be changed each time somebody who knows the password leaves the organisation. Passwords also protect the database from malicious corruption from people who may want to alter the information held.

 When using database software you will use the following skills:

- Planning
- Organising
- Communicating
- Using technology
- Checking
- Problem solving

These skills are covered in chapter 1.

There are a number of database packages available. The most commonly used is Microsoft Access so the examples used in this chapter relate to Microsoft Access. Whether you use this system, or another, the principles are the same.

Entering data

The purpose of databases is to store information in a way that allows it to be manipulated for a variety of purposes. You can obtain the data to enter into a database from a number of sources. You may be computerising existing paper-based information, or you may already have a database and be adding information to it from almost anywhere.

An existing database will constantly require updating so you will need access to the sources of information. These may hold confidential or sensitive data, and may be protected by the Data Protection Act 1998. Access to the information may be controlled by a password. If you are given the authority to setup or amend a password, use one that is easy to remember but difficult to guess. If you have to write it down, keep it somewhere that people are not likely to look for it. Be very careful that the data you enter is accurate.

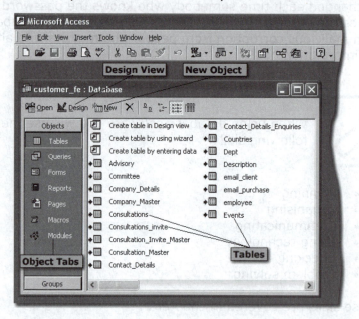

Some fields will make it difficult for you to enter the wrong sort of data, for instance you couldn't enter an address in a date of birth field, but you could enter an incorrect date of birth. This could result in someone not receiving information intended for people of their age group.

A database is made up of one or more tables. Each table is divided into 'fields' into which data is input. Fields have characteristics including:

- Name
- Size
- Type
- Format

The relevant characteristics should be used when creating a new field and can be modified in an existing database where necessary. Care must be taken to ensure that existing data is not corrupted when field characteristics are changed.

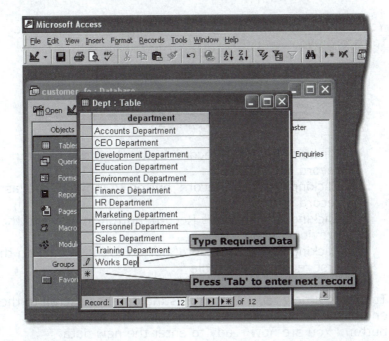

Each field contains one piece of information, for instance house number, road, town, county. The collected data about a person or topic forms a 'record'.

To enter data into an existing database:

- Click the 'Tables' option in the Objects bar
- Click the selected table
- Click 'Open' in the database window's toolbar

- If the table already contains records they will be visible, otherwise the table will be blank
- Type an entry into the selected field and press the 'Tab' key
- The cursor automatically moves to the next field. Type an entry into this field if required
- Continue entering data until you have completed all the necessary entries for that record
- When you have completed the record, a new blank row appears ready for the next record

In order to see all the records in a table there is a row of scroll buttons which you can use to move up and down the table quickly.

You can also use the navigation buttons to move from record to record by:

- Clicking the 'Next Record' button to move to the next record in the table
- Clicking the 'Last Record' button to move to the last record in the table
- Clicking the 'Previous Record' button to move to the previous record or
- Clicking the 'First Record' button to move back to the first record in the table

To create a new record in an existing database scroll to the end of the table and press tab or click the 'New Record' button. You are now ready to enter the new data.

It is critical that the information entered into the database is accurate, so one of the most important aspects of database work is checking data. Automated facilities such as spell check and data sorting are available.

Many people entering a list will use a ruler placed along the line they are entering to avoid errors. Some databases have cross-checking routines to prevent the input of inaccurate data. For instance age may have to be entered as well as date of birth, but these will not pick up all errors. The best check of accuracy is to check your own work as you go along and correct errors as you find them. Develop a routine for entering data that will help you avoid mistakes. Your subconscious will often alert you that you have missed a field if you are entering data in a routine fashion. If you discover a mistake in a field that you cannot amend, report it immediately. Remember the reports you get from the database will only be as accurate as the input. 'Garbage in Garbage out'.

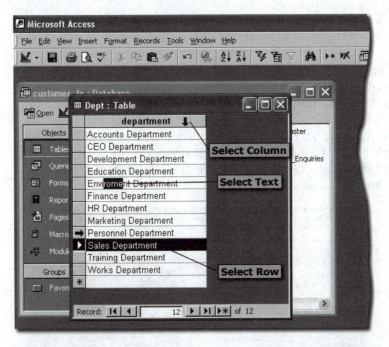

To edit or delete an existing entry in a field move the cursor to the field that you wish to amend. If you wish to replace all of the existing data in that field simply type the new information and the original data will be replaced. If you only wish to change part of the entry, for instance if you have mis-spelt the street name in an address field, click in the field and drag the cursor across the part of the entry you wish to amend.

To delete an entire record move the cursor to the 'Record Selector' column, on the left hand side of the screen. The record will be highlighted. To select a block of records hold down the 'Shift' key and move the cursor down to the last record of those that you wish to delete. Open the 'Edit' menu and select 'Delete Record'. Click 'Yes'.

Only carry out this action if you are sure that you wish to permanently delete this record.

If the table contains more columns than can fit on the screen you may want to freeze one or more columns that you need to work on so that these columns remain on the screen at all times.

To do this:

- Click in the column that you want to freeze
- Open the 'Format' menu and select 'Freeze Columns'

As you scroll to other fields the selected frozen column remains in the same place. To unfreeze the column, open the 'Format' menu and select 'Unfreeze Columns'.

Alternatively you can hide columns that you don't need to work on, or to allow you to print only certain columns from the table. You can hide a single column or a block of columns.

Click on the single column you wish to hide or click on the first column and drag across the other columns you wish to hide. Open the 'Format' menu and select 'Hide Columns'. To reveal hidden columns open the 'Format' menu and select 'Unhide Columns'.

When you first open a table all the columns will be the same width. You may need to vary the width of columns to suit the amount of information entered.

To do this:

- Place the cursor on the right edge of the column so that it appears like this ◄├►
- Click and drag the column border to the left or right to narrow or widen the column

You may want to change the order in which columns appear. In this case place the cursor in the column title you wish to move and drag it to its new location.

If the same data is going to appear in several records in the same table you may prefer to copy an entry from one field to another.

Move the cursor to the original entry, open the 'Edit' menu and select 'Copy'. Move the cursor to the field in which you wish the information to be placed, open the 'Edit' menu and select 'Paste'. To copy an entire record move the cursor to the 'Record Selector' column for that record open the 'Edit' menu and select 'Copy', move the cursor to the next blank row, open the 'Edit' menu and select 'Paste Append'. You can also use a similar technique to move a complete record. This time open the 'Edit' menu and select 'Cut' instead of 'Copy'.

The data you enter will initially be stored in the order in which you enter it, but it is likely you will want it in some other order, alphabetical or numerical for example. You can sort the data based on any of the fields in the table.

Put the cursor in the column containing the information by which you wish to sort it. If you wish to sort the data in ascending order, i.e. A-Z or 1-100, click 'Sort Ascending' on the standard toolbar. If you wish to sort the data in descending order, i.e. Z-A or 100-1, click 'Sort Descending'.

If you want to find a particular record in an extensive table you can search for the record using any particular field.

For instance, if you were looking for the details of a customer and all the information you had was that they were in Suffolk:

- Put the cursor in the column for County
- Open the 'Edit' menu and select 'Find'
- A dialog box will open with the 'Find' tab displayed
- In the 'Find What' field, type 'Suffolk'
- Click 'Find Next'. The first entry containing the word 'Suffolk' will be located. If this is the customer you are looking for click 'Cancel'. If not, click 'Find Next' and repeat until you find the correct customer

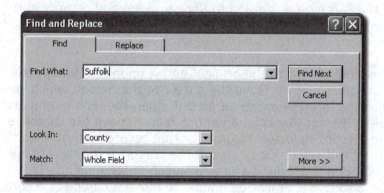

You may want to replace all instances of an entry wherever it appears in the table. For instance, if an area postcode changes you would need to change every address in that area.

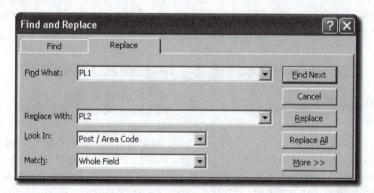

Quicker than going through every address and changing them individually you can:

- Put the cursor in the postcode column
- Open the 'Edit' menu and select 'Replace'
- A dialog box opens with the 'Replace' tab displayed
- In the 'Find What' field type the existing postcode
- In the 'Replace With' field type the new postcode
- Click the 'Find Next' button and the record with first matching entry will be located
- Click the 'Replace' button. The postcode will change. The next matching entry will be located
- Repeat until the last matching entry is reached then click 'OK'

What you need to know

The difference between a 'field' and a 'record'

How would you move a column?

The type of information to be entered on a database

What are the principles of The Data Protection Act?

What databases your organisation uses

Who is responsible for maintaining the databases?

Why accuracy is essential when entering data onto a database

What methods can you use for sorting information?

How to gain access to a password protected database

If your organisation had changed the specification of a product, how could you amend this in the database without having to look in every record?

The purpose of freezing columns

How do you hide unwanted columns?

How to re-size columns and rows

To sort a column alphabetically from A-Z do you use Sort Ascending or Sort Descending?

What the acronym GIGO stands for

Why is it not essential that data is entered into a database in strict alphabetical order?

Creating database queries

The main purpose of operating a database is to enable information to be found quickly. By running database queries you can ask the computer to search through the database and find all of the records that match particular criteria. For instance, all the customers who live in Somerset or all the male customers over 18 who bought a specific make of car. You can refine the search by applying filters which specify further criteria. You may want only to highlight customers over 18, living in Somerset who bought a Ford Mondeo with cash in 2005, for instance.

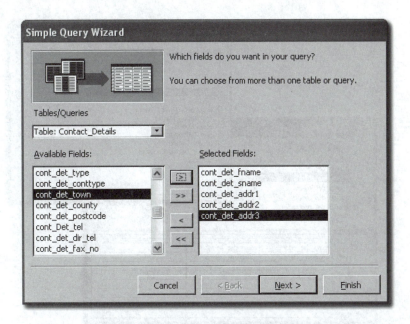

You can create a query one of two ways. You can use a
Wizard and:

- Click the 'Queries' button in the Objects bar
- Double click the 'Create query by using wizard' option
- Click the 'down arrow' next to the 'Tables/Queries'
  field and select the table on which you want to base
  the query
- The 'Available Fields' list includes all the fields in the
  selected table. Click the first field that you want to
  include in your query
- Click the 'Add' button
- Repeat until all the fields you want are added, then
  click the 'Next' button
- In the 'What title do you want for your query' field,
  type the name that you want to save your query
  under
- Click the 'Open the query to view information' option
  button
- Click the 'Finish' button

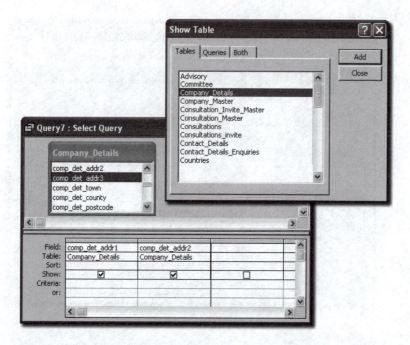

Alternatively you can start a query from scratch by:

- Clicking the 'Queries' button in the objects bar
- Double click the 'Create Query in Design view' option
- Select the table on which you want to base your query
- Click the 'Add' button to add a list of fields in the selected table to the 'Design' window
- Click the 'Close' button in the 'Show Table' dialog box
- Click in the 'Field' box in the lower half of the 'Query Design' window
- Click the down arrow in the 'Field' box and choose the first field you want to add to your query
- Repeat until the fields you want are added. Open the 'File' menu and select 'Save'
- Type the name that you want to save your query under in the 'Query Name' field of the 'Save As' dialog box and click 'OK'

Once you have the query structure set up you will be able to enter the criteria that will enable the query to select the records you want.

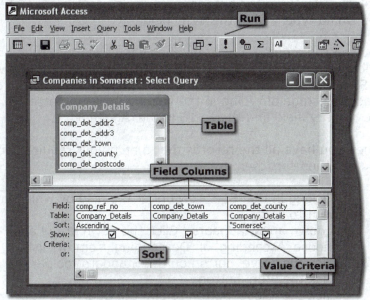

Select the query that you wish to work with and:

- Click the 'Design' button in the toolbar in the database window
- The query design window will open. The top part of the window contains the tables on which the query is based. The bottom part of the window contains a grid that displays each of the fields you selected as well as the table in which each field sits
- Use the 'Sort' row to specify which field is used to sort the query in either Ascending or Descending order
- Type the value you want to match into the 'criteria' row. For instance, type 'Somerset' in the 'County' field to find all the entries for people who live in Somerset
- Click the 'Save' button on the Standard toolbar to save the query design
- Click the 'Run' button to run the query
- A table will be displayed containing only those records that match the criteria, in this case people who live in Somerset
- To close the query design window click the 'Close' button

To run a query for a range of matches (for instance, customers over 18) follow the above steps until you reach the point where you are typing in the value you want to match. Then type the criteria expression. In our example you would type >18 in the 'Age' field.

You can run a query which matches values in more than one field. For instance, you can find customers over 18 who live in Somerset. To do this you follow the above steps until you reach the stage of typing in the value. Type 'Somerset' in the 'County' field and then >18 in the 'Age' field.

When you have all the records that match your requirements you can then sort them by:

- Clicking in the 'Sort' row under the field by which you want to sort
- A down arrow appears. Click the down arrow and choose 'Ascending' or 'Descending' from the list
- Click the 'Save' button on the Standard toolbar
- Click the 'Run' button
- Click the 'Close' button to end the query

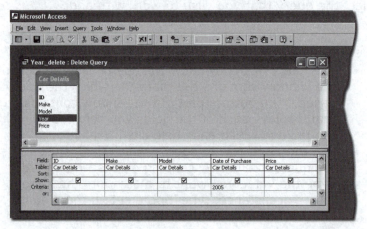

You can also use queries to delete records from your database more efficiently than going through them one-by-one. For instance, if you were using the database to market new cars, you might want to delete all customers who had purchased cars in 2005.

To do this:

- Open the 'Query' menu and select 'Delete Query'
- The design grid will show a 'Delete' row
- Enter the criteria for the records you want to delete, for instance, 2005 in the 'date of purchase' field
- Click the 'Save' button on the Standard toolbar
- Click the 'Run' button
- Click 'Yes' to delete the records

Beware of this process, as you cannot undo it

What you need to know

How to run a database query

> If you were asked to list all the customers in the Surrey area, would you know how to?

Methods of creating a query using a wizard

> Could you enter criteria to query for an exact match?

Why it is necessary to take extreme care when deleting records

> In what circumstances would you run a database query?

How to enter criteria to query for a range of matches

> How would you enter criteria to match more than one field?

Creating database reports

There will be times when you will be asked to produce a printed report from the information in the database. Use the techniques already described to select the range and layout of information to be printed. Once you have set up the report in the way you think is best, examine it on screen.

You may want to add a heading or a date, or vary the font to emphasise certain sections. If the report is going to cover several pages, print a sample page so that you and the person you are producing the report for can have a look and check the layout. You will then be able to print off a report which contains only the information that you choose, maybe the top 100 by date of birth or those who live in a particular area. Alternatively you may be going to send the report electronically. In this case save it as a file and attach it to an e-mail.

You can create an AutoReport or create a report using a wizard. There are several AutoReports available to create simple reports with either columnar (in columns) or tabular (in tables) layouts.

To use an AutoReport:

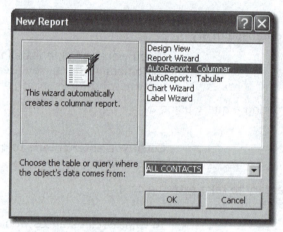

- Open the database and click the 'Reports' option in the 'Objects' bar
- Click the 'New' button in the Toolbar
- Click either 'AutoReport:Columnar' or 'AutoReport:Tabular' in the dialog box

- Click the down arrow next to the 'Choose the table or query' field and select the table you wish to use
- Click 'OK'

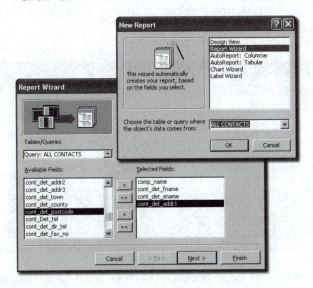

A report, either columnar or tabular as chosen, will be created and the first page displayed. To look at subsequent pages use the page buttons at the bottom of the page.

To create a report using a wizard:

- Open the database and click the 'Reports' option in the 'Objects' bar
- Double click the 'Create report by using wizard' option
- Click the down arrow next to the 'Tables/Queries' field and select the table that you wish to use
- In the 'Available Fields' list click the first field you want to include in the report
- Click the 'Add' button
- Repeat until you have all the fields you want then click the 'Next' button
- A drop-down list will ask you how the fields in the report should be sorted. Choose the first sort field and repeat for any additional fields you want to use to sort
- Click the 'Next' button
- In the 'Layout' area select from the 'Columnar', 'Tabular', or 'Justified' options
- In the 'Orientation' area select either 'Portrait' or 'Landscape'

- Click the 'Next' button
- Select a style from the options in the list
- Click the 'Next' button
- Type a name for the report in the 'What title do you want for your report' field
- Click the 'Finish' button

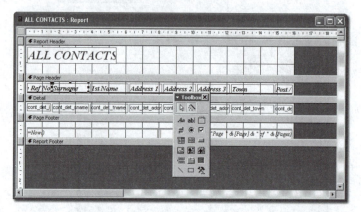

Before printing off your report you may want to make some alterations to it, such as adding labels, headers and footers, drawings or pictures.

This is done by clicking the 'Reports' option in the 'Objects' bar and selecting the report you want to amend. Click the 'Design' button in the database window's toolbar. The report opens in Design view and is divided into Report Header, Page Header, Detail Area, Page Footer and Report Footer. Items can be added to each of these sections.

At any stage during the production of a report you can amend the format of the text. There are various options available in the format menu. It is possible to format:

- **Characters** - by selecting 'font' you can change the *STYLE*, colour and Size of letters, **embolden** them, *italicise* them, <u>underline</u> them
- **Pages** - you can change the size, orientation and margins of pages, add page numbers, headers and footers or the date and time. You can insert page breaks to indicate where a new page should begin, or columns to divide the page vertically

If you use a format for part of the report and want to use it again later, you can select 'styles and formatting' and the software will show you what you have used previously.

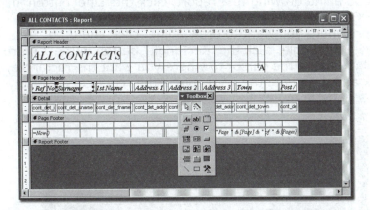

To add labels open the report in the Design view and:

- Click the 'Label' button in the 'Control' toolbox
- The cursor becomes '+A'. Move the cursor to the place in the report where you want a label
- Click and drag to draw a text box for the label
- Put the cursor inside the text box and type the label
- Click the 'Save' button

The placement of the label affects where it appears in the report. For instance, if the label is in the 'Details' section it will appear with the detailed information for each record in the report; if it is in the page header, it will appear at the top of every page.

Headers and footers will have been added by AutoReport or the Report Wizard. You may want to add labels or page numbers to the headers and footers, so you may need to re-size the header or footer section.

To re-size a header, put the cursor on the header section divider line, click and drag. To add page numbers click in the header or footer then open the 'Insert' menu and select 'Page Numbers'. Select the required 'Format', 'Position' and 'Alignment' options then click 'OK'. To add the date and time open the 'Insert' menu and select 'Date and Time'. Click the 'Include Date' and 'Include Time' check boxes and click 'OK'. You can add text to the header or footer by adding a new label and placing it in the header or footer, then following the instructions above.

To add a line drawing to a report, click the 'Line' button in the 'Control' toolbox, move the cursor to the area on the report where you want to draw a line, click and drag. To draw a rectangle, click the 'Rectangle' button in the 'Control' toolbox, move the cursor to where you want the rectangle, click and drag until the rectangle is the required size. To

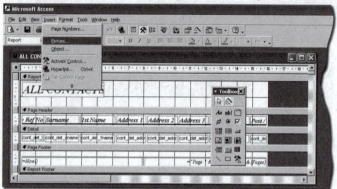

draw a straight line or a perfect square, hold down the 'Shift' key as you drag.

You may want to include a picture in the report such as a Company logo. Open the 'Insert' menu and select 'Picture'. The Insert Picture dialog box opens. Use the 'Look in' drop-down list or the 'Places' bar and open the folder where the picture you want to add is filed. Click the picture you want. Click 'OK'. If necessary move or re-size the picture.

After making all of the required modifications it is a good idea to preview what the report will look like before printing it. At this stage you can check whether the report is formatted and laid out appropriately.

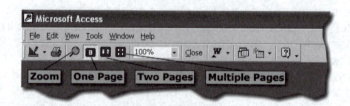

Select the report you want to preview and:

- Click the 'Preview' button
- If necessary, click the 'Maximise' button
- To look at further pages, click the 'Page' button
- To view more than one page at a time, click the 'Two Pages' or 'Multiple Pages' button
- Click the 'Close' button

Make any changes necessary then:

- Open the 'File' menu and select 'Print'
- In the 'Print Range' area enter the numbers of the pages that you want to print
- In the 'Number of Copies' field enter the number of copies that you want to print
- Click 'OK'

What you need to know

How to preview a report prior to printing it

Can you name two ways of creating a report?

Methods of adding page numbers to a report

What is the difference between a columnar and a tabular report?

How to add labels to a report

Could you draw a rectangle on a report?

Ways to re-size a picture that you have put into a report

If you were asked to add the date and time to each page of a report, would you know how to?

Your organisation's protocols for naming reports

Would you be able to add your company logo to a report?

Managing the database

You shouldn't find many problems in actually using the system. If you do, you could be searching against criteria which the system doesn't recognise, searching for deleted or corrupted data or entering data in an inappropriate format. In this case check your manual, handbook or the program's help facility. The main problems that you may encounter are saving files with the wrong name, saving a file with a name that has already been used (which will delete the original file), or a system failure. The first two can be avoided by taking care in naming files, the last can best be prevented by backing up files regularly. This can be done by saving them onto discs and storing the discs safely, thus improving efficiency.

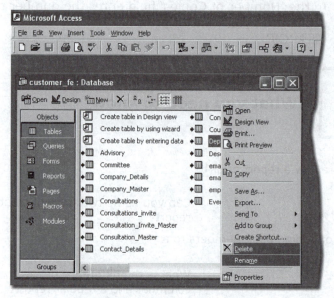

If you decide that the name you have used to save a file is wrong, click the object type in the Objects bar. For instance to rename a report click 'Reports'. From the list that will be displayed right click the report you want to rename and select 'Rename' in the shortcut menu. Type the correct name for the report and press 'Enter'.

From time-to-time you will want to delete objects from the database. Remember if you delete a table you will delete all the data in the table.

To delete an object from a database, click the object type in the Objects bar. For instance to delete a query:

- Click 'Queries'
- Right click the query you want to delete from the list that will be displayed and
- select 'Delete' in the shortcut menu
- Click 'Yes'

You may want to protect the database by giving it a password so that only certain people have access to it.

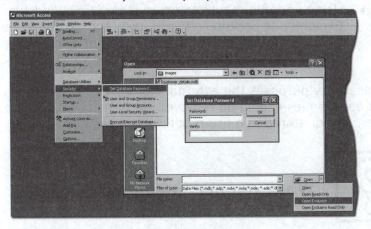

To do this:

- Select 'Open' from the 'File' menu
- Open the folder that contains the database from the 'Look in' drop-down list or the 'Places' bar
- Click on the database
- Click the down arrow next to the 'Open' button
- Select 'Open Exclusive'
- Select 'Security' from the 'Tools' menu
- Select 'Set Database Password'
- Type the password in the 'Password' field
- Press 'Tab'
- Type the password in the 'Verify' field
- Click 'OK'

The worst possible disaster that could befall your database would be for all of the information held in it to be lost due to circumstances beyond your control such as a computer crash or power surge for instance. For this reason it is vital that you back up your data frequently on to an external storage device such as a floppy disk, CD Rom, memory stick or external hard drive. This creates a separate file containing all of your data which can be re-loaded should the worst happen.

To back up a database:

- Click the 'Save' button
- Close the database. If you are in a multi-user environment, confirm that all users have closed the database
- Using your file management system (e.g. Windows Explorer) or backup software, copy the database file to a backup medium such as a CD-Rom or memory stick

For security purposes the external storage device containing the backup files should be removed from the premises overnight or stored in a fire-proof, locked cabinet.

 What you need to know

Your organisation's procedures for backing up databases

Why are some databases password protected and others not?

The authority needed to access password protected databases

Does your organisation have a system for naming databases?

Why it is important to back up databases

What types of external storage devices are available in your organisation?

The maintenance of databases may appear to be one of the most routine functions of the office, but many other people depend on the database being accurate and up to date to carry out their tasks. Many departments could not function at all without an accurate database, and the organisation could be liable to prosecution under the Data Protection Act 1998.

Good use of the features of databases will improve the efficiency and smooth-running of your department or organisation

Are you ready for assessment?

To achieve this unit of a Level 2 Business & Administration qualification you will need to demonstrate that you are competent in the following:

- Create fields for entering data with the required field characteristics, such as name, type, size and format
- Modify field characteristics in a simple (e.g. single table, non relational) database while maintaining the integrity of existing data, such as name, type and size
- Use appropriate tools and techniques to format data that is text and numbers
- Format reports from simple (e.g. single table, non relational) databases using appropriate tools and techniques for page layout, such as page size, page orientation, page numbering, headers and footers and margins
- Use automated facilities for checking data and reports, such as spell checking and sorting data
- Check reports are formatted and laid out appropriately
- Create and use multiple criteria queries to extract data
- Plan and produce reports from single (e.g. single table, non relational)
- Set up short cuts

(Remember that you will need the skills listed at the beginning of this chapter and that these are covered in chapter 1.)

Your Assessor will need you to produce evidence from a variety of sources. If you carry out the activities that follow they will provide some of the evidence for you.

Activity 1
You have been asked to create a database for a major marketing campaign in your organisation. Make assumptions about the scope and nature of the marketing campaign in line with your own organisation's needs. Design an outline database identifying the fields you are going to create, using field characteristics such as name, type, size and format. Write a brief report explaining what you have done and why.

Activity 2

Keep a work diary over the period of a month. Identify which databases you have been working on, the type of work you have completed and the range of database functions you have learned to use. Keep a copy of a database record you have produced and short cuts which you have set up.

Activity 3

Create a database containing at least 50 records each of at least tenfields. This can be based on any set of information of your choosing, for instance; names, addresses, telephone numbers, likes and dislikes of friends and family; the averages of your local or favourite cricket team; your CD collection; customer records not currently kept in a database. Use your imagination and see what you can come up with. Format the data using appropriate tools and techniques, and check the accuracy using sort data.

Activity 4

Using the database you have created, modify the field characteristics being careful to maintain the integrity of existing data. Set up three different database queries, each matching values in at least two fields. Sort the records appropriately and print a report using appropriate tools and techniques for page layout such as page size, page orientation, page numbering, headers and footers, and margins. Check the report using automated facilities such as spell check.

Activity 5

What do you understand by the following database software terms:

AutoReport

Database

Field

Label

Object

Object bar

Query

Record

Record Selector

Report

Sort

Table

Wizard

Remember: While gathering evidence for this unit, evidence **may** be generated for units 110, 201, 202, 208, 209, 210, 212, 213 and 225.

CHAPTER 19
UNIT 217 – Presentation software 2

Presentation software is used to produce a series of slides that can be projected or shown on a screen to be viewed by any number of people simultaneously. Slides may consist of text, images, graphs, charts, tables, video, sound and even animation. There are a number of ways of presenting slide shows. Slides can either be shown consecutively or can be merged each into the next or made to appear word-by-word or line-by-line.

When producing a slide show for somebody else to present it is important to listen carefully to exactly what information they want the slide show to communicate. When you feel that you have created what has been asked for it is important to check with the presenter that the slide show content and format serves their purpose.

Slide shows can be used for a number of purposes:

- Sales promotion
- Training
- Passing on of information

The advantages include:

- The opportunity to present to a larger audience
- Reduced risk of inconsistency as the message doesn't have to be repeated a number of times to smaller groups
- Less misunderstanding as the presenter can explain the information
- The possibility of revealing information one piece at a time and checking understanding before moving on
- The ability to be delivered consistently by different presenters

It is possible to communicate far more information with the help of visual aids than simply in written form. The detail can be covered by the addition of handouts.

 When using presentation software you will use the following skills:

- Planning
- Organising
- Summarising
- Writing
- Communicating
- Using technology
- Checking

These skills are covered in chapter 1.

Before you start

You will need to sit down with the presenter and take notes so that you can remember exactly what they want. There are several questions you will need to ask them in order to gain the information. The first is, what is the purpose of the presentation? It may be:

- A sales presentation aimed at customers or potential customers
- A training presentation for employees
- A presentation to management of a suggested change in procedures

- A presentation of results
- A tender for a contract
- A bid for funding
- An update on a project

The next question is, what is to be included? The presentation may include:

- Text
- Graphics
- Animation
- Images
- Charts
- Tables

You will then want to know how long the presentation is to last and in what order the information is to be given. Also:

- The format of the slides
- Whether speaker notes are required
- Whether handouts are required for the audience

What you need to know

The different types of presentations you may be asked to create

What questions do you need to ask before planning a presentation?

What questioning techniques can be used

What types of information may be included in a presentation?

Creating a presentation

In order to create a presentation you will need to use a software package. The most commonly used package is PowerPoint, so the following instructions are based on this.

The first step to creating a presentation is to open the PowerPoint program and familiarise yourself with the screen. On the screen you will see the 'Menu bar', the 'Standard' and 'Formatting' toolbars at the top and the Drawing toolbar at the bottom.

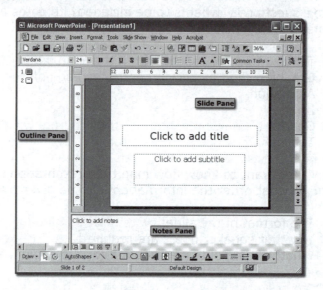

The screen shows three panes:

- The Slide Pane is where you enter the text, images, background colour etc
- The Outline Pane shows the text entered on the slides. Text can be added to or edited and new slides added
- The Notes Pane holds the notes that you may want to print for the presenter

The PowerPoint display has six views:

- Normal view where the Slide Pane dominates, the Outline Pane is open on the left hand side of the screen and the Notes Pane is open at the bottom of the screen
- Outline view where the Outline Pane dominates. This view is useful when you want to concentrate on the text
- Slide view reduces the Outline Pane to a strip showing numbered symbols for the slides. This is useful when you want to work on the layout or insert objects

- Slide Sorter view where the whole working area of the screen is used for small images (thumbnails) of the slides. This is useful when you want to re-arrange the order of the slides
- Slide Show view allows you to run the presentation
- Notes Page view shows the slide and its notes as they will appear when printed

The first five views are reached from the Status bar, Notes Page view is reached by clicking on Notes Page on the View menu.

When you start a new presentation, the program will give the file a generic name such as 'presentation1'. To name your presentation click on 'Save As' in the 'File' menu. Give the presentation a name that will make it easy to find at a later date.

Your organisation may have a system for naming files, such as the originator's initials followed by the date, for example.

You are now ready to start creating slides. The best way to start is to open the New Slide dialog box and select an AutoLayout. When you click 'OK' a slide will appear on the screen. Replace the 'click to add text' with your own text. Double-click in any object frame to add an object. Text on a slide is edited and formatted exactly the same as in a word processed document, except that you cannot type on a slide. Text is entered inside a text box. These are created from the Text box tool on the Drawing toolbar, or you can start with a slide containing a text placeholder. The text box/placeholder can be moved and resized as required, by clicking and dragging on its border.

- Put your cursor on the 'Click to add text' and click, the prompt will disappear and you can type in your text
- Highlight your text using the 'click and drag' method
- Format the text by using the toolbar buttons and the font and size drop-down lists

- Drag on the outline of the box to move the box to where you want it
- Drag on a 'handle' to change the size of the box

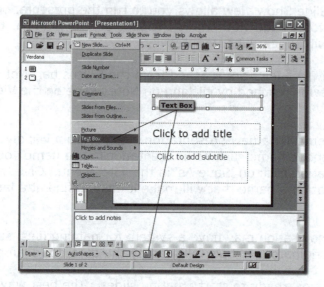

Text placeholders come in two types – titles and subtitles, and body text. Body text initially appears as bulleted lists as this is the most likely format you will require. You can change the bullets' style, size and colour, replace them with numbers or not use them at all.

- Select a slide with a bullets placeholder
- Put your cursor inside the text box, type the first point and press 'Enter'
- This will return you to the beginning of the next line where you will find your second bullet point
- Repeat until you have entered all your points. Do not press 'Enter' after entering the last point
- Highlight all the text using the 'click and drag' method you are then ready to change the bullets
- If you don't want bullets at all, click the 'Bullets' button on the Formatting toolbar
- If you want to replace the bullets with numbers click the 'Numbering' button on the Formatting toolbar
- If you want to change the style of the bullet points, click on 'Format' and select 'Bullets and Numbering' from the drop-down menu

- Select the style you want and click on it. You can also change the size and colour if you wish
- Click on 'OK'

You may want to add images from files and Clip Art images to your presentation. To add an image from a file:

- Open the Insert menu scroll down to 'Picture' this will open a further menu, select 'From File'
- Select the picture to put into your presentation
- Double click on the picture and it will be placed in the slide
- The picture may need to be re-sized or moved by right-clicking the image and formatting the picture or by dragging the re-size handles

To insert an image from Clip Art either start from an AutoLayout containing a Clip Art object and double click on the object or:

- Open the Insert menu scroll down to 'Picture' this will open a further menu, select 'Clip Art'
- Select a picture from the gallery
- Right click on the picture and from the drop-down menu select 'Show Picture Toolbar'
- From this toolbar you can manipulate your picture, either by changing the colour, brightness and contrast, or by compressing, rotating or cropping your picture or by adding a border

Often you will want uniformity across all the slides in the presentation. There are a number of ways of formatting the whole presentation. The Master Slide sets the colours, text formats, images and footers that can be shown in all the slides (unless they are changed individually). You can do anything to a Master Slide that you can do to an individual slide, the difference is it will affect all the slides in the presentation. To edit the Master Slide:

- Open the View menu, point to Master and select Slide Master
- Select the title text or a bullet level
- Edit the font, style, size and colour by using the Format menu in the normal way
- If you want the same image on every slide insert it onto the Master Slide

- If you want to add a footer click into the Footer area and add your text
- Click 'Close' on the Master toolbar

You can apply a colour scheme by:

- Clicking on the Format menu and selecting Slide Colour Scheme
- Select a scheme and click 'Preview'
- Click 'Apply to All'

You can set a background colour or design by:

- Clicking on the Format menu and selecting Background
- Select a colour from the selection on the drop-down palette
- Click 'More Colours' for a wider range
- Click 'Fill Effects' to set a gradient, textured or patterned background. You can at this point insert a picture as the background to all the slides
- Click 'Apply to All'

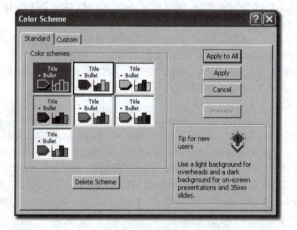

You can use a Design Template which has a background design, colour scheme and text styles. These can be used from the start of a new presentation or be applied to an existing presentation.

To start from a design template:

- Click on the File menu and select New
- Go to the Design Templates tab of the New Presentation dialog box
- Choose a template and click on it

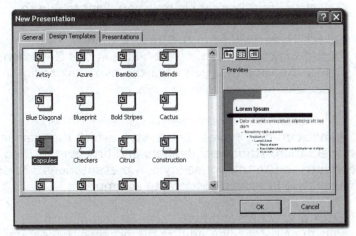

To apply a design template to an existing presentation:

- Click on the Format menu and select Apply Design Template
- At the Apply Design Template dialog box select a template
- Click 'Apply'

It is also possible to enhance presentations by adding animation, which means that text can be made to appear word-by-word or line-by-line in a variety of interesting ways:

- Click on the Format menu and select Apply Design Template
- At the Apply Design Template dialog box select Animation Schemes
- Choose a scheme
- Click 'Apply to All Slides'

You can also add hyperlinks to your presentation. Hyperlinks allow the presenter to jump from one slide directly to a later slide by clicking on a particular section of text or image, or they can link to a website or file outside the presentation. To create a hyperlink in your presentation:

- Select the text or graphic that you want to use to create the hyperlink
- Select 'Hyperlink' from the 'Insert' toolbar
- In the 'Link To' option, select 'Place in this Document'
- Select the slide that you want the hyperlink to link to
- Click 'OK'

Your organisation may have a house style which they use in all documentation, stationery, leaflets and brochures. If so it is a good idea to use the house style in presentations. To set up a house style in PowerPoint create a template:

- Start a new presentation
- Edit the Master Slide adding the organisation's name and logo as required
- Open the File menu and select Save As
- At the Save As dialog box, select Design Template (*.pot) in the 'Save As' type field
- Name the file and click 'save'

 What you need to know

Whether your organisation has a house style

What is the main purpose of a Master Slide?

How to change the style of bullet points

What is Clip Art?

How you can use a picture as a background

If you were asked to insert a graph into a presentation, would you know how to?

Checking and previewing the presentation

Before handing over the slide show to the presenter it is essential that you check it not only for spelling and grammar, but also for layout, continuity and that the images are of an appropriate size in comparison to the text.

To ensure consistency of your presentation, you can use the style checker function, which will check for consistency between all slides in the presentation as well as the text size and layout of your text boxes. To use this function:

- Select 'Options' from the 'Tools' menu
- Click on the 'Spelling and Styling' tab
- Click on the 'Check Style' box. At this stage you will be given the option of turning on the office assistant, if it is not already enabled. You cannot do a style check without the office assistant on
- Click on the 'Style Options' button and select the case, punctuation and visual characteristics of your presentation that you want the style checker to examine
- Click 'OK' to return to 'Options'
- Click 'OK' to return to your presentation

The style checker will automatically generate a light bulb icon next to any text that does not meet the criteria you have specified in style check.

When you are satisfied that the slide show is technically correct and as well presented as you can make it, you will need to run it for the presenter by:

- Clicking on Slide Show
- Selecting View Show
- Clicking through the slide show

Make any alterations needed and then check with the presenter what printing is required. In PowerPoint you can print:

- The slides as they appear on the screen
- The notes by themselves
- Slides with accompanying notes as handouts
- The text of the presentation as an outline

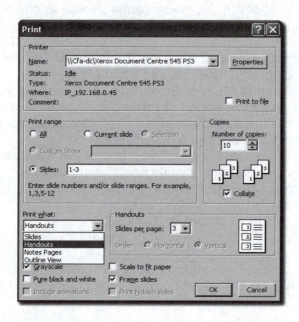

You can select which slides to print and how many copies. If you simply want to print all the slides, click the print icon. If you want to choose what to print:
- Open the File menu and select Print
- Set the range of slides to print
- Set the number of copies
- Select the Print what option – Slides, Handouts, Notes Pages or Outline View
- For handouts set the number per page
- Set the other options as required
- Click 'OK'

Save the presentation onto a disk and hand it over to the presenter with the printed documents requested.

What you need to know

Why it is important to check the slide
show before running it for the presenter

> Other than spelling and grammar what
> should you check a slide show for?

The printouts that are required

> If you were asked to print all even
> numbered slides, would you know how
> to do it?

How to run the slide show

> How can you change the order of the
> slides?

Modern presentation techniques have come a long way since
the overhead projector or 'chalk and talk'. It is now possible
to make a seamless presentation at the click of a button,
rather than changing transparencies every few seconds.
Most users of presentation software will use Microsoft
PowerPoint, and the details above are based on this
software, but there are other packages available. These will
produce similar results, but the detailed pathways will be
different.

Good use of the features of presentation software will enable you to make your presentations memorable

Are you ready for assessment?

To achieve this unit of a Level 2 Business & Administration qualification you will need to demonstrate that you are competent in the following:

- Use appropriate techniques to handle, organise and save files
- Link information in the same type of software
- Add information from one type of software to information produced using different software, such as a spreadsheet graph to a word processing document, text to an image file, picture to a presentation slide or simple information from a database onto a website
- Use a wide range of editing techniques appropriately for more complex presentations such as inserting objects and other resources, resizing images and changing the position or orientation of other objects
- Use proofreading techniques to check that text and images look professional
- Check text formatting techniques are used appropriately
- Check images and other objects are positioned and edited appropriately
- Format complex presentations using appropriate tools and techniques, such as changing colour schemes for slides or using an organisational house style
- Choose an appropriate method and presentation style to suit audience needs
- Choose, use and adjust templates for presentations
- Save a presentation as a slide show
- Print speaker notes

Remember that you will need the skills listed at the beginning of this chapter and that these are covered in chapter 1.

Your Assessor will need you to produce evidence from a variety of sources. If you carry out the activities that follow they will provide some of the evidence for you.

Activity 1

What options would you find on the 'insert' menu?
What is the purpose of bullet points?
How do you change bullet points to numbers?
Does your organisation have a standard template for presentations?
How many views are there in the PowerPoint display?

Activity 2

Keep a work diary over a period of a month recording which presentation software functions you have learned to use.

Activity 3

You have been asked to produce a slide show for an important presentation. How would you make the slide show interesting?

Activity 4

Create a presentation from a design template to induct a new member of staff to the department. You will need slides which cover terms and conditions and health and safety. Make the presentation as interesting as possible to encourage the new staff member that this is the place that they want to spend the rest of their working life by including pictures, text and objects. Save the presentation as "staff induction". Produce handouts and keep a copy.

Activity 5

Amend the presentation you created to add training opportunities and the organisation's rules and regulations. Resize the images originally used and change the position or orientation of the objects introduced. Amend the colour scheme used and ensure that your organisation's house style is being correctly used. Check that the text and images look professional.

Remember: While gathering evidence for this unit, evidence **may** be generated for units 110, 201, 202 and 225.

CHAPTER 20
UNIT 218 Specialist or bespoke software 2

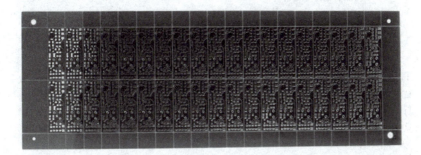

Almost all tasks that are required to be carried out in the administrative function can nowadays be carried out by computer. Some tasks such as the writing of letters, the storing and sorting of information and simple calculations can be carried out by standard software, often already on the hard drive of the computer. More complex tasks will require software specifically written to meet the needs of the business. Where the needs are fairly straightforward they can be met by specialist software; where they are specific to the organisation they will be met by bespoke software.

Specialist software includes:

- Accounts applications
- Logistics planning applications
- Computer aided designs (CAD) applications
- Computer animation applications
- Digital video editing applications
- Music composition and editing applications
- Project management applications

These can be bought 'off the shelf'.

Where specialist software does not fully meet the organisation's requirements it may be necessary to develop bespoke software, that is, software which is written specifically for the organisation to meet particular requirements. As every organisation is unique it is not always possible to customise specialist software to exactly fit what is required. In this case the organisation has to commission bespoke software from a software developer. Examples of this may be:

- Customer relationship management
- Stock control
- Plan control
- Engineering diagnostics
- Credit management
- Sales analysis

The software developer will discuss with the organisation the exact requirements so that the software application makes the organisation more efficient and better able to provide an effective service. Bespoke software may be used anywhere; you may find it in solicitors' offices being used to help with legal case management in a high volume 'production' environment to produce standard letters and merge case data; in local health authorities to collect and analyse data; in doctors' surgeries to record data, help with referrals and provide statistical analysis.

 When using specialist and bespoke software you will use the following skills:

- Planning
- Organising
- Using Technology
- Checking

These skills are covered in chapter 1.

Software application

Clearly it would be impossible to cover every conceivable application of software in the modern administration environment. In this section we will look at the most common and briefly describe their features.

Accounts applications

These basically imitate manual accounts systems. In the same way that accounts departments used to keep a series of books, each of which had its function, accounting software operates through a series of components which are parallels of these functions. These will include:

- Purchase ledger
- Sales ledger

- Nominal ledger
- Cash book

Transactions such as invoices raised and received, cheques raised and payments received are entered and the software completes the accounting process. It is important to remember that every entry affects a multitude of other records. For instance, entering a payment of a telephone bill by cheque will amend the supplier's account, the bank balance, the telephone expense code and the VAT account immediately, and have an effect on the month-end and year-end accounts.

Computer aided designs (CAD) applications

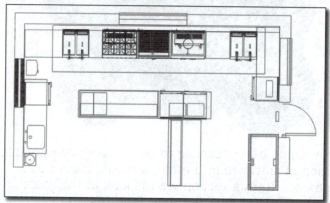

Computer aided design software greatly speeds up the whole process of design and enables testing and analysis to take place without the need to build a succession of prototypes.

Among the areas of design in which CAD has been extensively developed are:

- Architectural design
- Planning applications
- Garden design
- Engineering
- Aircraft design
- Car design

CAD helps designers to visualise their designs to scale. This can even be in three dimensions, so that amendments can be made instantly and alternatives can be tested against each other.

The software enables you to enlarge or reduce the scale of shapes; draw circles, curves, regular and irregular shapes; select and rotate shapes; use patterns and shading and show measurements.

Computer animation applications

Before the advent of computer animation software there were two ways to produce animated movement. Either a succession of drawings were made in each of which the characters had made minute movements, and these were then filmed to give the illusion of continuous movement (like Mickey Mouse or The Simpsons); or physical models were filmed, then moved very slightly and filmed again until a complete film is created (like Wallace and Grommit or Chicken Run).

Both of these ways are extremely time consuming and therefore expensive. Computer animation involves drawing three dimensional models and sets on the computer. This can be done by:

- Scanning images using digital photography
- Scanning wire-frame models which can be built up into coloured and textured form
- Producing sets and furnishings using CAD

Now the finished computer animated product looks much more realistic and can actually be significantly cheaper.

Digital video editing applications

The advantages of digital video are that it does not degrade over time and there is no generation loss. However many copies you make the quality is as good as the original. Digital video is stored in a format that can be understood by computers, which means it can be edited, manipulated, cleaned up or have special effects added.

Digital video editing software has many similarities to word processing software. It can be 'cut and pasted' without damaging the picture quality. Among the benefits of digital video editing software are:

- Improved programme finish
- Choice of programme styles
- Greater user satisfaction
- Backgrounds can be enhanced (cloudy days can look bright)
- Location appearance can be improved
- People can be made to look more glamorous

Videos can be enhanced by adding text, audio, interactive menus or transition effects. This enables you to produce more interesting and effective video presentations.

Music composition and editing applications

Music composition and editing software is a kind of musical word processing. It is used to record, edit, arrange and publish music. Generally speaking there are three types of music composition and editing software:

- **Notation programs** - These turn compositions into printed sheet music. Music can be saved for editing or transposed to another vocal or instrumental range. Arrangements using traditional notation, guitar tablature or drum tracks can be produced
- **Sequencers** - These are used to create compositions by recording the separate parts onto individual tracks and using the sequencer to bring them together. You can start and stop at any point and change tempos or instruments at will. It is possible to produce music beyond your own ability and record it
- **Auto-accompaniment programs** - These are basically backing tracks that you can play along with, but with the advantage of having the facility to alter the tempo. It makes practising a more fulfilling experience. You can try out different styles and harmonies, improve creativity and learn to play along with other instruments

If you are looking to create printed music you would choose notation programs; to create CDs you would choose sequencers; to create backing tracks you would choose auto-accompaniment programs.

Logistics planning applications

Logistics is the management of the flow of goods either through an organisation or from an organisation to its customers. Logistics software is used for:

- **Strategic planning** - Working out how many lorries, how many trailers and how many drivers you need, the necessary shift patterns to balance the number of drivers with the workload, the best routes to make deliveries to all the required drops in the minimum time and mileage
- **Daily planning** - Re-scheduling in response to delays, breakdowns or staff shortages. Seasonal variations, return loads and consolidation of loads will also affect the daily plans
- **Cost minimisation** - Analysing the point at which adding further resources such as extra lorries or drivers no longer increases the profit to be made. Calculating the comparative costs of in-house servicing against out-sourcing

Efficient use of the software enables you to see at a glance where every lorry is, what it is carrying and the drivers' hours. It enables you to react to problems such as staff sickness, road works and mechanical problems.

Project management applications

A project is a 'series of activities designed to achieve a specific outcome in a set budget and timescale'. Prior to the development of project management software the monitoring of budgets and schedules was a time consuming activity as every variation required a number of amendments which had to be made by hand. Specialist project management software can provide:

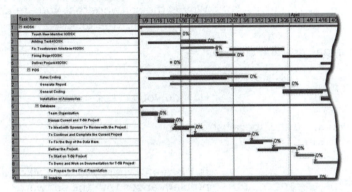

- Gantt charts - Time is marked out in columns, with individual tasks represented as arrows or solid bars terminating at dots. The length and positions show the start date and duration of tasks
- Critical path analysis - The critical path is the longest sequence of dependent activities that lead to the completion of the plan. Any delay of a stage in the critical path will delay completion of the whole plan, unless later activities are speeded up
- Automatic or manual re-scheduling of tasks
- Time recording and task completion tracking
- Task routing to team members on completion of previous tasks
- Individual work schedules for team members

This software helps you to manage the time element of the project; the budget element is managed on either spreadsheet or accounting software.

What you need to know

What the functions are of the various applications

Why is the software that you are using appropriate for the task?

The advantages of using specialist software

How do you access software?

Whether you are using specialist or bespoke software

Is there an expert you can call on if a problem arises with the software?

Skills and techniques

With all software packages there are certain basic skills and techniques that are required. Mastering these will enable you to produce high-quality work with whichever specialist application you use. As specialist and bespoke software covers such a vast range, it is not possible to tell you about every command in each application, but the following are basic techniques that will be found in many different packages.

Handling files

A feature common to all software programs is the need to create, file and produce documents. Some of the general commands for these actions are:

- **New** (Ctrl+n) - This is used to open a completely blank file when you wish to start a new task
- **Open** (Ctrl+o) - This is used to open an already existing file so that you can amend it or continue working on it
- **Save** (Ctrl+s) - This is used to save the file so that the data you have input is not lost if the whole system crashes
- **Save as** - This is used when you are ready to name the file. Use a reliable file-naming system so that you can easily retrieve the file later
- **Print** (Ctrl+p) - This is used to print a hardcopy of a file or part of it

Combining information

Documents such as reports and presentations can be enhanced with the use of other applications. Images, charts, movies and data can be imported into other documents.

- **Insert** - This is used to bring an object from one package into another, for instance a spreadsheet graph to a word processing document; text to an image file; picture to a presentation slide or simple information from a database onto a website
- **Size** - This is used to alter the size of an object or image
- **Position** - This is used to specify a precise location on the page

Entering, editing and processing information

Documents and files can be easily edited by moving, deleting and copying text, images and other elements.

- **Delete** - This is used to erase data previously entered
- **Cut** (Ctrl+x) - This is also used to erase data previously entered. It can be used in combination with the 'paste' instruction to move data
- **Copy** (Ctrl+c) - This is used in combination with the 'paste' instruction to duplicate previously entered data
- **Paste** (Ctrl+v) - This is used in combination with either the 'cut' or 'copy' instruction. Paste will add the last data selected to the file
- **Drag and drop** - This is used to move selected items from one location to another
- **Find and replace** (Ctrl+f) - This is used to replace all examples of selected text with an alternative. For instance all references to 'motor car' with 'vehicle'

Checking information

Whatever application you are using it is essential that you check the accuracy of the input. Remember the acronym GIGO, 'garbage in, garbage out'. Among the checks to be made are:

- The accuracy of text
- That figures are entered correctly
- The labeling and size of images, charts and diagrams

What you need to know

How to choose and use appropriate tools
and functions for simple tasks

What functions can you use to move
data from one position to another?

How to select and use appropriate tools
and functions for complex tasks

What function would you use to add a graph to a word processing document?

Techniques for handling, organising and saving files

How would you re-name an existing file?

The variety of specialist and bespoke software available is almost endless. Selecting the application that exactly meets the organisation's requirements will probably be the task of a technical specialist. Your role is likely to be to learn how to make the most effective use of the packages provided. Use the manual to get the best out of the available functions.

As with most things in life, when you buy software, you get what you pay for

Are you ready for assessment?

To achieve this unit of a Level 2 Business & Administration qualification you will need to demonstrate that you are competent in the following:

- Use appropriate techniques to handle, organise and save files
- Link information with the same kind of software
- Add information from one type of software to information produced using different software, such as a spreadsheet graph to a word processing document, text to an image file, a picture to a presentation file or simple information from a database onto a website
- Carry out more complex tasks using appropriate tools and techniques for entering, editing and processing information
- Use appropriate techniques to check more complex information

(Remember that you will need the skills listed at the beginning of this chapter and that these are covered in chapter 1.)

Your Assessor will need you to produce evidence from a variety of sources. If you carry out the activities that follow they will provide some of the evidence for you.

Activity 1
Write a simple 'how to' guide on a specialist or bespoke software application to help a new user.

Activity 2
Carry out two projects that fully demonstrate the use of specialist or bespoke software application that you use regularly. The projects should include:

- Using appropriate techniques to save files in appropriate folders and directories
- Importing information from both the same software and other software types
- Using appropriate tools and techniques for entering, editing, processing and checking information

Activity 3
Write reports on the projects explaining the stages that you went through and the advantages of using the software application.

Activity 4
Keep a diary over the period of a month recording all of the specialist or bespoke software that you have used and the new functions that you have used.

Activity 5
For the specialist software you are using, research five commercially available alternative packages and list the advantages of your current application over each.

Remember: While gathering evidence for this unit, evidence **may** be generated for units 110, 201, 202, 212, 214, 215, 216, 217 and 225.

CHAPTER 21
UNIT 219 Use a telephone system

Every business uses the telephone to communicate, both externally with its customers and suppliers and internally with other parts of the organisation. The way in which telephone calls are made and answered is very important. Make sure you have all the necessary information to hand before making a call. Remember when answering the phone that external callers will base their impression of the organisation on what they hear. Remember to:

- Be polite, amiable and above all helpful
- Use the caller's name
- Be patient and considerate
- Seek further information
- Make notes
- Do not rush the caller
- Never make promises you can't keep

This could have a lasting effect on their dealings with your organisation. Friendly but efficient is the impression you are aiming to make. Particular attention should be paid to how you:

- Transfer incoming calls, ensuring that the caller is not left on hold longer than is absolutely necessary
- Deal with messages that you take, recording enough detail to allow an efficient return call to be made
- Leave messages on answering machines, by being clear and precise

Most business lines and many residential lines will have some form of voicemail, whether this is an answering machine or a telephone company's service such as BT's 1571. You may find leaving a message daunting, especially if you are not expecting to. The important thing is to speak clearly and make sure your message is concise while delivering all of the necessary information. Remember to end your message with 'Thank you' or 'Goodbye' so the recipient knows the message is ended.

If you are recording an outgoing message include as much information as possible while being reasonably brief. Always give a name, a location and if possible, an alternative number the caller can use.

 When using a telephone system you will need the following skills:

- Questioning
- Listening
- Researching
- Communicating
- Presenting yourself
- Summarising
- Using technology
- Problem solving

These skills are covered in chapter 1.

Making calls

Before making a call consider whether the telephone is the best way of communicating. It will usually be the best method if you need an instant response, or if you need to exchange opinions with someone to get agreement. While most people nowadays carry a mobile phone, giving you access to them when they are away from their workplace, they may be in the car or on a train, and variable reception or background noise may make communication difficult. If however you need a written record, to discuss something complex, or a confidential issue is involved, there are better methods than using the telephone.

When you decide that a telephone call is necessary, you will obviously have to find the name and number of the person you wish to call. You will find it much easier if you can speak directly to the right person. There are a number of ways of finding out who this person is. You may already have had communication from them, if not, a colleague may be able to help. Failing that, a call to the company reception may be the quickest way. Internal databases, which may be held on computer or manually, will help with regular contacts. For a call to anyone else some form of Directory Enquiries may be used. Numbers are available on Internet websites, a variety of telephone services or paper based telephone directories.

It will make a very bad impression on the person you are calling if you are not clear what you are calling about, so always state the reason for the call. Make sure you have all the information that you need to pass on or all the questions you need to ask prepared before you make the call. You may want to make a list of the main points to be covered.

Now you know the person's name and telephone number you are ready to make the call. On a standard telephone you will just pick up the handset and dial the number. Most telephones however, have a number of features which you may need to use:

- **Speed dialling** – Numbers used regularly can be replaced by pre-programmed versions
- **Speaker phones** – You speak through a microphone and listen through a loud speaker without picking up the handset. This leaves your hands free to turn over pages and also allows other people to join in the conversation
- **Last number re-dial** – Calls back the last number dialled

An internal call may mean you only dialling the extension number; a local call requires only the telephone number while a long distance call may need you to dial an international or area code as well as the number. When your call is answered ask for the person you want to speak to. Remember to smile!

Say who you are and what organisation you are calling from:

- Speak clearly and slowly in as simple terms as possible
- Hold the receiver a little way away from your mouth so that you do not appear to be shouting
- Don't discuss the call with someone else with your hand over the receiver, you can still be heard
- Never hold another conversation while you are on the phone
- If you have to use technical terms or pass on names and addresses repeat any words that may be difficult
- If asking for information use open questions and clarify your understanding
- Try not to be side tracked. The person you are calling may not want to discuss what you want to talk to them about, for instance if you are calling to chase a late payment or delivery
- Don't let the person at the other end distract you always listen carefully
- Remember *why* you made the call and make sure you get your point across. It will waste your time and theirs if you hold a meandering conversation without getting to the point
- While keeping in mind that time is money, remember you should be focused without being abrupt

When you make a call you represent your organisation so remember to give a positive impression. The person at the other end will judge what they hear, what is said and how it sounds. The impression they form of you and the organisation may influence whether they do business with you. Be polite at all times. If you need to get your point across, be *assertive* but not aggressive.

One of the disadvantages of telephone calls is that there is no record of what was agreed. By the end of a long and complicated call you may be sure that you have reached an agreement, while the person you are speaking to may be equally sure that an entirely different agreement has been reached. Make notes of key points during the call. You can then summarise the main points of the conversation before ending the call. This will give the other person a chance to confirm or deny your understanding of what has been agreed.

 ## What you need to know

Where to find contact names, telephone and extension numbers of people you need to call

> Could you find the extension number of the security department if you were asked?

How you are expected to address people on the phone (do you call them 'Sir/Madam' or is it OK to call them 'mate/love'? If their names are known, do you refer to them by their first name or their family name?)

> Do you know why it is OK to call people on the phone by their first name in some situations but unacceptable in others?

How to use the features of the telephone system available in your organisation

> Can you explain the difference between being assertive and being aggressive?

Techniques for structuring a call to include
a beginning, a middle and an end

Why is it important always to be polite
when making a call?

Receiving calls

Answering the phone at work is completely different from
answering it at home. At work it needs to be answered in a
professional manner. Your organisation will probably have a
standard format for answering calls, for example:

- Telephone rings – pick up within five rings
- Say 'Good morning/afternoon Berry School of Dance
  Donna speaking, how may I help you?'

Use it, it may not be your personal style but it is the
company style. The purpose of answering the phone within
an agreed number of rings is to provide the customer with a
prompt response, not to make you run across the office.

When you pick up the phone the whole organisation may be
judged on how you deal with that call. It may not be
convenient to you to answer the phone at that moment, but
the caller has called because it is convenient to them:

- Remember to smile when you answer the phone, it
  will project a positive image
- Don't answer the phone while eating, chewing gum or
  yawning
- Don't forget that the first few syllables may be missed
  so say 'good morning/afternoon' before giving your
  name
- Find out who is calling and what they want. You will
  need to know more than simply the caller's name. In
  order to decide the best way to deal with the call you
  will need to know whether the caller is a customer, a
  colleague, somebody trying to sell you something or
  an official
- Listen carefully and try to help the caller
- If you are unable to help, suggest an alternative
- Remember that if you put the handset down, the
  caller will still be able to hear anything that is said
  nearby unless you use a mute or secrecy button
- If you put the caller on hold, reassure them every 30
  seconds or so that you are still there

Whoever it is, the call is important to the caller, they need to know you are listening and showing an interest. You can do this by inserting words such as 'really', 'indeed', 'I see' or simply 'mmm' to re-assure the caller you are still listening.

When you know what the caller wants you will be able to decide whether you can help them or not. Whenever possible, you should aim to deal with the call yourself. To do this you will need to have access to the latest information, as out-of-date information is of little use to anyone.

However, there are some things that you should not tell anyone over the phone if you are to protect the organisation's confidentiality and security. For instance, never disclose any sensitive information about the organisation, colleagues' personal details or anything that may be a risk to security. Your organisation will have rules about what information can be given.

If you are in doubt whether to disclose something, or the information will take some time to gather, offer to call back, agreeing a time and if necessary ask for advice before returning the call. Make sure you return the call at the agreed time. If you don't have the necessary information by then, call back, apologise and arrange another time for the call. Remember the Data Protection Act 1998 covers information given over the telephone as well as in writing.

Sometimes a caller will be speaking to the wrong person. It is important to remember that they have *not* 'come through to the wrong department'. They have been *put* through to the wrong department. Offer to transfer the call if you are unable to help. It is up to you to relay the information you have already gained to the person you are transferring the call to. The caller should not have to repeat themselves.

Your telephone system may have a number of features which you will need to know how to use when transferring calls:

- **Group hunting** – this enables a call to be transferred to a group of extensions. The first available extension will ring
- **Call diversion** – this automatically transfers calls to another extension if someone is away from their desk

- **Music on hold** - if you have to put the caller on hold, perhaps because you need to find out who to transfer them to, check regularly that they are happy to continue to hold. Do not leave them listening to silence or 'hold' music for several minutes

If you cannot transfer them reasonably quickly, offer to get somebody to call them back. *Make sure somebody does call them back.*

You may answer a phone on somebody else's desk if you are alone in the office or happen to be passing when the desk is unmanned, or you may have a feature such as 'Call pick-up' which enables you to answer another extension from your own phone. In these situations:

- Make sure you have a pen and paper near the phone so you can write down
    - who called and when
    - who they wanted to speak to
    - any message they want to leave

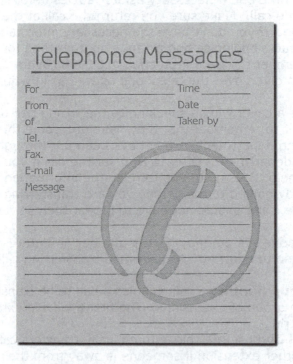

- what action you have agreed will be taken
- Confirm with the caller the message that you are going to pass on

If you tell the caller someone will call them back within an hour and you don't tell your colleague you have promised that, your colleague is likely to get a very unfriendly response when they call back the next day. As well as this, the caller will have formed a negative opinion about your organisation because of the service they have received.

It is just as important when receiving calls as it is when making calls to summarise the outcomes of the conversation so that both parties know and agree what has been said. Don't rely on your memory. Make sure that you write down what has been agreed. Remember to end the call by saying 'Thank you for calling'.

What you need to know

Your organisation's preferred style for answering the phone

> Does your organisation have a standard for how quickly the phone must be answered?

Why you handle a call from a customer differently from one from a colleague

> Does your telephone system indicate whether a call is internal or external?

What information can and cannot be given over the phone

> Can you explain how to use listening skills on the phone?

How to transfer a call

> Why is it necessary to smile when answering the phone?

The information needed when taking a message

> Why should you always have a pen and paper near the phone?

Dealing with message systems

When you leave your phone make sure your voicemail or answer phone is activated and your message is up-to-date. Your message should be simple and accurate, for instance:

> 'I'm sorry I am not available to take your call at the moment, please leave your name and telephone number and I will return your call as soon as possible.'

The one thing more frustrating than getting a continuous ringing when making a call is to get a message saying you will be back at 2pm and you are not. If a caller rings at 2.10pm they will not be pleased to hear that you should have been back ten minutes ago. If you are going to be on holiday it may be a good idea to leave a message on your voicemail to let callers know when you will be back, for instance:

> 'I'm sorry I am not available to take your call. I am on holiday from 16th July to 30th July. If you need to speak to somebody before then, please call extension 216.'

When coming back to your phone the first thing you must do is check the system for messages. If you leave it until later you may miss a vital message. This could have all sorts of consequences: lost business, you run the risk of annoying customers or you could even miss an invitation or an appointment that it may be too late to keep. Not all messages will be straightforward. Some people find leaving messages on machines difficult:

- Nervous callers leave gaps in the message while they think what to say
- Some try to leave too long a message and get cut off
- They may forget to say who they are or what their number is

When you have listened to your messages, write them down but don't just forget them, respond to them. Call back those that need a reply, being sure that you have got all the information that the caller wants. Remember to deal with the messages that don't need a call back as well. Almost every message will require some sort of response. Pass on the information or record the fact that the call was received.

Delete messages when you have dealt with them. There are three reasons why this is important:

- If you do not it will take longer and longer to get to any new messages as you will have to listen to all of the old ones first
- Once messages have been dealt with they are no longer useful
- There is a risk that somebody else will listen to the message and deal with it again, thinking that it is still current; for instance a customer may receive two deliveries for the same order

If you are prepared in advance for any call you need to make, it will not throw you off balance if you are answered by a recorded message. *DO NOT HANG UP*. You have all the information in front of you, leave a message on the system. Make sure you don't speak too quickly and be clear and precise. Remember to include your name and telephone number, the name of your organisation and only enough information to allow the recipient to prepare before returning the call. For instance,

> 'Hello, this is Donna from The Berry School of Dance, my number is 2556635, can you call me back about the costumes that have been ordered, thanks.'

What you need to know

Why it is important to leave a simple and
accurate message

> Could you improve the message on
> your voicemail/answer phone?

How to check your system for messages

> How would you explain to a new
> member of staff the timescales for
> responding to messages?

The system for dealing with messages
that don't need an immediate call back

> What could be the consequences of not
> deleting messages?

How do delete messages once they have
been dealt with

> If you had to leave a message on a
> supplier's answer phone asking them to
> contact the buyer to discuss an order,
> what information would you give?

In conclusion all telephone calls, whether internal or external,
must be given due importance. Callers will receive an
impression of the organisation from the way you answer the
phone. Make sure you are polite, receptive and let the caller
know you are listening. If you are giving information keep it
relevant and accurate, if you are receiving information have
a pen and paper handy. Don't 'lose' callers when transferring
them or leave them to repeat themselves. Use message
systems efficiently, both your own and other people's.

All telephone calls are important, they are not an interruption to your work they are a vital part of it

Are you ready for assessment?

To achieve this unit of a Level 2 Business & Administration qualification you will need to demonstrate that you are competent in the following:

- Identify the purpose of the call
- Obtain the name and numbers of the person to be contacted
- Make contact with the person
- Communicate information to achieve the purpose of the call
- Project a positive image of yourself and your organisation
- Summarise the outcomes of the conversation before ending the call
- Answer the phone according to your organisation's procedures
- Identify the caller, where they are calling from and what they need
- Provide accurate and up-to-date information whilst protecting confidentiality and security
- Transfer calls where requested
- Take and relay messages according to the caller's needs
- Keep your message system up-to-date
- Check the system for callers' messages
- Respond to callers' messages within agreed timescales
- Delete messages when you have dealt with them
- Leave recorded messages on other people's systems that achieve their purpose

(Remember that you will need the skills listed at the beginning of this chapter and that these are covered in chapter 1.)

Your Assessor will need you to produce evidence from a variety of sources. If you carry out the activities that follow they will provide some of the evidence for you.

Activity 1

Which of the following would you use to indicate to a caller that you are listening?

Really?
Yeah well
Mmmmm
Right
Flippin' 'eck
Blimey!

Activity 2

Keep a work diary over the period of a month recording all of the incoming and outgoing calls you deal with, their requirements and how you met them, indicating any confidentiality issues involved.

Activity 3

You have been asked to make an appointment for your Managing Director. What information do you need before making the call?

Activity 4

If your organisation has an internal telephone directory, find a copy and highlight your extension on it. If it doesn't, create one.

Activity 5

Write an account of an important message left on your system, detailing the action you took and the result of the action. Explain the possible consequences if you had not taken the appropriate action promptly.

Activity 6

You are working as a legal secretary in a solicitor's office. When you return from lunch there is a message from Mrs Roberts asking you to call her back with information on the progress of her husband's bankruptcy hearing. What action should you take?

Remember: While gathering evidence for this unit, evidence **may** be generated for units 110, 201, 202 and 225.

CHAPTER 22
UNIT 220 – Operate office equipment

In a modern office there is a wide range of equipment in use. This will include:

- **Computers** - These are no longer simply super typewriters. Many are now multi-media machines. They are capable of everything from producing a simple letter to putting a man on the moon. They may have peripherals attached such as printers, scanners, digital cameras, modems or speakers. Complex as they are, they rely on simple resources such as paper and cartridges for the printer to produce their best results
- **Telephones** - The humble telephone has come a long way in recent years. Once an expensive and cumbersome means of communication it is now available to carry around and use almost anywhere. Telephones can now be used to take photographs, send pictures and enable the caller to be seen by the receiver. Text messages can be sent, conference calls held where three or more people can join in and voice messages can be left. Although less expensive now than before, telephone calls can still be a major expense if you do not prepare before making the call. Make sure you have the right telephone number to hand, you have considered what you wish to say, and have the means to make a note of what is said
- **Photocopiers** - Although work produced on computers can often be printed off directly, large

runs, complex jobs or copies from other sources are best done on a photocopier. Modern photocopiers can do much more than simply reproduce a copy of the original. They can enlarge or reduce, produce multiple copies, collate and staple documents, produce double-sided copies, colour copies, and even enhance the original so that the copy is actually superior. Before starting a run, make sure the machine is stocked with paper and either toner or print cartridges

- **Fax machines** - Fax is short for facsimile. A fax machine sends a copy of an original document over the telephone line to another fax machine or a computer with a fax facility. The recipient's telephone number is dialled and the start button pressed, and a copy of the original will appear at the other end. Incoming faxes may be received automatically, or may require the receive button to be pressed when the telephone rings. Paper and an ink source are needed to print out incoming faxes

- **Franking machines** - Basically these are machines which print the cost of postage onto envelopes or labels, and replace postage stamps. The postage is paid for in advance either by visiting the Post Office or, more recently, by downloading credit over the telephone line. Care must be taken when using a franking machine as any mistakes cannot be rectified. Once the franking is printed, the credit has been used. Post should be weighed before being franked to check that the correct amount of postage is used. Always check that there is sufficient credit available, and that you have adhesive labels to use on packages that won't fit into the machine

- **Shredders** - An increasing amount of paperwork is confidential and will need to be destroyed rather than being thrown away. A shredder will cut the paper into strips or squares which will be virtually impossible to read. Obviously care should be taken not to shred any document until you are sure that it is ready to be destroyed. Attempting to stick it back together is a thankless task! Care must also be taken not to get clothing or hair trapped in the shredder
- **Calculators** - People have been using mechanical devices to help them with calculations since before the Chinese invented the abacus. Modern calculators can carry out a wide range of calculations at the press of a few buttons. You will probably have been using them since you were at school. Office calculators differ only slightly from pocket calculators. They may have a print function so that calculations can be

checked and a record kept. Make sure there is sufficient paper and ink before starting a task

- **Laminators** - Some documents need to be protected from the elements. A laminator will encapsulate the document inside plastic. Business cards, ID cards, luggage tags, telephone lists, training notes, glossy prints, photos and maps are examples of items that may be laminated. The item is placed in a pouch and the laminator seals the item

When you are new to an organisation, some of the equipment may be familiar from your previous experience, but you are bound to be faced with equipment that you have not come across before – just when you think you have it all under control, something new will be delivered!

Before operating any unfamiliar equipment, make sure you have received the necessary training. This may be from:

- Attending training courses
- Using distance-learning materials
- Getting a more experienced colleague to show you

While operating the equipment take care to work as efficiently as possible, remembering that a well-maintained piece of equipment will give better results.

When you have finished using the equipment check your work and leave the equipment ready for the next user.

 When operating office equipment you will need the following skills:

- Communicating
- Problem solving
- Planning
- Organising
- Using technology

These skills are covered in chapter 1.

Before operating equipment

It is important to know what each piece of equipment in the office is used for, and what other materials are required, in order that you can use the equipment and resources in the most efficient way. You will probably already be familiar with some of the equipment mentioned above. It is likely that you will come across most, if not, all of it during your working life. Don't expect to know how to use it all without being shown or trained. A valuable resource in getting to know an unfamiliar piece of equipment is the operating manual.

Why do manufacturers bother to give you a manual? Because it contains the most efficient and cost effective way of using the equipment. Many people seem to believe the manual is the last resort if you cannot figure out how to make a machine work. A lot of time can be saved if you follow the manufacturer's operating instructions by reading the manual before you start. The manual contains vital safety and operating information, which, if ignored, can invalidate the warranty. There may also be a number of functions or time-saving features that you will not discover by chance. The manual will usually include a troubleshooting guide, so that when the equipment doesn't work you can quickly find out why. Keep the manual close to the equipment for easy reference.

 ## What you need to know

What equipment is in use in your office

> Do you know where to get stationery for the equipment?

Whether you need authority to use any of the equipment

> Where would you find the postage costs for a variety of outgoing mail?

What functions the equipment in use in your office offers

If required, could you produce multiple photocopies, back-to-back, in full colour, stapled and collated?

How to use the equipment available

Would you be able to identify documents for laminating or shredding?

Where the manuals are kept for each piece of equipment

Is somebody in your office responsible for keeping the manuals up-to-date?

Why you should refer to the manual before using the equipment

Could you find and use the trouble shooting sections for each machine?

Who to ask if you don't understand the manual

Why is it necessary to refer to the manual before operating equipment?

While operating equipment

Most office equipment will need some sort of consumables. These will include:

- **Paper** - This comes in a range of quality measured by weight, including headed, letter, copy and photographic paper. Use the right quality for the intended purpose
- **Envelopes** - Letters to external addresses will need good quality envelopes while internal memos may be sent using internal ones which can be used a number of times. Consideration should be given to the size needed: a document shouldn't be folded more than twice. Documents with several pages should be placed flat in their envelope
- **Cartridges** - These are used in ink-jet printers and come in black, multi-colour, single colour and photo quality versions. Use the right cartridge for the right job
- **Toner** - This is used in laser printers and photocopiers and comes in black and single colour versions

- **Ribbons** - These are used in dot matrix printers, printing calculators, fax machines and typewriters
- **Labels** - These are used in franking machines for letters and parcels that are too bulky to frank directly; computer printers as address labels and file labels. Specially printed labels are used in laminators to create security passes and visitor passes
- **Pouches** - These are used in laminators to protect the contents
- **Floppy disks and CDs** - These are used in computers to store files

All of these are relatively expensive items, so you should take care to waste as few resources as possible. While it is essential always to have sufficient stock, care must be taken to avoid over ordering which may result in you having obsolete stock left over when equipment changes. Careful storage of consumables will also prevent waste through damage. Probably the biggest source of waste in an office comes from unwanted copies being produced. If you are producing a number of copies of a document it is worth running off one and checking it before creating a large number which have to be thrown away.

Almost all waste produced by operating office equipment can be recycled, in many cases saving money on replacements. Think before you throw anything away. Remember to shred any confidential documents before recycling.

All office equipment will operate more efficiently if it is kept clean. Most will have instructions in the manual on cleaning procedures to keep the equipment clean and hygienic, and some will have self-cleaning functions. Standards of cleanliness should be sufficient to ensure that they meet health and safety requirements. Care should be taken when undertaking cleaning on particular equipment, for instance remembering not to attempt to clean electrical equipment using water. Equipment which regularly comes into contact with people, for instance telephone handsets and keyboards, needs to be cleaned with antiseptic to prevent germs being transferred from one person to another.

The manual provided with the equipment will contain a guide to help you deal with problems according to the manufacturer's instructions. This may include a helpline number to call or addresses of service centres. Most equipment should only be maintained or repaired by qualified service engineers, as attempting to remedy a fault yourself could easily damage the machine further and invalidate the warranty. The manufacturer will also recommend particular consumables to be used with the machine. These should be adhered to wherever possible, as use of non-standard resources may also invalidate the manufacturer's warranty or reduce the efficiency of the equipment.

 ## What you need to know

What consumables your organisation uses

> Do you know which consumables are recyclable?

Where and how consumables are stored in your organisation

> Why is it important to keep waste to a minimum?

Who is responsible for monitoring the use of consumables within your organisation

> Do you ensure that your copying is accurate before undertaking a large copying task?

What the procedure is for re-ordering
consumables

Why must some documents be
shredded before recycling?

How to keep equipment clean and
hygienic

Do you know what cleaning materials
can safely be used on each piece of
equipment?

What health and safety implications relate
to the cleaning of equipment

Where are cleaning materials stored in
your organisation?

How often cleaning should be undertaken
on each piece of equipment

Who is responsible for supervising the
safe storage and use of cleaning
products?

Who to call in the event of an equipment
breakdown

What is the reporting procedure in your
organisation if equipment fails?

Where to find contact numbers for service
centres

Why do equipment manufacturers
recommend particular consumables for
their machines?

Whether your organisation has an internal
maintenance department

In the event of a serious photocopy
failure during a large copying task, who
would you inform?

After operating equipment

When you are given a task, check exactly what is required in order to make sure the final product meets the requirements. You need to know if you are producing a finished article which is going out to customers, or a rough draft for internal use. Are copies required in colour or black and white? Should copies be single or double-sided? If you know exactly what standard of work is required you will be able to check for yourself whether you have met it. If there is a deadline, and for any reason you are unable to meet it, report the fact immediately. It is too late to know that a deadline will not be met when the deadline is reached.

When you have finished using a piece of equipment, leave it, any resources you have been using and the work area ready for the next user. For instance:

- Do not leave paperclips or pieces of paper on the photocopier
- Put the telephone handset back on its base when you have finished with it
- Ensure that the franking machine is not set on a high value when you have finished using it
- Stocks of paper should be stored flat and tidily
- If you use the last sheet of paper, the ink cartridge runs out or you use the last laminator pouch, replace them for the next user

Just think ahead and think how you would feel if you came to use equipment and you had to go looking for the resources you needed.

What you need to know

Why it is important to leave the work area
ready for the next user

> Why should you always re-set the
> franking machine after use?

The financial implications of not ensuring
that equipment is adequately prepared for
future use

> How do you re-set the franking
> machine?

How to re-stock paper and toner in the
photocopier, printer and fax machine

> Why should you not throw away used
> paperclips?

When beginning a task, the standard of
work required

> To whom should problems with
> deadlines be reported?

The deadline for each task before starting
the task

> When should you report delays which
> may affect meeting deadlines?

What different standards of work are
required in your organisation for different
types of work

> Why are deadlines so important in
> business?

Why it is important to store paper flat

> State two reasons for putting the
> telephone back on its base

Once you have mastered the use of the various types of office equipment, your working life and the working lives of your colleagues will be easier. Tasks will be carried out more efficiently and the standard of work you can achieve will be higher, so remember to take every opportunity to learn how to use any new equipment that becomes available. The more skilled you are the greater your prospects will be and the more valuable you will be to your organisation.

You will improve your visibility and worth to your employers by mastering the use of all the office equipment

Are you ready for assessment?

To achieve this unit of a Level 2 Business & Administration qualification you will need to demonstrate that you are competent in the following:

- Locate and select the equipment and resources you need for the task
- Follow the manufacturer's operating instructions
- Waste as few resources as possible
- Keep the equipment clean and hygienic
- Deal with equipment and resource problems according to the manufacturer's instructions
- Make sure the final product meets required standards and deadlines
- Make sure the equipment, resources and work area are ready for next user

(Remember that you will need the skills listed at the beginning of this chapter and that these are covered in chapter 1.)

Your Assessor will need you to produce evidence from a variety of sources. If you carry out the activities that follow they will provide some of the evidence for you.

Activity 1
What is fax an abbreviation for?

Which piece of office equipment would you use

- To produce a letter?
- To produce 1,000 copies of a leaflet?
- To stamp envelopes and parcels?
- To encapsulate a document?

When a new piece of office equipment is delivered, what is the first thing you should do?

Where in the instruction manual would you find the best advice to resolve a problem with office equipment?

Activity 2

Keep a work diary over a period of a month recording what office equipment you have used and the training you have received.

Activity 3

Put together a list of all the operating manuals for equipment in your office and where they are kept.

Activity 4

A new photocopier is delivered and installed in your office. You are asked to produce 200 colour, double-sided brochures by 5.00pm. When you start the task at 4.05pm, the paper jams causing the photocopier to break down. What do you do?

Activity 5

You are responsible for the outgoing post. Today you have the following to despatch:

- A parcel weighing 1kilo 47gms to be posted to Norwich first class
- A package weighing 437gms to be posted to Canada by air mail
- Seven letters to go first class
- 34 letters to go second class

Find out how much postage would be required on each. What is the maximum weight of each letter before it exceeds the minimum postage?

Activity 6

If there is any equipment in your office that you have not been trained to use, speak to your supervisor about getting trained to use it.

Remember: While gathering evidence for this unit, evidence **may** be generated for units 110, 201, 202, 219 and 225

CHAPTER 23
UNITS 221/222/223 Prepare text

Every organisation, whether it be a doctor's surgery, solicitor's office, bank, factory, shop, leisure centre or garage, will have one thing in common - the need to produce text-based documents. These will include memos, letters, reports and minutes of meetings and will be produced from a variety of sources including shorthand notes, audio recordings and handwritten drafts.

Whenever you are producing written documents it is important that you are able to spell, use grammar correctly and punctuate so that the finished product both gives a good impression of your organisation and, more importantly, conveys the intended message.

If you have trouble with your spelling, there are only two ways to improve – read more books and practice. The following are 30 of the words most commonly misspelled. If you learn how to spell these, you will be able to spell most everyday words.

accommodate	description	privilege
achievement	embarrass	proceed
acknowledgement	extension	recommend
analysis	gauge	separate
benefited	guarantee	slight
calendar	height	supersede
commitment	judgement	through
convenient	occurrence	unconscious
criticism	possession	weight
delicious	precede	yacht

Of course, if you are using a word processor with the spell check facility operating, it will tell you if you have misspelled most of these words. The spell check cannot, however, differentiate between words that are spelt correctly but used incorrectly; for instance, if you spelt 'through' as 'threw' the spell checker would not notice. Some of the most commonly confused words are:

- We are pleased to <u>accept</u> your donation.
  Everyone made a donation <u>except</u> Mr. Jones.
- Never listen to <u>advice</u> from your parents.
  I would <u>advise</u> you always to listen to your parents.
- The increase in interest rates will <u>affect</u> everyone.
  The <u>effect</u> of the increase was felt by everyone.
- She thought she was <u>eligible</u> for a grant.
  The letter she received was <u>illegible</u>.
- You must <u>ensure</u> that your car is <u>insured</u>.
- Lowestoft is <u>farther</u> east than Birmingham.
  I need <u>further</u> information on the location of Hull.
- There are <u>fewer</u> days in February than in June.
  It is <u>less</u> likely to rain today than it was yesterday.
- My <u>personal</u> opinion is that it will rain today.
  The HR Department deals with <u>personnel</u>.
- I visited the local doctor's <u>practice</u> this morning.
  I need to <u>practise</u> my spelling more often.
- The <u>principal</u> cause of heart disease is overeating.
  The Minister resigned over a matter of <u>principle</u>.
- The traffic on the M6 was <u>stationary</u> for two hours.
  We need to order some more <u>stationery</u> this week.
- This week's sales were better <u>than</u> last week's.
  We will look at this week's plan, <u>then</u> next week's.
- The girls picked up <u>their</u> handbags.
  The boys will be over <u>there</u> tomorrow.
  <u>They're</u> planning to visit next week.

People often think that grammar is either extremely complicated or that it no longer matters. In fact it is relatively simple and incorrect grammar can lead to serious misunderstandings. For example, 'Use both lanes when turning right' actually requires drivers to straddle the two lanes – a highly dangerous manoeuvre. The correct instruction should be 'Use either lane when turning right'.

There are five parts of speech which you need to know:

- **Nouns** - these are the names of things, for instance 'book', 'television', 'Sunday', 'Norfolk'
- **Pronouns** - these are used instead of nouns, for instance 'he', 'she', 'they', 'it'
- **Verbs** - these are doing words, for instance 'run', 'eat', 'listen', 'speak'
- **Adverbs** - these give more information about the verb, for instance 'run quickly', 'eat slowly', listen carefully', 'speak clearly'
- **Adjectives** - these describe nouns, for instance 'interesting book', 'reality television', 'lazy Sunday', 'flat Norfolk'

Sentences are formed by linking parts of speech together. Simple sentences contain a subject and a verb; for instance 'I am.' 'The new vicar thought he spoke clearly' is a sentence that contains all of the five parts of speech listed above. Can you identify the five parts of speech? Sentences must start with a capital letter and end with a full stop, question mark or exclamation mark. Capital letters are also used to indicate proper names (Ahmed, Francesca, Belgrade, Africa), titles (Mr., Mrs., Lord, Sir, Dr.), days of the week and months of the year and acronyms (RAF, CIA, FBI, MI5, RAC).

A paragraph is formed by linking two or more sentences about the same subject. When the subject changes, start a new paragraph. For instance, this paragraph is about paragraphs, the previous paragraph was about sentences.

Correct punctuation is important if people are to understand what you are trying to tell them. For instance, if you say 'Fred, the dog is ill' you are telling someone called Fred that the dog is unwell. If you say 'Fred the dog is ill' you are telling someone that the dog called Fred is unwell. There are three punctuation marks that you need to use correctly at all times:

- **Full stops (.)** - these are used to mark the end of a sentence or after abbreviations
- **Commas (,)** - these are used to separate words in a list or phrases in a sentence, or to make sentences easier to read
- **Apostrophes (')** - there are two uses of the apostrophe; to replace a missing letter, 'I'm, he's, don't' or to indicate something belongs to someone, 'Jim's book, Pauline's shoes, women's clothing, babies' bottles'

Whatever sort of document is produced, regardless of the source, it is important that it is checked for accuracy before being distributed. Copies of both the finished document and the source must be stored safely and securely.

In this chapter we will look at preparing text from notes, shorthand and audio instruction. We will look first at those areas that are common to all three and then at the unique features of each in turn.

 When preparing text you will need the following skills:

- Questioning
- Listening
- Reading
- Writing
- Using technology
- Checking
- Managing time

These skills are covered in chapter 1.

Preparing and producing text

Whatever source material you are planning to use, you will be producing documents in one of the following formats:

Memos are used internally within the organisation, but this does not mean they are informal. They:

- May be addressed to more than one recipient
- Will usually not include addresses or signatures
- Will simply state the date, name of the recipient, the name of the sender and the content
- May have the recipient and sender's job titles and departments
- Will usually be produced on a template which reflects the organisation's house style

The use of memos is declining in the UK as e-mail communication becomes more popular. However, most organisations still use memos for important internal messages.

MEMORANDUM

To: All Department Managers

From: Human Resources

Date: 15th August 2005

Subject: Bank Holiday Pay

Staff required to work on the Bank Holiday Monday August 29th will receive double-time plus a day off in lieu providing Monday is one of their normal working days.

Staff working on the Bank Holiday Monday when Monday is not one of their normal working days will also receive an extra day off in lieu.

Business letters are usually printed on paper headed with the organisation's own address and business details. While there is a recognised format to letter writing, each organisation will adopt its own house style. There is a convention that business letters are produced fully blocked and with open punctuation. This means:

- All parts of the document start at the left hand margin
- All punctuation except that in the body of the letter which is essential for grammatical accuracy and ease of understanding is omitted

Business letters are also laid out in a fixed sequence;

- References (this is optional)
- Date
- Name and address of recipient
- Salutation
- Heading (this is optional)
- Opening remarks
- Main message
- Action or results
- Closing remarks
- Compliments

A letter addressed to:

Mrs Jayne Wilcox
12 Manver's Street
London
SW19 7ER

can be sent using the following salutations and complimentary closure:

| Dear Jayne | Dear Mrs Wilcox | Dear Madam |
| Kind regards | Yours sincerely | Yours faithfully |

Someone who knows Jayne Wilcox may well choose to address her as Jayne. If a sender does not know Jayne very well they may feel more comfortable addressing her as Mrs Wilcox. The most formal way to address Jayne is to use the term Madam. This might be done by people who do not know Jayne at all. You will notice that as the salutation becomes more formal so does the complimentary close.

In business, letters are used as a formal means of communication between individuals in different organisations. Over the last few years many organisations have found the volume of letters produced and received each day has dropped because of the increased use of e-mail communications. However, many important external communications are still made by letter.

Mrs Jayne Wilcox
12 Manver's Street
London
SW19 7ER

20/05/2005

Dear Mrs Wilcox

Re: Complaint Letter 17/05/2005

Thank you for your letter dated 17th May regarding your complaint about the service you received on the 5th May 2005.

I am sorry to hear that you have been disappointed by the level of service you have received from our staff. We pride ourselves on putting customer satisfaction first and I can assure you that I will investigate your complaint fully.

I will be in touch soon by writing. In the meantime if I can be of any further assistance or you require any further information then please do not hesitate to contact me on 020 7091 9620.

Yours sincerely

A Hawkins

A Hawkins
Customer Services Manager

Reports are usually produced in response to a request for information. They may be formal or informal depending on the audience. A report to the Board will generally be more formal than a report to the members of a club. The common thread is that they are written to inform the reader of facts about a subject. The depth of information contained in a report will depend on the purpose of the report and its intended audience.

The type of report that you are most likely to be asked to produce from scratch is a research report. This will involve analysing and interpreting the findings, drawing appropriate conclusions and making suitable recommendations.

All reports will follow a similar structure, however detailed they may be:

- **Front page** - this contains the title of the report, the name of the author and the date
- **Contents** - a list of the subjects covered
- **Executive summary** - a brief outline of the report which can stand alone
- **Background information** - this gives the reasons that the report was produced
- **Methodology** - this tells you how the report was produced (surveys, questionnaires or research)
- **Findings** - there are a number of ways of presenting the findings of a report. These include:

  - by importance (beginning with the central idea)
  - by chronology (in order of events starting either with the latest or the first)
  - by sequence (where one idea follows from another)
  - by comparison (where two ideas are compared in alternate paragraphs)

- **Conclusion** - this section states what the research has led to, and how. Conclusions should be drawn from the information included in the report
- **Recommendations** - actions to be taken as a result of the conclusion
- **Acknowledgements** - in this section the contribution of others to the report is recorded
- **Bibliography** - source material should be referred to, listed alphabetically by author giving the date of publication
- **Appendices** - there may be information referred to in the report which is too detailed to be given in full without distracting from the purpose of the report. The full information is given in an appendix

Minutes of meetings are a written record of what took place at a meeting. They can be recorded in a number of different forms:

- **Verbatim** - everything is recorded word for word
- **Narrative** - a summary of the meeting including discussions and conclusions. Formal resolutions are recorded verbatim
- **Resolution** - a resolution is a motion which has been voted on and passed. Details of the proposer and seconder are recorded with a verbatim recording of the resolution
- **Action** - the agenda item, the outcome or action required and the name of the person or persons responsible for carrying out the action are recorded. The discussions are not recorded

Whichever form of minutes is used they must contain everything of importance.

Minutes of Social Club Meeting held on 19th May 2004
West Hotel, Pendleton. 2.30pm.

Those present

Bill Banstow	Chair
Mike Willis	Secretary
Pete Axty	Treasurer
Carol Carter	
Brian Williams	
Kevin Bissle	
Janet Hewitt	

Apologies for absence were received from: Michael Ford

Minutes of the last meeting were approved.

There were no matters arising.

The Chair reported that discussion with management had commenced with regard to the possibility of using the staff canteen for future events.

The Treasurer reported that there were seven subscriptions still outstanding. It was agreed that letters be written to the appropriate members advising them that if payment was not received by 6th June their membership would be terminated.

A.O.B.

Carol Carter suggested that a staff outing to the seaside in August could be arranged.

It was agreed that she would look into the costings of such an event.

The next meeting will be on 16th June 2004 at 2.30pm at the West Hotel, Pendleton.

Whichever form of minutes is used they must contain everything of importance.

It is important to agree the standard of the finished product required and the deadline for producing it. If, having agreed a deadline, you experience difficulties, remember to report the problem immediately. It is too late to be told that a deadline will not be met when the deadline has already passed.

At any stage during the production of a document, formatting text may be necessary. There are various options available in the format menu.

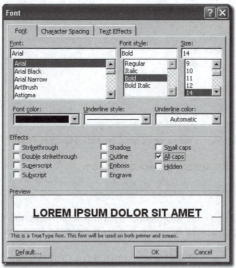

It is possible to format

- **Characters** - By selecting 'font' you can change the **STYLE**, colour and SIZE of letters, **embolden** them, *italicise* them, <u>underline</u> them, change the s p a c i n g , or add various text effects

- **Paragraphs** - You can align text using the centre or justify options, or by selecting 'bullets and numbering' add bullet points or numbers. You can make other amendments by selecting 'borders and shading', or by altering the line spacing, tabs and indents
- **Pages** - You can change the size, orientation and margins of pages, or add page numbers, headers and footers or the date and time. You can insert page breaks to indicate where a new page should begin, or columns to divide the page vertically
- Sections - As you will see from the examples above it is not necessary for the whole of a document to be in the same format. By highlighting individual sections of a document you can apply different formats

If you use a format for part of the document and want to use it again later, you can select 'styles and formatting' and the software will show you what you have used previously in the document.

What you need to know

The different uses of memos, reports, minutes and letters

What is meant by fully blocked?

The importance of meeting deadlines

What type of document will always have a signature?

How to spell, punctuate and use grammar accurately

What forms can minutes take?

The sequence in which reports are presented

What do you understand by an 'executive summary'?

The sequence in which business letters
are laid out

What punctuation is used in a letter
using open punctuation?

How to use the format menu

If you were asked to emphasise a
sentence in a report how would you do
it?

Checking and editing text

There will be occasions while inputting text when the writer's
intention will not be entirely clear. You may be listening to
an audio tape or transcribing shorthand notes when you
come to a word or phrase that you could interpret in more
than one way. Always check with the writer as soon as
possible. It is much better to ask and get it right at this
point than to guess and have to change it later.

In many circumstances you will need to produce a 'draft'
copy so that the originator can check that what you have
produced matches what they intended. Before even
producing the draft, though, you should check your work and
correct any errors that you can find.

Most word processing packages contain spell checking and
grammar checking facilities. Use these first to correct the
more glaring errors, but do not rely on them entirely. They
tend to use American spelling and grammar, so will accept
'color' and reject 'colour', for instance.

When the automatic checking is complete, read the
document carefully to look for missed errors, and also for
correct use of paragraphs, headings and subheadings, style
and formatting. Be particularly careful to proof read
numbers, dates, times and amounts. Check for errors
between similar words such as 'affect' and 'effect' or 'less'
and 'fewer'.

When you are satisfied that there are no further errors that
you can correct, print a draft copy of the document and pass
it to the originator for them to proof read. This means not
only looking for any typing errors but also for errors of

context and content. They will mark up the draft indicating any required changes. These may come about as a result of:

- **Input errors** - if you have carried out your checks thoroughly these should be few
- **Errors in the source material** - if you have produced the text from audio instruction or from someone else's notes, you may have faithfully produced what the source contained, only for the originator to find that there were errors
- **Amendments to the content** - particularly if the originator has dictated the content verbally, it is possible that on seeing the finished product they have second thoughts about the best way to convey the information

So, if your draft comes back covered in red ink, don't feel that you have necessarily produced a poor document. The chances are that the changes have been made by the originator to improve the overall effect.

Probably the greatest advantage that the word processor has over the typewriter is the opportunity to edit. In the bad old days when you got your draft back you had to recreate it from scratch. This meant the chances were that you would make different errors the second time. Nowadays at least the parts of the text that you wish to keep are still there.

You should therefore make the most efficient use of the technology available to make the alterations that have been requested. Functions in common use in most word processing packages include:

- **Delete** - this allows you to delete a letter, to delete a whole word at a time use 'ctrl+delete'
- **Cut** (Ctrl+x) - you can highlight a piece of text and cut it from the document
- **Copy** (Ctrl+c) - This is used in combination with the 'paste' instruction to duplicate previously entered text
- **Paste** (Ctrl+v) - This is used in combination with either the 'cut' or 'copy' instruction. Paste will add the last text selected to the file
- **Copy and paste** - allows you to highlight a piece of text and add it to another location
- **Find and replace** (Ctrl+f) - this function is used to change all the examples of a particular word to

another word (for instance if you are asked to write a report and you use the word 'company' several times and are then asked to substitute the word 'organisation' there is no need to re-type use 'find and replace' to change all the examples)

- **Inserting special characters and symbols** - this enables you to use a wide range of non-Arabic letters and other signs e.g. ©, é, 'Ω, %

Mṃinutes of Social Club Meeting held on 19th May 2004, West Hotel, Pendleton. 2.30.PM

Those present

Bill Banstow	Chair
Mike Willis	Secretary
Pete Axty	Treasurer
Carol Carter	
Brian Williams	
Kevin Bissle	
Janet Hewitt	

Apologies for absense were recieved from: Michael Ford

Mṃinutes of the last meeting were approved.

There were no matters arising.

The Chairman reported that discussion with management had commenced with regard to the possibility of using the staff canteen for future events.

The treasurer reported that there were seven subscriptions still outstanding. It was agreed that letters be written to the appropriate members advising them that if payment was not received by 6th June their membership would be terminated.

A.O.B.

Carol Carter suggested that a staff outing to the seaside in Aug could be arranged.
It was agreed that she would look into the costings of such an event.

The next meeting will be on 16th June 2004 at 2.30pm at the West Hotel, Pendleton

---

Having made all the requested alterations, produce a final draft and pass that to the originator. Hopefully their proofreading this time will result in no further amendments. You will then be able to print off the requested number of copies to the quality standard requested, not forgetting an extra copy for the file.

What you need to know

How to proof read your own work

What is meant by proofreading?

Printers' correction symbols

What is a noun?

Uses of full stops, commas and apostrophes

What is an adverb?

The functions available to edit text

Why should you produce a final draft?

The importance of raising any queries with the originator before producing the draft

What types of amendments might be made to a draft?

Storing the text

Every document that you produce will need to be stored in some way. Your computer will have its own in-built sorting and storing mechanisms. You will need to be able to store information accurately in approved locations and find it again quickly. Most systems will include a facility to store the information in folders within the main directory. These should be used to group files together to speed up retrieval.

Paper copies will have to be stored manually. There are a number of different methods that can be used:

- **Alphabetical** - filed in order from A–Z. Files starting with the same letter are filed in order of the second letter (Aa, Ab, Ac) and so on. People's names are filed by their surnames, and if more than one has the same surname, by their first names. Names starting with 'The' are filed by ignoring the 'The'
- **Numerical** - files are given numbers and filed from 1 to infinity. This is useful for information which naturally lends itself to being filed this way (purchase orders, sales invoices, for instance)
- **Alpha-numerical** - files have a combination of letters and numbers. Examples include postal codes, National Insurance numbers, car registration numbers, etc. These are usually large data bases as they hold more information than numerical systems and are more flexible than alphabetical systems. The order of filing depends on the sequence of the file name. If file names start with letters followed by numbers, they are filed in alphabetical order first, and numerical order within each letter
- **Chronological** - this is most often used within one of the other methods. For instance, each customer's records are filed alphabetically, but the information within the file is stored chronologically, usually with the latest at the front. This enables a picture of the activity to be gained. However, it can be used based on dates of birth or start dates

Some information may be marked 'confidential'. Make sure you know exactly what is meant by 'confidential' in your organisation. It may mean senior staff are allowed access, it may mean only the person who created the document is permitted to read it. Access to information about individuals is covered by the Data Protection Act and you must be very careful to comply with its requirements.

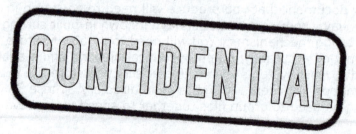

As well as the completed document you will need to file the original source material in case it needs to be referred to at a later date. Your organisation may have its own system of referencing documents or you may create your own. If you put the same reference that you have given the completed document onto the source material, you will be able to track the source should any query arise later. The source material therefore needs to be stored in a logical manner:

- Hand written notes can be attached to the file copy of the completed document
- Shorthand note books should be stored chronologically with the start and end date written on the front
- Audio tapes should be stored chronologically and labelled with the date

You will then be able to find the source material by locating the completed document in the filing system and using the combination of reference and date.

What you need to know

Your organisation's referencing system

Why is the source material filed as well as the completed document?

Why it is important to be able to locate the source material if requested

How would you store customer letters?

How to store electronic files in folders

What does 'confidential' mean in terms of text storage?

Unit 221 – Prepare text from notes

The great advantage of longhand notes is that they can be prepared anywhere, by anybody without any special training; on the bus on the way to work, on the train on the way back from a meeting, during a meeting. The important thing is to make sufficient notes that if you are preparing text from them yourself you will remember all of the details that you want to include or if someone else is to prepare the text they will understand exactly what you want to say.

ASAP

When preparing text from notes that you have made yourself, you should have no problem reading them back. On the other hand if you are preparing text from someone else's notes this may be more difficult. Read through the notes to make sure that you understand what is intended. You will not just be typing the notes verbatim, you will be required to sort them into sentences and paragraphs. Sort the notes into the order that you are going to type them. This may mean making your own notes on them to remind you which part comes next. The more often you prepare text from notes given by a particular person, the easier it will become to read the writing and understand the meaning of them.

Unit 222 – Prepare text from shorthand

The advantages of being able to take shorthand notes are that you can either take dictation verbatim or make more detailed notes for your own use than you could in long hand.

Shorthand is a skill that takes some time to learn, but once you have become proficient it will save you a lot of time.

When taking shorthand notes you will be sitting in one place for some time so it is important that you are comfortable. Hold your shorthand notebook in a position that you find most convenient, this may be on your lap or on the desk. Make sure you have a sharp pencil (and a spare in case of accidents). Listen very carefully to what is being said to you, if you miss a word or don't fully understand, ask immediately. It is much easier for the person giving dictation to clarify as they go along than to wait until the end. If you build up a rapport with the person giving dictation you will find it easier to understand what they mean and efficiently record it.

Unit 223 – Prepare text from recorded audio instruction

The advantages of using audio equipment are that a verbatim transcript will be produced and that there will be no problem in deciphering the hand writing of the person who produces it. Although it may take a little while to get used to the equipment, once you have mastered the necessary co-ordination you will find it relatively simple.

When preparing text from recorded audio instruction it is advisable to sit with a straight back. Make sure that your foot is comfortable on the foot pedal and that the headset fits properly. Listen carefully to what is being said, using the foot pedal stop the machine and type in what you have heard. Some people will give instruction onto the tape such as 'comma', 'full stop', 'paragraph' or 'new page'. Follow these instructions even if they seem to contradict the layout that you would expect for the document you are producing. The more often you use audio equipment the less often you will have to use the foot pedal.

Whatever source you are producing text from, the more often you do it the easier it becomes

Are you ready for assessment?

To achieve this unit of a Level 2 Business & Administration qualification you will need to demonstrate that you are competent in the following:

Prepare text from notes

- Agree the purpose, format, quality standards and deadlines for the text
- Input the text at the speed and level of accuracy required by your organisation
- Format the text, making efficient use of the technology available
- Check for accuracy, editing and correcting as necessary
- Seek clarification when necessary
- Store the text and the original notes safely and securely in approved locations
- Present the text in the required format within agreed deadlines and quality standards

Your Assessor will need you to produce evidence from a variety of sources. If you carry out the activities that follow they will provide some of the evidence for you.

Activity 1
Choose a piece of text that contains at least 1,000 words. Switch off the spell check function on your computer. Type the text for ten minutes. After ten minutes stop and calculate your typing speed using the following method:

Count the total number of characters typed including spaces.
Divide the answer by 5 (average length of word).
This gives the gross number of words typed.

Divide the answer by ten (time spent typing).
This gives the gross words per minute (wpm).
Count the number of mis-typed words.
Deduct the number of mis-typed words from the gross wpm.
This gives the net wpm.
If your computer has a word count facility make sure that you use the characters (with spaces) figure.

Activity 2

Attend a meeting (this could be a team meeting at work, a social club meeting, a meeting at college) and take longhand notes of what is said. Produce a short typed report from your notes. Time yourself inputting the text and count the number of words. Proof read the document and calculate the net words per minute.

Activity 3

You work in an Estate Agent's office in Burnley. When you arrive at work you find the following note:

A new house has just come onto the market can you type the details? 112 Bestonic Street semi situated in a pop. and est. res. location convenient for local schools and shops and town centre, vestibule, entrance hall, lounge, dining room, three bedrooms CH gas garage, upvc DG throughout fully fitted kitchen cloakroom on ground family bath on 1st gardens front and rear

Lounge 8.1x3.48
Dining room 4.72x4.22
Kitchen 2.39x4.5
Bed 1 3.12x4.62
Bed 2 3.61x2.95
Bed 3 3.42x4.56

Make sure you point out that the house has a large well looked after garden, council tax band B photo to follow

Activity 4

Proof read and correct the following and produce a corrected version. Switch off the spell check function on your computer.

Our ref: DT/GY/1256

Mr G Willims
Apart 21
The shore
Manchster
M6 7yu

23.06.023

Dear nr Williams

Account number 45678956 –Flat 24 tge maltings, Manchester

Thankyou for you're recent enqiry regarding your mortgage, and the interst rates available to you. I am enclosing a quotition showing what yur new payments would be at a new rate of interst. Yhjis has been calculated on and Interest only Basis.

At the moment you're monthly payments is ^189.23 vased ib a rate if 6.75%. Should you decide to except our offer (details)attached, your new repayments would be approx $206.93. The admin fee of £120.00 gas veeb added ti tyour balance for quotation's pyrposes only.

This offer is valid for 14 day's from the date of the enclosed quotation. you should of receved further details yesterday.

Transferring yourmortgage onto the new rate couldnt be easier, Simply return the Deed of Variation enclosed, signed by all partied to the mortgage.

We will charge you the aministration fee of £120.00. This sum can be added to the loan or may be paid by check if you wish.

If you have any questions, plesse contact me on 02356 56998 Monday to Friday between 9.00pm and 5.00pm.

Yours faithfyully

W Gaines
Consultant Mortgage Provider

(Remember that you will need the skills listed at the beginning of this chapter and that these are covered in chapter 1.)

Are you ready for assessment?

To achieve this unit of a Level 2 Business & Administration qualification you will need to demonstrate that you are competent in the following:

Prepare text from shorthand

- Agree the purpose, format, quality standards and deadlines for the text
- Take dictation using shorthand at a minimum speed of 60 words per minute
- Clarify points you are unsure about
- Input and format the text from your shorthand notes
- Make efficient use of the technology available
- Check for accuracy, editing and correcting as necessary
- Store the text and the original shorthand notes safely and securely in approved locations
- Present the text in the required format within agreed deadlines and quality standards

Your Assessor will need you to produce evidence from a variety of sources. If you carry out the activities that follow they will provide some of the evidence for you.

Activity 1

Choose a piece of text that contains at least 1,000 words. Switch off the spell check function on your computer. Type the text for ten minutes. After ten minutes stop and calculate your typing speed using the following method.

Count the total number of characters typed including spaces.
Divide the answer by 5 (average length of word).
This gives the gross number of words typed.
Divide the answer by 10 (time spent typing).
This gives the gross words per minute (wpm).
Count the number of mis-typed words.
Deduct the number of mis-typed words from the gross wpm.
This gives the net wpm.

If your computer has a word count facility make sure that you use the characters (with spaces) figure.

Activity 2

Ask a colleague to read a document containing at least 600 words to you at dictation speed. (This should take no more than ten minutes.) Take notes in shorthand. Type the document from your notes. Proof read your version against the original.

Activity 3

Proof read and correct the following and produce a corrected version. Switch off the spell check function on your computer.

Our ref: DT/GY/1256

Mr G Willims
Apart 21
The shore
Manchster
M6 7yu

23.06.023

Dear nr Williams

Account number 45678956 –Flat 24 tge maltings, Manchester

Thankyou for you're recent enqiry regarding your mortgage, and the interst rates available to you. I am enclosing a quotition showing what yur new payments would be at a new rate of interst. Yhjis has been calculated on and Interest only Basis.

At the moment you're monthly payments is ^189.23 vased ib a rate if 6.75%. Should you decide to except our offer (details)attached, your new repayments would be approx $206.93. The admin fee of £120.00 gas veeb added ti tyour balance for quotation's pyrposes only.

This offer is valid for 14 day's from the date of the enclosed quotation. you should of receved further details yesterday.

Transferring yourmortgage onto the new rate couldnt be easier, Simply return the Deed of Variation enclosed, signed by all partied to the mortgage.

We will charge you the aministration fee of £120.00. This sum can be added to the loan or may be paid by check if you wish.

If you have any questions, plesse contact me on 02356 56998 Monday to Friday between 9.00pm and 5.00pm.

Yours faithfyully

W Gaines
Consultant Mortgage Provider

Activity 4
You work in an Estate Agent's office in Burnley. When you arrive at work you find the following note:

A new house has just come onto the market can you type the details? 112 Bestonic Street semi situated in a pop. and est. res. location convenient for local schools and shops and town centre, vestibule, entrance hall, lounge, dining room, three bedrooms CH gas garage, upvc DG throughout fully fitted kitchen cloakroom on ground family bath on 1st gardens front and rear.

Lounge 8.1x3.48
Dining room 4.72x4.22
Kitchen 2.39x4.5
Bed 1 3.12x4.62
Bed 2 3.61x2.95
Bed 3 3.42x4.56

Make sure you point out that the house has a large well looked after garden, council tax band B photo to follow

Transcribe this into shorthand and then type up the note in full. Ask your supervisor, team leader or manager to check your work.

(Remember that you will need the skills listed at the beginning of this chapter and that these are covered in chapter 1.)

Are you ready for assessment?

To achieve this unit of a Level 2 Business & Administration qualification you will need to demonstrate that you are competent in the following:

Prepare text from recorded audio instruction

- Agree the purpose, format quality standards and deadlines for the transcription
- Input the text from the audio recording at a minimum speed of 40 words per minute
- Format the text making efficient use of the technology available
- Check content for accuracy, editing and correcting as necessary
- Seek clarification when necessary
- Store the text and the original recording safely and securely in approved locations
- Present the text in the required format within agreed deadlines and quality standards

(Remember that you will need the skills listed at the beginning of this chapter and that these are covered in chapter 1.)

Your Assessor will need you to produce evidence from a variety of sources. If you carry out the activities that follow they will provide some of the evidence for you.

Activity 1

Choose a piece of text that contains at least 1,000 words. Switch off the spell check function on your computer. Type the text for ten minutes. After ten minutes stop and calculate your typing speed using the following method.

Count the total number of characters typed including spaces.
Divide the answer by 5 (average length of word).
This gives the gross number of words typed.
Divide the answer by 10 (time spent typing).
This gives the gross words per minute (wpm).
Count the number of mis-typed words.

Deduct the number of mis-typed words from the gross wpm.
This gives the net wpm.

If your computer has a word count facility make sure that you use the characters (with spaces) figure.

Activity 2

Proof read and correct the following and produce a corrected version. Switch off the spell check function on your computer.

Our ref: DT/GY/1256

Mr G Willims
Apart 21
The shore
Manchster
M6 7yu

23.06.023

Dear nr Williams

Account number 45678956 –Flat 24 tge maltings, Manchester

Thankyou for you're recent enqiry regarding your mortgage, and the interst rates available to you. I am enclosing a quotition showing what yur new payments would be at a new rate of interst. Yhjis has been calculated on and Interest only Basis.

At the moment you're monthly payments is ^189.23 vased ib a rate if 6.75%. Should you decide to except our offer (details)attached, your new repayments would be approx $206.93. The admin fee of £120.00 gas veeb added ti tyour balance for quotation's pyrposes only.

This offer is valid for 14 day's from the date of the enclosed quotation. you should of receved further details yesterday.

Transferring yourmortgage onto the new rate couldnt be easier, Simply return the Deed of Variation enclosed, signed by all partied to the mortgage.

We will charge you the aministration fee of £120.00. This sum can be added to the loan or may be paid by check if you wish.

If you have any questions, plesse contact me on 02356 56998 Monday to Friday between 9.00pm and 5.00pm.

Yours faithfyully

W Gaines
Consultant Mortgage Provider

Activity 3
Using any pre-recorded text (a talking book, for instance) type for ten minutes. Ask a colleague to proof read your version against the recording. Count the number of words you have typed and calculate the net words per minute.

Remember: While gathering evidence for these units, evidence **may** be generated for units 110, 201, 202, 212, 214, 224 and 225.

CHAPTER 24
UNIT 224 – Produce documents

The layout and accuracy of documents produced in any organisation is very important. The key to this is the amount of preparation that you put into it. Most organisations have an agreed policy about the way their documents look to ensure consistency and quality, often referred to as the 'house-style'. The type of document you are asked to produce will determine the style you should use. Before actually starting to produce any document make sure you have all the resources you will need and that you have considered the most appropriate layout to use.

It has been said that first impressions are made within thirty seconds, and the first impression a potential customer gets of your organisation could have a vital effect on their decision whether to do business with your company. A well presented, correctly spelt, grammatical and accurately punctuated document will create a positive impression which will last.

There is a wide range of software available that will help you to produce the highest quality documents possible. Remember that there are a number of different features that can be added such as images, graphs, tables or diagrams. These should be used with care however, and in agreement with the author of the document. You will also need to follow your organisation's agreed procedures.

After producing your document it should be checked carefully, errors in spelling or grammar could have a potentially disastrous effect. If in doubt about the intended meaning, refer back to the author. During production regularly save the document, giving it a file name in accordance with your organisation's policy. When you are entirely happy with the results give the author the opportunity to check that the document meets their requirements.

Both during the production of documents and subsequently, it is important to bear in mind the question of confidentiality and the security of the information contained. Any personal information may be subject to the Data Protection Act 1998, and there may also be commercially sensitive information which would be valuable to a competitor.

Before being printed off the document will need to be stored electronically, after production it will need to be stored in hard copy. In both formats the important thing is that it can be found easily.

 When producing documents you will need the following skills:

- Questioning
- Listening
- Reading
- Organising
- Writing
- Using technology
- Checking
- Managing time

These skills are covered in chapter 1.

Preparing the document

There are several types of documents you may be asked to produce, these may include:

- **Memos** - These are used internally within the organisation. They will usually not include addresses or signatures, this does not mean they are informal. They may be addressed to more than one recipient

---

MEMORANDUM

To: All selling staff

From: Sales Manager

Date: 27th August 2005

Subject: Sales targets

Last week saw total sales of £127,436, an increase of 3.1% on last year.
This week we have a challenging target of £148,000, or 3.7% on last year.
This will require 100% effort from all of us, but I am confident we can do it.

REMEMBER THE PROMOTION ON DISPOSABLE BARBECUES.

- **Faxes** - A fax is a document transmitted over the telephone line. It may include a memo or a letter. Many organisations use a cover sheet to precede the document to include the name and fax numbers of the sender and recipient, and the number of pages being sent

---

FACSIMILE

To:	Peter Robinson
	Motor Vehicle Repairs
Fax No:	02274 55369
From:	Ronald R. Barker
	Paving Co. Ltd.
Fax No:	02564 33465
No of Pages:	1 plus this cover sheet

- **Letters** - These will usually be written on paper headed with the organisation's address. Your organisation will probably have its own 'house-style' for letters

---

Matthew and Son Builders
Allington Place
West Billington
WB1 1AD
Tel:0224 566854

Our ref: GM/RA/124
Your ref: VH/AK

17 March 2005

Mr V Harmison
Oval Walk
West Billington
WB2 1AX

Dear Mr Harmison

Thank you for your letter dated 14 March 2005 accepting our quotation to extend your office building.

The work will commence on Monday next and will be completed within 6 working weeks.

If you have any queries please do not hesitate to contact me.

Yours sincerely
Matthew and Son Builders

G Matthew

Graham Matthew
Director

- **Reports** - There are a wide variety of report types. The common thread is that they are written to inform the reader of facts about a subject. They will often include an executive summary which states the main points.

Preparation made at an early stage will save you time later. If your organisation has a 'house-style' (the layout of a document) make sure that you use it. You may be able to set up templates for standard documents on your computer, this will save time when you are asked to produce the same type of document at a later date. Whatever type of document you produce you must confirm the purpose, content, style, quality standards and deadline. You will need to know the deadline for document in order to prioritise your work.

To produce any document you need a computer, a printer and paper. For letters and some memos you will need envelopes. You will need to consider the purpose of the document to make sure you have the resources you need. These may include:

- **Paper** – Headed, letter quality or copy quality
- **Printer** – Media (which gives you a choice of paper), quality settings (best, normal or draft) and colour or black and white
- **Envelopes** - Letters to external addresses will need good quality envelopes while internal memos may be sent using internal envelopes which can be used a number of times. Consideration should be given to the size of envelope needed. A document shouldn't be folded more than twice to fit into an envelope. Documents with several pages should be placed flat in an envelope

Gather the information you need to include in the document. This may come from any number of sources, including the letter you are replying to, previous reports, databases, the Internet and other files. Having decided the content, you will need to organise it so that you can find it when you need it. It may be useful to produce a first draft so you can see where the content fits into the whole. For a long or complex document you may want to draft the topics or headings to organise the content before writing the detail. You will then want to consider:

- The size of paper to use. Most documents are printed on A4 paper (210mm x 297mm) but you may want to consider A5 (half of A4) for memos, leaflets and brochures or A3 (twice A4) for posters
- Whether to present your document in portrait or landscape form. Most standard documents are presented in portrait form, landscape is used for tables and spreadsheets where it is helpful to be able to see the full row of information at a glance

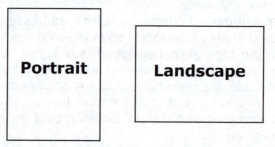

- Any diagrams or tables you may want to insert into your document. Diagrams will usually be imported from elsewhere, tables are produced from the 'table' menu

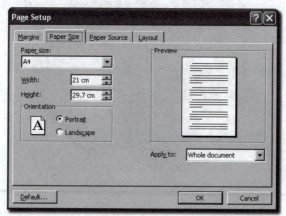

What you need to know

Where to find relevant content

> Do you know how what options are available on your printer?

How to prioritise tasks

> Do you know how to select options on your printer?

What types of documents you are required to produce

> Can you access databases?

How to layout a formal letter

> Does your organisation have its own 'house-style'?

Producing the document

Probably the greatest advantage that the word processor has over the typewriter is the opportunity to edit. Functions of the word processor in common use include:

- **Delete** - This allows you to delete a single letter at a time. To delete a whole word at a time use 'ctrl+delete'
- **Paste** (Ctrl+v) - This is used in combination with either the 'cut' or 'copy' instruction. Paste will add the last data selected to the document
- **Cut** (Ctrl+x) - You can highlight a piece of text and remove it from the document. This command then allows you to paste the text elsewhere in the document
- **Copy** (Ctrl+c) - This is used in combination with the 'paste' instruction to duplicate previously entered data
- **Find and replace** (Ctrl+f) - This function is used to change all the examples of a particular word to another word. For instance if you are asked to write a report and you use the word 'company' several times and are then asked to substitute the word

'organisation' there is no need to retype it, use 'find and replace' to change all the examples

- **Inserting special characters and symbols** - This enables you to use a wide range of non-Arabic letters and other signs e.g. ©, é, 'Ω, %
- **Mail merge -** This function is useful if the same letter is going to several recipients, it allows you to change the name and address without having to re-type the whole letter
- **Track changes** - Any changes that are made to text will be highlighted

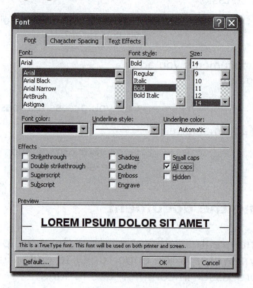

At any stage during the production of a document you can amend the format of the text. There are various options available in the format menu. It is possible to format characters, pages or whole sections. If you use a format for part of the document and want to use it again later, you can select 'styles and formatting' and the software will show you what you have used previously in the document.

Whatever you have been asked for you will be required to produce it in the agreed style. The style will differ between:

- **Memos** - These will usually simply state the name of the recipient, the name of the sender and the content. They may have the recipient and sender's job titles and departments
- **Letters** - There is a convention that business letters are produced fully blocked and with open punctuation.

Fully blocked means all parts of the document start at the left hand margin. Open punctuation omits all punctuation except that in the body of the letter which is essential for grammatical accuracy and ease of understanding. Business letters are also laid out in a fixed sequence; salutation (e.g. Dear Sir or Madam), opening, main message, action or results, closing, compliments (e.g. Yours faithfully) and signature

- **Reports** - There are a number of ways of ordering the contents of a report. These include;
    - **by importance** - beginning with the central idea
    - **by chronology** - in order of events starting either with the latest or the first
    - **by sequence** - where one idea follows from another
    - **by comparison** - where two ideas are compared in alternate paragraphs

If you are producing a lengthy or complex document you may need to give each page a header and footer, or page number. A title can be put onto each page with a page number. It is also possible to number paragraphs and include an index or table of contents to help the reader find their way around the document.

Any picture, diagram or table already held on your hard drive or on a disk can be imported. You can also import objects from other software on your computer, or through a connected scanner or digital camera, or from the internet. Care will need to be taken when importing non-text objects. In a letter 'less is more' where pictures and diagrams are concerned. In a report pictures and diagrams can certainly add to the impact, but you must take care that they are used only when they are relevant and can add to the content. Their positioning and size must also be carefully considered. Beware of the use of images for their own sake.

What you need to know

How to use your word processing package

> If you were asked to find the word 'pencil' in a document and replace it with 'pen' would you know which function to use?

When the use of images is appropriate

> Could you find appropriate images for a report on the Cricket World Cup?

The differences between the layout of memos, letters and reports

> Would you be able to manipulate images to fit the purpose?

Checking the document

When you have completed the document it is essential that you check it for accuracy, then edit and correct as necessary. Most word processing packages contain spell checking and grammar checking facilities. Use these first to correct the more glaring errors, but do not rely on them entirely. They tend to use American spelling and grammar, so will accept 'color' and reject 'colour', for instance. When the automatic checking is complete, *read* the document carefully to look for missed errors, and also for correct use of paragraphs, headings and subheadings, style and formatting. You may find it useful to remember the 'Five Cs' when checking your documents

- **Conciseness** – Minimise the amount of words you use to get your point across?
- **Completeness** - Is everything the reader needs there?
- **Courtesy** - Have you been polite to the reader?
- **Clarity** - Will the reader understand your point?
- **Correctness** - Are all statements accurate and true?

Be particularly careful to proof read numbers, dates, times and amounts. Check for errors between similar words such as 'affect' and 'effect' or 'less' and 'fewer'.

While you can check the document for spelling, punctuation and grammar, only the author can check for the accuracy of statements and details so you may need to seek clarification. For example, if the author has dictated 'we will sell petrol only to people in a metal container' you should suggest re-wording this to clarify that it is not necessary for the purchasers of petrol to be inside a metal container at the time of purchase.

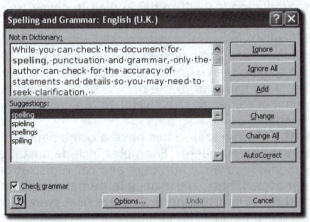

You will need to present the document by the agreed deadline and in the style required. If unforeseen circumstances mean that you need to change the style or content, or that you will be unable to meet the agreed deadline, it is important that you report the fact as soon as the situation arises. It is too late to be told that a deadline will not be met when the deadline arrives. It is not acceptable to lower the agreed quality standards in order to meet the deadline.

Documents may be stored in hard copy or electronically. Your organisation will have a system for filing hard copies. Electronically the document can be stored by using the 'save as' function on the word processor and naming the document appropriately. There may be a system for naming files such as the originator's initials followed by the date, for example. You may group files into folders for ease of retrieval. Confidential or sensitive documents may be password protected.

With paper records it will be necessary to store the document safely and securely. There are a number of different methods that can be used:

- **Alphabetical** - Filed in order from A–Z. Files starting with the same letter are filed in order of the second letter (Aa, Ab, Ac) and so on. People's names are filed by their surnames, and if more than one has the same surname by their first names. Names starting with 'The' are filed by ignoring the 'The'
- **Numerical** - Files are given numbers and filed from 1 to infinity. This is useful for information which naturally lends itself to being filed this way (purchase orders, sales invoices, for instance). There is a difficulty where, for instance, all customers are given numbers and their records filed numerically. If you don't know the customer's number you can't find their file. This can lead to the necessity of keeping an alphabetical list to cross-refer to the customer's number
- **Alpha-numerical** - Files have a combination of letters and numbers. Examples include postal codes, National Insurance numbers and car registration numbers. These are usually large databases as they hold more information than numerical systems and are more flexible than alphabetical systems. The order of filing depends on the sequence of the file name. If file names start with letters followed by numbers, they are filed in alphabetical order first, and numerical order within each letter
- **Chronological** - This is most often used within one of the other methods. For instance, each customer's records are filed alphabetically, but the information within the file is stored chronologically, usually with the latest at the front. This enables a picture of the activity to be gained

Whichever method is adopted if the information is not stored accurately it will be extremely difficult to find.

What you need to know

The use of spell check and grammar check

> What are the 5 C's?

How to spell, punctuate and use correct grammar

> If you were filing vehicle records by registration number which filing method would you use?

Your organisation's convention for naming electronic files

> Do you know which filing methods are in use in your organisation?

The benefits of placing electronic files in folders

> Do you know the difference between 'there', 'they're' and 'their'?

When you are producing any document, ask yourself 'who is this for?' Knowing your reader shapes the tone and content of documents. Remember to write to the reader but not down to the reader. Don't allow yourself to believe that correct spelling, punctuation and grammar are old-fashioned conventions. They enable you to communicate your ideas accurately and articulately to your reader. Without them it is easy for your meaning to be misunderstood.

Good looking documents give a positive impression

Are you ready for assessment?

To achieve this unit of a Level 2 Business & Administration qualification you will need to demonstrate that you are competent in the following:

- Confirm the purpose, content, style, quality standards and deadlines for the document
- Prepare the resources you need
- Organise the content you need
- Make efficient use of the technology available
- Produce the document in the agreed style
- Integrate non-text objects in the agreed layout
- Check for accuracy, editing and correcting as necessary
- Seek clarification when necessary
- Store the document safely and securely in an approved location
- Present the document in the required format within agreed deadlines and quality standard

(Remember that you will need the skills listed at the beginning of this chapter and that these are covered in chapter 1.)

Your Assessor will need you to produce evidence from a variety of sources. If you carry out the activities that follow they will provide some of the evidence for you.

Activity 1

What sort of document would you use to advise colleagues of the date and location of a meeting?

True or false, a letter should contain as many images as possible to improve the effect?

What would you call a rough outline of a long and complex document?

True or false, a letter opening 'Dear Sir or Madam' should close 'Yours sincerely'?

Activity 2

Write a report to your supervisor suggesting ways in which your current filing systems can be improved. Consider which is the best way to order the contents of the report.

Activity 3

Which of the following are correct?

Would we have less problems if we had fewer departments?
Neither Edinburgh or Glasgow is in England.
The customers are always right.
The customer's always right.
The ship's crew was up to its full complement.
The customer's are always right.

Activity 4

Select a number of documents that you have produced which you feel demonstrate your competence in using correct layout, spelling, punctuation and grammar. Consider the question of confidentiality in making your selection.

Activity 5

Which of the following documents are likely to be confidential?

Letter of dismissal
Report on fraud within the organisation
Memo stating date and time of a meeting
Fax copy of an invoice
Minutes of staff meeting
Study on potential redundancies

Activity 6

You have been given the following hand-written notice and asked to type it up and place it on the notice board. Correct the errors in spelling, punctuation and grammar and produce a finished notice. Underneath list the spelling errors which would not be picked up by the computer using the spell check function.

Mr. Wilson will not be avalaible to give the lecture on Friday 15th she is sick he wil be replaiced by Mr, Jefferson who will now be giving the lecture on Adminastration in the motor industry. The thyme of the lectur has also changed it will knot be at 11.00 am butt at 14.00 pm. The locasion has not changed it'll still be held on the 5th flaw in the charity room.

Activity 7

What are the following abbreviations of?

abbrev.
adv.
Biochem.
cent.
cm.
Educ.
eg
ie
k
km
mm
N.Z.
pl.n.
R.C.
sq.
UK

Remember: While gathering evidence for this unit, evidence **may** be generated for units 110, 201, 202, 212, 214, 221, 222, 223 and 225.

CHAPTER 25
UNIT 225 –Work effectively with other people

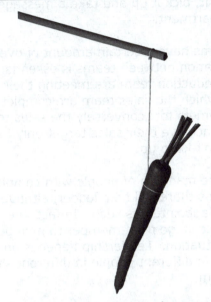

The core of every organisation is the people who work within it. Whether it is a multi-national company or a small office, work will be organised in such a way that goals can be achieved much more effectively by people working together in teams. There will be a variety of types of team within any business:

- **'Permanent' teams** - such as the sales team, the management team, the production team and the accounts team
- **'Ad-hoc' teams** - brought together to carry out specific tasks, such as a project team, a store opening team, stock-taking teams
- **'Unofficial' teams** - made up of your personal contacts both within and outside of the organisation, which you will use as a network to get things done

At any one time you may be working in a permanent team, an unofficial team and an ad-hoc team. For instance, if you are a member of the production team carrying out stock-taking while using your contact with the management team to arrange for additional staff to help. The important thing to remember is that the whole organisation is one big team that should override any internal divisions between departments.

If people work effectively together the business will thrive. If people are working against each other all the time it will cause friction and nothing effective will be achieved. If you are passing a telephone that is ringing and there is nobody else free to answer it, pick it up and take a message, even if it is not in your department.

The majority of teams have a certain amount of overlap, so effective communication between teams is essential. It is not helpful if the production team are meeting their targets turning out goods which the sales team are completely unable to find customers for; conversely the sales team may be working hard to achieve their sales target only to find the production team can't keep up.

Successful teams are made up of people with complementary abilities. In all teams there will be a leader, although they may not have been appointed as such. In fact, the leadership role may change from member to member depending on the situation. Leadership depends on power, which can be found in different people in different situations. Power can come from:

- **Authority** - The appointed leader
- **Budgets -** If you control the team budget you have power over decision making
- **Knowledge** - If you have particular expertise within the team your opinions will be given weight
- **Charisma** - Some people just have the ability to influence others
- **Incentives** - If you are in a position to decide who gets the best assignments, the desk overlooking the window or first choice of holiday dates, you will be able to exert some control
- **Who you know** - The opportunity to influence people outside the team, on behalf of the team

Other roles within the team will involve:

- **The innovator** - Comes up with new ideas
- **The peacemaker** - Mediates between people with strongly held opposing views
- **The co-ordinator** - Takes the ideas and gets on with the team's task
- **The analyst** - Keeps the team on track and sees the overall picture

- **The dissenter** - Disagrees with the majority view and keeps the team open-minded

Just as leadership changes from member to member according to the situation, so do the roles within the team. Today's analyst may be tomorrow's co-ordinator.

The trick is to recognise what your particular abilities are, and what the abilities of other team members are, and use these where they will be most effective. Care must be taken not to offend people's sensibilities as their view of their own abilities may be different from yours.

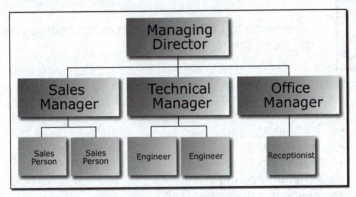

In some organisations teams are arranged competitively in an attempt to motivate the members to achieve goals. This needs careful handling as it can have a negative effect. Team-members become de-motivated if their team is consistently unsuccessful, or if teams do not co-operate with each other in an attempt to 'win'. However the teams are arranged the purpose is to achieve the objectives set. It is important that all members of the team know whether they are meeting those objectives or not.

No matter how well organised the team there will be problems from time to time. If you can anticipate problems before they happen, you will be able to work out a solution so that the difficulty can be overcome as soon as it arises. You will be halfway to solving the problem if you can accurately identify what the problem is. Often we attempt to solve what we think is the problem only to find that the real problem remains.

The key to working effectively with others is communication. A word of encouragement when things are not going well, or a 'thank you' and a 'well done' when they are, will work much better with most people than constant criticism. Usually people are not doing things badly deliberately. It is much more likely that they are overworked or being asked to achieve something beyond their abilities.

It is possible to get so involved in team building, team dynamics and effective communication that you forget the overriding objective of all business; producing work to the required standard by the given deadline.

 When working effectively with other people you will need the following skills:

- Communicating
- Team working
- Planning
- Negotiating
- Managing time
- Problem solving
- Resolving disagreement

These skills are covered in chapter 1.

Personal effectiveness

In order to work effectively with other people you must first be working effectively in your own right. An important aspect is personal presentation. Appearance matters, people judge on appearance and you should dress suitably for where you work. When choosing your outfit for work you should consider:

- Can you be identified as a member of staff?
- Will your colleagues, clients and customers feel comfortable with the way you look?
- Are your clothes practical for the type of work you will be doing?
- Are your shoes comfortable enough to wear all day?
- Are any accessories you plan to wear suitable?

Other important considerations are personal hygiene and hair. Ask yourself if you would want to work next to you all day.

Having showered, dressed and brushed your hair you are ready to make your way to work. Make sure that you leave home in plenty of time to arrive at work early. This gives you time to settle into your day without being rushed. You will feel ready for work, rather than feeling you're trying to catch up all day. Use this time to plan your day and write your to-do lists.

If you find that you are going to be late, let someone know. Don't think that you will be able to use an excuse no one has heard before, they don't exist. Look at the real reasons that have made you late and address them. Do you need to get out of bed earlier, catch an earlier bus, get your clothes ready the night before? However well prepared you are there will always be the occasion when an unforeseeable circumstance means you will be late. If you have a good timekeeping record, people will accept the occasional unavoidable lateness.

0900 AM

As well as good timekeeping, good attendance is also very important. If you are the sort of person who 'enjoys ill health' your colleagues will have to cover for the work that you are not doing. They will be happy to do this if you are genuinely unwell but will soon get tired of it if you take every second Friday off. You may be tempted to take a day off if you are faced with a task that you don't want to do. It is much better to deal with the problem head on by talking to colleagues or your supervisor about the task than to try to avoid it altogether. This will only delay the inevitable, eventually you are going to have to do it. Seek more training so that you feel more confident about handling it.

You are at work only for a few hours a day, try to concentrate on what you are there for. Behave positively and colleagues, customers and even you, yourself, will be affected by your attitude. Colleagues will see you as a valued member of the team and the workload will be shared; customers will be left with a positive impression; you will find work is more enjoyable and opportunities to progress are more likely to be offered to people with a positive attitude.

You will probably be working with both men and women of varying ages and backgrounds, certainly of differing personalities. Some of them will be from different cultural backgrounds and all will have different abilities and talents. To maintain successful working relationships with all of them will require that you temper your style of communication to match their personality. Don't look on this as you always changing your style and not being yourself; the person you are talking to will also be tempering their style to match your personality. Other people will probably be keen to offer you advice, especially if they have been in the job for a lot longer than you have. Try to listen to what they have to say, while at the same time avoiding offering advice unless you are asked for it. If you are asked to give your advice, think carefully and make it relevant. Your judgement is being relied on, so prove worthy of the compliment.

Something else people will freely offer is criticism. This can be hurtful, especially if it is unexpected or worse, unjustified. Try to look objectively at the criticism and ask yourself if it is deserved. If it is, take steps to correct the situation. Everybody makes mistakes and if they are not pointed out you will not get the opportunity to correct them or avoid repeating them. If the criticism is not deserved, challenge it. Be sure of your facts and present them politely.

From time to time you may encounter problems with individuals you work with. Communication is the key to resolving these. Often the cause is a misunderstanding which can be easily resolved by being open. The critical thing is to talk to the person you feel you have the problem with, not to everybody else behind their back. Only if the problem appears to be beyond your ability to resolve should you consider taking it to a third person.

You will find far fewer problems if you are motivated and work well in a team. Keep yourself busy and use your initiative. There is always something that needs doing and it is much less boring to be busy. Think about what you can do next, if you have finished all today's tasks can you make a start on tomorrow's, or does somebody else need a hand finishing theirs?

 What you need to know

Your organisation's dress code

What are the advantages to you of good timekeeping?

Who to report to if you are sick

What must you do if you realise you are going to be late for work?

The advantages of a positive attitude

What steps should you take if you are regularly late for work?

How to deal with personal problems

What do you understand by the word 'empathy'?

How to accept constructive criticism

When should you offer advice?

Team working

A team is a collection of people but a collection of people is not always a team. The best teams are made up of a wide mix of people. Look for opportunities to be appointed to a team as this will enable you to use your abilities alongside those of others. Although the team will be expected to work effectively straight away, in reality this is unlikely as team members have to get to know each other, find ways of working together and will produce results only after they have had some time together. This process can be described as:

- **Forming** - People get to know each other as team members and discuss how they will work together, how they will be organised, what each person's role in the team is. There may be a lot of activity but very little progress made during this stage
- **Storming** - Conflict starts to occur between team members as the team realise that the task may be more difficult than they thought, and the roles each identified for themselves may be challenged by others. People become frustrated and feel de-motivated. There is very little creativity
- **Norming** - After the storming stage it is necessary to go back to the answers that were found to the questions in the forming stage and review the decisions that were taken. They will certainly have been revised. The team will now be in a position to take decisions about how the team is organised, how

decisions are taken, acceptable behaviour, conflict resolution and how specialisms will be developed

- **Performing** - This is the stage at which the team is actually starting to achieve the purpose for which it was put together. Previously the team will have been wasting much of its energy on sorting themselves out, now they can concentrate on their goal. An effective team produces synergy. This means their performance as a team is greater than the sum of their individual performance. It is sometimes written as 1+1+1=4. Of course, it is usually at this point that somebody leaves the team and the whole process has to be started again

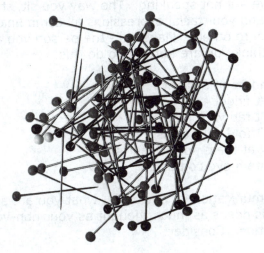

Team building, therefore, is a never-ending process. There are a great many important factors in building a successful team. These include:

- Making sure you don't let team members down. If you cannot do something you have offered to do, tell them why
- Sharing credit and blame. The good results will have been achieved by the team, not individual members; bad results must be the fault of the team, not individual members
- Sharing goals and planning objectives, priorities and responsibilities
- Listening to other team members. It's unlikely that you will be the only one who is right
- Respecting others and yourself
- Being assertive not aggressive when conflict arises

When you are working within a team you will need to be able to communicate effectively. Effective teams are those where all the members feel able to talk to each other openly whenever they have anything to say. An average person has a working vocabulary of some 60,000 words, so should find no difficulty in expressing themselves verbally. They also have the ability to use non-verbal communication to get their meaning across. 80% of what we communicate is through body language; 13% through the way we say things and only 7% through the actual words we use.

Non-verbal communication means the 'messages' we send out when we are not speaking. The way you sit, stand, fold your arms and your facial expressions all communicate the way you feel to others. Make sure the person you are talking to doesn't think you are bored. To do this:

- Stand or sit upright
- Don't fidget
- Don't tap your feet
- Don't fold your arms
- Look at them not at your shoes
- Maintain eye contact

Verbal communication is, obviously, what you are actually saying. This needs as much thought as your non-verbal communication. Consider:

- What you are saying
- The speed at which you are saying it
- The tone of voice you are using
- The volume at which you are speaking

Remember also, that communication is a two-way street. You need to be able to listen to what is being said to you too. How can you show someone that you are listening to them? You can use the following listening techniques:

- Look at the person who is speaking
- Lean towards them
- Keep still
- Nod your head occasionally
- Mirror their facial expression
- Say things like 'mmm', 'I see', 'right'

You must also ask questions to clarify what is being said. There are a number of questioning techniques, but the basic two to understand are:

- **Open questions** - These are questions which begin with 'who', 'when', 'where', 'what', 'how' and 'why' and therefore cannot be answered 'yes' or 'no'. They are used to gain information
- **Closed questions** - These are questions which begin with 'do', 'can', 'will' and 'may' and therefore can be answered 'yes' or 'no'. They are used to gain confirmation

A good example of the difference between open and closed questions is:

- 'May I help you?' A closed question which invites the answer 'No'.
- 'How may I help you?' An open question which requires a fuller answer

Use a mix of open and closed questions to find out what you need to know.

Working effectively with people is a skill that you will need to develop as it is something you do all the time. Unless you are working in complete isolation there is always interaction with others. This is true not only of the team that you work in but also everybody else in the organisation and many outside of it. Co-operating with others enables you to achieve more, which makes your work more enjoyable. Very few of us actually thrive on conflict, successful organisations are those where everybody works in harmony.

What you need to know

The important factors involved in team-building

> Why are the best teams made up of a diverse group of people?

Why communication with colleagues is essential

> What do you understand by the word 'synergy'?

How to agree quality measures with your colleagues

> What is the difference between open and closed questions?

The sources of leadership power

> What different roles are there in a successful team?

The stages of team formation

> How do you tell if someone is listening?

A successful team is one in which all members are pulling in the same direction with the same purpose

Are you ready for assessment?

To achieve this unit of a Level 2 Business & Administration qualification you will need to demonstrate that you are competent in the following:

- Communicate effectively with other people
- Welcome opportunities to work with other people when this will achieve a positive outcome
- Share work goals and plan work objectives, priorities and responsibilities together
- Work in a way that makes best use of your abilities and the abilities of others
- Show respect for individuals
- Produce quality work on time
- Identify and solve problems
- Share feedback with others on the achievement of objectives

(Remember that you will need the skills listed at the beginning of this chapter and that these are covered in chapter 1.)

Your Assessor will need you to produce evidence from a variety of sources. If you carry out the activities that follow they will provide some of the evidence for you.

Activity 1
Think about a team that you are a member of. This may be a work team or a team in which you are involved outside of work. Write a report explaining how the team went through the forming, storming, norming, performing process.

Activity 2
Identify an improvement that could be achieved in your workplace if members of your team were to co-operate in changing the status quo. List the stages that you would go through to achieve the desired result, stating what the necessary change is, how it would improve the workplace, who would be affected, what actions would need to be taken, who by, whose approval would be needed, whose co-operation would be needed, how you would obtain their commitment, how you would monitor the result.

Activity 3

You are included in a team that has been brought together for the sole purpose of managing the move from your current location to a new purpose built office five miles away. One member of the team is consistently negative, raising objections to every suggestion while offering no ideas of their own. The van won't be big enough, the phones will never be connected on time, the photocopier is too heavy to move, the paperwork will get in a mess and will never be sorted again, why don't we just stay where we are? There is no possibility of them being removed from the team, write an account of how would you deal with the situation?

Activity 4

You have been asked to join a team to market a new product which is a completely new avenue for the organisation. The first meeting of the team is to take place next Wednesday. Prepare your notes for the meeting listing the questions you think need to be answered.

Activity 5

You have been on a course to learn how to operate a new piece of equipment. Your task is to train the rest of your team to use it. Choosing a piece of equipment that you are familiar with, write step-by-step instructions for its use. Give the instructions to somebody who doesn't know how to use the equipment and ask them to follow them, word for word.

Remember: While gathering evidence for this unit, evidence **may** be generated for all other units at Level 2.

Index